The Immigrant Heritage of America Series

Cecyle S. Neidle, *Editor*

ASIANS IN AMERICA:

Filipinos, Koreans, and East Indians

By H. BRETT MELENDY
University of Hawaii

TWAYNE PUBLISHERS
A DIVISION OF G. K. HALL & CO., BOSTON

Library of Congress Cataloging in Publication Data

Melendy, Howard Brett.
  Asians in America.

  (The Immigrant heritage of America series)
  Bibliography: pp. 299–325.
  Includes index.
  1. Filipino Americans. 2. Korean Americans. 3. East Indian
Americans. I. Title.
E184.F4M44   301.45′19′5073   77-9268
ISBN 0-8057-8414-4

For
My Parents,
HOWARD and PEARL MELENDY

Contents

Preface

Since the 1850's, people from many different nations have migrated eastward across the Pacific Ocean to the mainland United States and Hawaii. Most Americans tended to categorize them in general terms such as Asians or Orientals. The fact of the matter is that these people have come from different civilizations with unique societies and traditions. The first such immigrants started coming from China and Japan. During the twentieth century, Filipinos, Koreans, and East Indians joined the flow to the United States and Hawaii. Americans have had a difficult time distinguishing between American Indians and immigrants from India. In reality, immigrants now come from three separate nations—Bangladesh, India, and Pakistan. To simplify the narrative, the term *East Indian* has been used throughout to refer to residents of these three nations. The reader should remember that the term is used for convenience only and does not imply that these people are the same, culturally or politically.

In the last ten years, immigrants from these five countries have been in the forefront of new immigrants arriving each year at the doors of the United States. Other Asian countries, old and new, also provide newcomers. Most Americans of the 1970's still remember vividly the influx of Vietnam refugees and the mixed reactions these people found in the United States.

The intent of this book is to examine the three distinct immigrant groups, the Filipinos, Koreans, and East Indians, in order to understand their motivations for migrating and to observe their similar encounters with white America. The first immigrants came primarily to be short-term unskilled laborers on the Pacific Coast and in Hawaii or as students. Most planned to return home after only a short stay. The book looks at what happened to their plans. The flow of immigration during the twentieth century is depicted and analyzed. Equally important is the story of how the different waves of immigrants adapted economically to life in the United States and of their struggles for jobs, for equality, and for American citizenship. The people of these five nations were, until 1946–47, all subjects of imperial systems. Their struggle for the independence of their homeland is an important story as is their effort to create homes in the United States.

Filipinos, Koreans, and East Indians, as do other Asian groups in the United States, view themselves as separate ethnic groups in America's pluralistic society. Unlike many European immigrants, they have not seen themselves becoming readily amalgamated, or accepting the label of a hyphenate group as have Italian-Americans or German-Americans. Recent scholarship in writing of Asian immigrants does not use the hyphen, acknowledging their continuing ethnicity. Editorial policy for *The Immigrant Heritage of America Series*, however, had determined to identify all immigrant groups with a hyphen. In this instance, then, the use of the hyphenate form is a matter of style and not substance.

The assistance given by the staffs of the Library of Congress, the National Archives, the libraries of San José State University, Stanford University, University of California, University of Hawaii, University of Oregon, and University of Washington is deeply acknowledged.

I am particularly indebted to the Bancroft Library at the University of California, the California Section of the California State Library, and the Documents Room and Hawaiian Collection, University of Hawaii Library.

The financial support given in part by the American Philosophical Society through two grants (1962 and 1974) and the San José State University Foundation has been of significant assistance. I am also indebted to Brenda, Darcie, and Lisa Melendy for their assistance in bibliographical endeavors and other technical help. The University of Hawaii History Department secretarial corps has assisted me constantly in the production of the final typescript—my fond *mahalo* to each of them.

Appreciation is happily acknowledged to the following publishers who have given permission to use materials to which

Preface

they hold the copyrights: Caxton Printers, Ltd. for *I Have Lived with the American People* by Manuel Buaken; *Honolulu* for "When Will the Filipinos Become a Political Power?" by Elisabeth H. Bell; *Sociology and Social Research* for "American Attitudes toward Filipinos," "Filipino Immigrant Attitudes" by Emory S. Bogardus, and "Social Adjustments of Filipinos in America" by D. F. Gonzalo.

I am exceedingly grateful for the support of many of my colleagues in history in California and Hawaii but particularly to Michael Onorato of California State University, Fullerton, and to Gerald Wheeler of San José State University for their assistance with materials from the Philippines. I must acknowledge, too, the help given by Cecyle S. Neidle, Editor of the Twayne Immigrant Heritage of America series for her advice and careful editing.

This book could not have reached fruition without the support and assistance of my wife, Marian. Most of all, I acknowledge my lifelong debt to my parents who have sustained me in my several enterprises.

H. BRETT MELENDY

Honolulu, Hawaii
October, 1976

About the Author

H. Brett Melendy was born in Eureka, California, attended its public schools and Humboldt State College. He received his A.B. in English, M.A. in Education, and Ph.D. in History .from Stanford University.

He first taught in public schools in Fresno, California, including Fresno City College. He joined the History faculty at San José State University, serving as its chairman from 1958–1969. He also served in several administrative capacities at San José State. In 1970, he became Professor of History and Vice President for Community Colleges at the University of Hawaii. Since 1973, he has been full time in the Department of History.

In addition to *Asians in America*, Melendy has authored *The Oriental Americans*, co-authored *The Governors of California*, contributed to *The Asian American, Counterpoint: Perspectives on Asian America, Letters in Exile,* and *Racism in California.* He has also written articles for several historical journals.

List of Tables

PART I

FILIPINO-AMERICANS

CHAPTER I

The Filipinos' Homeland

IMMIGRATION to the United States from all of Asia changed dramatically on October 3, 1965. At the base of the Statue of Liberty that day, President Lyndon B. Johnson signed into law the end to the national origins immigration system which had regulated the flow of immigrants into the United States since the 1920's and had effectively limited the entry of Asians. Now, with this change, people from all corners of the world could request admittance.[1] The impact of this new law upon immigrants and upon the United States was very significant and brought both benefits and liabilities. Large numbers of immigrants arrived at various ports of entry for the same reasons that had propelled countless multitudes of others to the United States earlier: economic gain, social improvement, and a freer political existence. The dreams were the same; unfortunately for many newcomers of the 1960's–1970's, the consequences were also the same. Many found themselves trapped in an economic rat race; others suffered from the results of prejudice and intolerance. For all, political freedom in the long run meant little without economic opportunity and social justice.

In the ten years following President Johnson's signing of the new law, Asian immigration annually formed a major part of the total of new arrivals into the United States. During the first years of the twentieth century, China and Japan had provided most of the Far East's share of immigrants. India, Pakistan, Korea, and the Philippines had provided relatively few immigrants before 1965. By the 1970's, however, these countries had become significant and major contributors to the new flow coming to America. The increase in just fourteen years, as shown in Table I, was both substantial and dramatic.

In order to understand more clearly the aspirations and the fears of these Asian immigrants as well as the driving motivation

17

TABLE I
ASIAN IMMIGRATION
TO THE UNITED STATES, 1960, 1970 & 1974

COUNTRY	1960[a]	1970[b]	1974[c]
China and Taiwan	3,681	14,093	18,055
Hong Kong	475	3,863	4,629
India	391	10,114	12,779
Pakistan	N.A.[d]	1,528	2,570
Japan	5,471	4,485	4,860
Korea	1,507	9,314	28,028
Philippines	2,954	31,203	32,857

[a]U.S. Department of Justice, Immigration and Naturalization
Service, *Annual Report, 1961*, p. 43.
[b]Ibid., *1971*, p. 54.   [c]Ibid., *1974*, p. 3.
[d]N.A. = Not available.

that led so many to migrate to the United States, a knowledge of
the homelands and of the cultures of the East Indians, Filipinos,
and Koreans is essential. Geography has always played an important part in shaping economic, political, and cultural forces
for all national groups.

✿   ✿   ✿   ✿   ✿

The Philippine Islands, rising from the world's deepest ocean
off the eastern edge of southeast Asia, are part of the fiery rim
of the Pacific where earthquakes and volcanic activity are still
common phenomena. An archipelago of about 7,100 islands,
the Philippines stretch for 1,152 miles in a north-south arc from
the Batan Islands in the north, sixty-five miles from Taiwan,
to the Sulu Archipelago in the south, only thirty miles from
Borneo; its widest east-west dimensions are 682 miles.[2] Generally, the islands, both large and small, have high rising mountains, surrounded by coral reef shorelines.

The eleven islands of Luzon, Mindanao, Samar, Negros, Palawan, Panay, Mindoro, Leyte, Cebu, Bohol, and Masbate com-
prise the major land masses, constituting about 95 percent of
the total land area of the Philippines. Luzon, 489 miles in
length and with a maximum width of about 138 miles, and
Mindanao, ninety miles long and sixty miles wide, together
form 67 percent of the country's land. The Philippines' land area

is 115,707 square miles, just slightly larger than the state of Arizona.

The archipelago can be visualized most easily when divided into four groupings. The first, and largest, is the island of Luzon in the north. The second, also the next largest island, is Mindanao—located in the southeast. The third, arranged around the Visayan Sea, consists of the islands of Samar, Leyte, Bohol, Cebu, Negros, Panay, and Masbate. The fourth group consists of two clusters stretching from the other island groups southwesterly to Borneo—the Palawan Islands and the Sulu Islands.[3]

Immigrants, for several centuries, sought out the islands' valleys and plains. By 1960, 25 percent of the nation's population was located on Luzon between the Lingayen Gulf in the northwest through the province of Laguna in the south. Population density was the highest in the Visayan Islands where 35 percent of the people lived. The island of Cebu had more than four hundred people per square mile. The large islands of Palawan, Mindanao, and Mindoro had less than twenty-five per square mile. Based on actual land utilization, it has been estimated that Cebu and the two provinces of Ilocos Norte and Ilocos Sur on Luzon had population concentrations of 1,750 people per cultivated square mile.[4]

Climatic conditions have played an important role in determining the life style in the islands. The Philippines, located between the latitudes of 4° and 21°, have a climate which is about the same throughout the islands—any differences can be attributed to latitude and elevation. The climate, classified as maritime and tropical, is marked by high humidity, high temperatures, scattered clouds, and light winds. Superimposed on these weather conditions are the northeast and southwest monsoons which bring heavy rains.

Another major factor affecting the climate is the *baguio* or typhoon. From July through September, winds, originating in the Pacific, sweep eastward across the islands of Luzon and Samar. From October through December, the typhoon track moves south into the Visayan Sea area. During this season, these storms bring high winds and heavy rains for short periods of time.[5]

Throughout history, climate has been a major determinant in

how and where people cultivated the soil. For centuries, agriculture, ranging from subsistence farming to export plantations, has been the backbone of the Philippine economy. In 1960, although over 65 percent of all Filipino workers were employed in some form of agriculture, only 15 percent of the land area was cultivated. The principal domestic crops were rice and corn while abaca (Manila hemp), copra, sugar, and tobacco were major export crops.[6]

One of the Philippines' long-standing problems has been land utilization. The share tenant system has tied most people to the soil. One reason for the Hukbalahap uprising following independence in 1946 was the fact that over 70 percent of the crops went to the *caciqueor*, the landlord, while the farmer was continually crushed by debts with no relief in sight. The problem of land reform remains high on the Philippine agenda. Coupled with the weight of tenancy has been a system of inadequate agricultural methods. Through most of the twentieth century, the yield per acre of the two basic foods, rice and corn, ranked among the lowest in the world.

Land utilization problems had great impact upon the people of the Northern Luzon provinces, particularly Ilocos Norte and Ilocos Sur. Upper-class farmers were frequently forced to reduce their acreage through sale or mortgage in order to provide for their families. People moved farther inland or into the upper reaches of Luzon's Cagayan Valley searching for additional lands. With annexation by the United States, these overpopulated provinces, the homeland of the Ilocanos, saw migration to Hawaii or to the mainland United States as one solution to both population and economic difficulties.[7]

The migration of different peoples to the islands has affected the evolution of the Philippine culture. Present-day Filipinos have diverse origins. From the time of European control, the islands have been called the Philippines, named after Prince Philip of Spain who, later as Philip II, pushed for greater Spanish influence in the islands. One of the earliest immigrant groups was the Little People, named Negritoes by the Spanish. Short in stature, under five feet, they were dark-skinned and had negroid features. From the time of their arrival some 25,000 years ago, the Negritoes lived throughout the islands. They

retreated inland as other people came. In the 1970's, they occupied the mountain interiors of the islands of Mindanao and
Palawan while on Luzon they lived in the provinces of Mountain
and Zambales.

Between 4000 B.C. and 3000 B.C. the first influx of Indonesians
from the Asian continent arrived. A second Indonesian invasion
started about 1000 B.C. and lasted five hundred years. Both
groups spread throughout the islands and, unlike the earlier
Negritoes, assimilated with subsequent immigrants. The present-
day Ilongots are one result of such intermixing.

The immigration of the Malays, an Iron Age people, begun
early in the third century, reached its peak in the thirteenth
century and continued at a high level through the fourteenth
century. From these Malays have descended the Bontoks, Igorots,
and Tinguians, known to Spanish and American colonialists as
head-hunting pagans. By European standards, these first Malay
people, while extremely primitive, were far advanced over
earlier immigrants.

Those Malays in the second wave had some elements of an
alphabet and metal tools as part of their culture. More peaceful
than their earlier migrating relatives, they were the ancestors
of most present-day Filipino Christians. Some members of this
second group brought Mohammedanism with them as they
moved into the southern islands during the fourteenth century.
Their descendants, militantly maintaining their identity and
religion, became known as the Moros.

Two Asian groups, the Chinese and Japanese, have played an
important part in the modern development of the Philippines.
Following the regularization of trade between China and the
islands by the fourteenth century, South China emigrants became successful entrepreneurs. At that time, most Filipinos
were not interested in commercial enterprise and this attitude
gave the Chinese a free hand. Their success made them powerful
economically and led them to control much of the nation's big
business. Consequently, during the twentieth century the Chinese
have faced hostilities and resentments which have resulted in
killings and official restrictions. Japanese immigration did not
become a major factor until after 1900 and the rise of industrial
Japan. Settlers first arrived in Mindanao where they developed

several large abaca plantations. Unlike other immigrant groups, the Japanese sought to remain homogeneous, rarely intermarrying. By 1940 they were scattered throughout the islands, mostly as craftsmen. Cabinetmaking and photography were two common occupations.[8]

European immigration came from Spain for about four hundred years but was of a transitory nature, for those who migrated did not plan on settling permanently in the islands. The same was true of American immigration in the twentieth century. European influx to the islands began in March, 1521, when Ferdinand Magellan's fleet reached the island of Samar. While Magellan claimed the islands for Spain and for the Catholic Church, Spanish influence in the Western Pacific remained at a low level until the reign of Philip II.[9] In 1565, nine years after Philip ascended the throne, a royal governor arrived to take firm control. First establishing himself on Cebu, the governor launched expeditions against other islands. From this beginning, Spanish authority became strong and lasting. In extending the empire, officials employed colonial methods developed in the Americas. As the Spanish control enlarged, the center of power was moved to Manila.

Spanish rule lasted from the sixteenth century until the Spanish-American War of 1898. The Spanish, endorsing European concepts of mercantilism and imperialism, considered the enrichment of Spain as the main purpose of the islands. But imperial success in planting a European culture and Christianity was achieved at the cost of alienating the Filipinos. The Spanish owned large estates and controlled the government from top to bottom while the Catholic Church, which also held large sections of land, monopolized education.

One important Spanish influence upon the Filipinos was the development of a class society. The Filipino upper class gained considerable experience in local government while at the same time acquiring large agricultural holdings. They quickly learned concepts of political bossism and how to use power and corruption to remain in control. The term *caciquism* came to be used to express this unsavory aspect of government, unsavory at least to those seeking democratic and participatory government. There is evidence that as a Filipino national government emerged and local politicians moved to the larger stage, *caciquism* became a national problem.[10]

During the last half of the nineteenth century, many local revolts against imperial corruption and racial discrimination occurred. The aim of these first revolts was reform, not independence. In the 1880's Jose Rizal, Philippine martyr and national hero, who received a European Jesuit medical education, wrote a novel while abroad, which pointed out the weaknesses of the Spanish colonial system and the church's ineffective educational program. After his return to the islands, he soon joined the Philippine nationalism movement. On July 3, 1892, Rizal founded *La Liga Filipina* (the Filipino League), dedicated to mutual defense and protection of all Filipinos against violence and injustice. The league advocated a moderate social reform program. When the Spanish banished Rizal, more radical revolutionaries assumed leadership of the league. After Rizal returned to the islands, he was captured and tried. Accused of being responsible for revolt and for killings, Rizal was found guilty and executed on the last day of 1896.[11]

With Rizal's death, twenty-seven-year-old Emilio Aguinaldo became the leader of the forces fighting the Spanish. After about two years of fighting and after organizing a Philippine national government, Aguinaldo met with American officials in Hong Kong and Singapore. He agreed that the Filipinos would join in the fight against the Spanish. These meetings started a series of misunderstandings between the people of the Philippines and the United States. Aguinaldo steadfastly maintained that United States diplomatic and military officers had agreed that there would be an independent Philippines. Officials, such as Admiral George Dewey and Consul General E. Spencer Pratt, later denied making such promises. Following the Spanish-American War, the United States ratified on February 6, 1899, the Treaty of Paris which transferred imperial control of the islands from Spain to the United States.

The United States started a relationship which lasted forty-seven years. The haunting question that began with the first conversations between Aguinaldo and Dewey was that of independence or United States control. The great American debate over the issue of imperialism did nothing to change the direction of the McKinley administration which moved to develop a Philippine commonwealth while using military forces to quell the Filipino revolution. Aguinaldo, captured on March 23, 1901, advised his followers to take oaths of allegiance to the United States. By July 4, 1902, the United States declared the insurrection over even though the Moros, who had been independent during Spanish colonial rule, continued to resist until 1913.[12]

The Moros never completely acknowledged allegiance to American rule or to the new Philippine nation after 1946. Even in the 1970's, these Muslims in the southern islands continued their fight for independence. The Moro National Liberation Front has called for an autonomous state consisting of the islands of Mindanao, Sulu, Palawan, and Basilan, which contained most of the nation's one and one-half million Muslims. Their demand is complicated by the fact that the majority of the inhabitants on the islands—some six million—are Christians.[13]

To institute United States control, President William McKinley sent several commissions to the islands. The most important of these, headed by William Howard Taft, began governing the islands on September 1, 1900. The instructions to this commission, written by Secretary of War Elihu Root, provided the basis of Philippine government for sixteen years. Between 1901 and 1913, American civilization probably made its strongest impact upon the islands. Democratic forms of government at local and provincial levels were established with Filipinos filling the offices. At the national level, an elected lower house shared in the governing process. A judicial system, based on American courts, was established while an American civil service was substituted for the Spanish one. Perhaps the most significant change in the long run was public education. Most communities had primary schools while each province had a high school. There were also several nationwide vocational schools and normal schools in addition to the University of the Philippines which was located in Manila. The old alliance of church and state was ended and religious freedom was guaranteed.[14]

At the turn of the century, Father Aglipay and his followers declared themselves independent of the Roman Catholic Church and formed the Philippine Independent Church. Several American churches responded to President McKinley's exhortation to send missionaries in order "to educate the Filipinos, and uplift and civilize and Christianize them, and by God's grace do the very best by them. . . ."[15]

One of the major causes of Filipino friction toward the Spanish had been the Friar Lands. The United States government purchased about 400,000 acres from the Catholic Church and sold the land in small parcels with easy payment terms, mostly to the former tenants. Throughout the islands, land surveys were carried out and a system of land titles created. Homestead land was made available from the public domain. Health officials instituted sanitation and medical programs. Agricultural experts improved farm methods and production. Franciscan, Dominican, Augustinian, and Recollect friars, Spanish by birth, were replaced by American and Filipino priests.[16]

But behind this imposed American form of government there still remained the Filipino desire for independence. Such hope was a clear and vocal objective of Filipino politicians, many of whom openly supported independence and opposed the developing American colonization. The American-backed party was the *Federalistas* while those favoring immediate independence were the *Nacionalistas*. From 1907 on, the *Nacionalistas* held control of elective offices from the local level through the Philippine Assembly. *Caciquism* (political bossism) was used to great advantage by a small number of wealthy party members to secure domination of the *Nacionalista* party.[17]

In 1916, President Woodrow Wilson signed the Jones Act which carried out his aim to turn the Philippines into an independent nation. By this act, total legislative power was vested in the Filipino people although executive control remained in the hands of the governor general, appointed by the President and confirmed by the United States Senate. Wilson's governor general, Francis B. Harrison, moved to implement the act by calling for independence at an early date. He willingly acquiesced to the sharing of his powers with Sergio Osmeña, Speaker of the House of Representatives, and Manuel Quezon, President of the Senate. By 1917, Osmeña and Quezon had gained virtual dictatorial control of the *Nacionalista* party. The Jones Act in-

advertently aided their political machine in consolidating its
power.

With the change in the United States from a Democratic national administration to a Republican one in 1921, independence
was no longer advocated in Washington, D.C. In fact, during
the governorships of Leonard Wood and Henry Stimson, the
position of governor general was strengthened with a sharp cur-
tailment of Filipino governmental powers.

Internally, Filipino political leaders argued and pushed constantly for independence. In 1921, reacting to the Wood and
Forbes Commission report that the Philippines were not ready
to be set free, island political parties adopted the slogan "Immediate, absolute, and complete independence." Although independence was a popular and natural issue, many Filipinos
including some highly placed leaders, also saw the advantage
of remaining within the United States' sphere because of free
trade benefits. By the early 1930's, many psychological and
economic influences, both in the Philippines and in the United
States, led American politicians to call for an independent
nation.[18]

On December 29, 1932, the United States Congress passed the
Gare-Hawes-Cutting Bill, granting Philippine independence, following a ten-year interim period. President Herbert Hoover
vetoed the bill, but Congress overrode his veto on January 17,
1933. The act called for the Philippines to develop a constitutional form of government, subject to the approval of the
President of the United States and the people of the islands.
Once approved, a national election for officials would be held
and the ten-year transitional period would begin. At the end
of ten years, the President would declare the islands independent and all public property, with the exception of certain
military bases, would be turned over to the new nation.

During the interim, American products were to be admitted
duty free to the islands, but Philippine exports to the United
States would face increasing tariff rates. One important aspect
of the law dealt with emigration to the United States as Filipinos
moved from the status of American nationals to that of foreigners and thus became subject during the ten-year transitory period
to an annual immigration quota of fifty. After that, the general

immigration laws of the United States would apply to Filipino immigrants.

In the judgment of many Filipino leaders, the law posed economic disaster for the islands since both the sugar and tobacco interests lost their benefits. Philippine political leadership split over acceptance of the independence act. In October, 1933, forces led by Manuel Quezon, rejected the measure which had the backing of Sergio Osmeña and Manuel Roxas. Quezon led a mission to Washington, D.C., to meet with representatives of the Roosevelt administration. The best terms Quezon could obtain was a modification of the earlier act. Key economic and immigration issues remained unchanged in the Tydings-McDuffie Act of March 23, 1934.

In May, 1934, the Philippine legislature accepted Quezon's recommendations and approved the act. One year later, the people approved the constitution and the first presidential election, in September, 1935, saw Quezon elected president and one of his chief political rivals, Osmeña, vice president. They were inaugurated on November 15, 1935, and the Commonwealth of the Philippines came into being, to last until independence came on July 4, 1946.[19]

The commonwealth actually governed for only six years. On December 8, 1941, the Japanese attacked the islands and conquered them in 1942. The territorial government, installed by this new invader, quickly collapsed when American and Filipino troops returned in 1944. On July 4, 1946, President Harry S. Truman proclaimed the independence of the Philippines. Manuel Roxas was elected as its president. But the new nation was not completely free; it still had economic ties with the United States. In April, 1946, Congress passed and Truman signed two acts—the Philippine Rehabilitation Act and the Philippine Trade Act. The former act helped rebuild the war-damaged islands by advancing four million dollars, but there was an important string—allocation of these funds was conditional upon the signing of a trade act. While the terms were more generous than the 1934 Tydings-McDuffie Act, the provisions kept the islands open to American enterprise in exchange for more specific trade provisions between the two nations. The Philippines, in need of the redevelopment funds, had little choice but to accept both

measures. The United States also enacted a Filipino Naturalization Act.[20]

Having attained independence, the Philippines struggled to
become a nation during the turmoil of a postwar world. The
new government was at once confronted with an internal armed
resistance in Luzon—the Hukbalahap revolt, but survived this time
of trial which lasted for almost eight years. Secretary of Defense
Ramon Magsaysay pushed a series of reforms to help the tenant
farmers, which took the steam out of the Huk movement. Inaugurated as President in 1953, Magsaysay negotiated more
favorable trade agreements with the United States. By 1955 the
Republic of the Philippines was considered a sturdy bastion of
democracy in the Far East, an example to be emulated by other
nations.[21]

During the 1970's, various groups conducted terrorist tactics
against the government. As in former times, Moros on Mindanao
continued to fight for their independence. On September 23,
1972, President Ferdinand E. Marcos declared martial law and
early in 1973 proclaimed a new constitution which increased
the powers of the president and lengthened the term of office.
This turmoil and suspension of individual freedoms came at a
time when immigration policies in the United States were liber-
alized. Many political opponents of Marcos found it expedient to
leave. The people of the islands found that this *caciquism* at
the national level gave them a feeling of personal insecurity.

Political activism during the twentieth century played a major
part in the lives of the Filipinos. But this was only one influence.
Another important factor has been the intermarriage between
different groups. During the Spanish and American imperial
periods, marriages between recent immigrants—Americans,
Chinese, and Spanish—with Filipinos whose ancestors had arrived earlier were common. Those Filipinos with Caucasian or
Chinese racial characteristics are known as mestizos.[22] The
heterogeneous mixing between all groups has continued and
out of this, a national group, the modern-day Filipinos, has
emerged.

An examination of the various subgroups of the archipelago
and their cultures provides an understanding of the differences in
the types of Filipino immigration to the United States. Language

has divided the people of the Philippines both at home and overseas. While the precise number of languages remains under dispute, linguists have identified at least eighty-seven different dialects. Those living on islands around the Visayan Sea are affiliated with the most common language—Visayan. In 1946, some 44 percent of the Filipinos spoke some variant of Visayan. The next largest language group, Tagalog, is located in central Luzon around Manila. After independence in the 1940's, Tagalog was made the national language of the new republic, even though only some 25 percent of the people spoke the language, a fact which has made other language groups quite unhappy.

Luzon, in addition to Tagalog, has two other major languages, Ilokano and Bicol. Fifteen percent of the people of Northern Luzon spoke the former while the latter language was spoken by 8 percent of the people, the Bicolanos of Southern Luzon. Throughout the islands about 27 percent, over seven million, spoke English while a decreasing percentage, two and one-half million, spoke Spanish.[23]

In addition to language diversity resulting from the country's ethnic complexity, there are several different religions. In 1946, some 80 percent of the people were Roman Catholic while 8 percent belonged to the Philippine Independent Church. The Moros, followers of Mohammed, comprised 4 percent of the total. The American missionary effort brought only 2 percent into the stream of Protestantism. The remaining 6 percent of the population was either Buddhist, pagan cultist, or atheist.[24]

Three and one-half centuries of Spanish rule provided the cement that bound together the diverse people who lived in the Philippines. The nation was populated by people living in rural areas, abiding by rural values. By 1960, 86 percent of the people still lived in towns and villages of less than five thousand people. Manila, the economic, social, and political center of the country, had over one million residents while its immediate neighbor, Quezon, the nation's capital, had almost 400,000 residents. But on island after island, families lived together in small, integrated villages known as *barrios*. Underlying these were kinship groups. Children were born into an immediate family of parents, brothers, and sisters, and they were all part of the extended kin of blood relatives, in-laws, and godparents. Young Filipinos, as part of a kin grouping, quickly gained a strong sense of identity.

Additionally, Filipinos had several other social relationships such as work-mates, village friends, and ritual kinsmen. Anthropologists have named this an "alliance system," an interwoven network of ego-centered groupings. The key to the system was acceptance of the individual by the group. The individual, for his part, had to work to keep congenial interpersonal relationships.[25]

In those *barrios* and towns where there are Catholic Churches, villagers frequently participate in colorful religious ceremonies. Christmas and Holy Week are festival times, with elaborate feasts, dancing, and music. Christenings, marriages, and deaths are also high occasions. Death calls for ceremonial rites culminating in a fiesta in which the "alliance system" pays final honor to the departed.[26]

Village routine, day in and day out, would become monotonous if villagers did not have festivals to celebrate, or if they did not devise other means of entertainment—partly for enjoyment, partly for religious and ritualistic purposes. Many Westerners, with Calvinistic upbringing, have condemned vigorously one Filipino pastime—gambling. Throughout the islands, a favorite form of gambling is cockfighting. Held mostly on Saturdays and Sundays in the town *galleras*, the cockfights provide the opportunity to wager.

The Filipinos of the 1920's and those emigrants of the 1960's and 1970's, driven by varying political and economic reasons into leaving their homes, brought their diverse cultural backgrounds from the villages to the United States. Unfortunately for most, they encountered similar political and economic difficulties as they sought to accommodate to life in America.

CHAPTER II

Filipino Immigration–Seeking a Share of the American Dream

FILIPINOS came to the United States during the twentieth century in three general waves. The earliest, starting in 1903 and lasting until World War II, brought many young men who came in search of university and collegiate education and then planned to return to the islands. The second influx lasted from 1907 to the 1930's when workers went to the Hawaiian Islands. Surplus labor and unemployment there put a brake on this immigration. During the 1920's Filipinos also arrived in Pacific Coast states from the Philippines and the Hawaiian Islands. After 1934, with immigration regulated, West Coast ports had virtually no new arrivals. In 1946, there was an additional brief flurry of arrivals in Hawaii anticipating Philippine independence. Between 1965 and 1974, Filipino immigration increased 949.7 percent as 210,269 immigrants entered the United States in that ten-year period. The 1965 immigration act changed completely Filipino immigration patterns. During these years, this third wave provided the United States with more newcomers than any other nation, with the exception of Mexico.[1]

During William Howard Taft's administration as the Philippines' first civil governor (1901–03), educational plans called for sending promising young Filipinos to the United States. This manifestation of the "white man's burden" gained the support of many Americans as a necessary obligation. For about twenty years, Filipino students were viewed by these Americans as disciples of democracy, who, having come for the true word, would return home to inculcate the American way of life among their own people.[2]

The educational program started in August, 1903, following approval of the *Pensionado* Act. The first group of one hundred,

31

the *Pensionados,* screened from twenty thousand applicants, departed in October; by 1910 all had returned. In 1907, 183 students were enrolled in forty-seven schools and colleges. The University of Illinois, with thirteen students, had the largest number; Purdue University had eleven. They had enrolled in a variety of professional programs: education (44), civil engineering (32), agriculture (23), mechanical engineering (19), and medicine (17). The students made an excellent reputation as serious scholars.[3]

Placed in American homes, the *Pensionados* learned about life in the United States as they·concentrated on their chosen educational specialty. Only one group, those at Knoxville, Tennessee, encountered any overt racial prejudice and had to be moved to another institution.

When the *Pensionados* returned to the Philippine Islands, they encountered confusion and jealousy on the part of other Filipinos and hostility on the part of the American colonials. The former felt that the students saw themselves as superior people, working only for self-aggrandizement, while the American reaction was that the returned students had forgotten their place in "established society." During the formative years of the commonwealth, these American-trained students played important roles in agriculture, business, education, engineering, and government as their education enabled them to achieve positions of authority.[4]

The *Pensionados'* achievements attracted others to the United States as independent students. Even so, Benicio Catapusan, a student himself, estimated that through 1924 only about three or four hundred students had been trained in the United States. After 1924, the number of students increased sharply for a time and then declined during the 1930's. Catapusan has reported that between 1910 and 1938 almost fourteen thousand Filipinos enrolled in a variety of educational institutions throughout the United States. But many factors, including in particular the high cost of living, prevented many students from succeeding and forced them to drift into unskilled work. A sizeable number were handicapped by language insufficiencies, inadequate academic preparation, and an inability to ascertain whether secondary schools, colleges, or universities were appropriate to their current stage of educational development. Many of these students, like college students everywhere, lacked the strength to withstand the discouragement that attended these difficulties and moved into the world of unskilled labor.[5] By 1940 few Filipinos were enrolled in collegiate institutions. Of those who had pursued academic careers, many graduated from major universities such as California, Columbia, Cornell, Harvard, Northwestern, Southern California, Stanford, and Yale, and returned to the islands to take their places with the *Pensionados* as provincial and national leaders.[6]

The bulk of Filipino immigration between 1907 and 1935 was comprised of young males under the age of thirty. Their migration to Alaska, Hawaii, and the western states contributed to the pool of cheap, unskilled labor.

During the days when Hawaii was first a kingdom and then an American territory, plantation owners in the mid-Pacific islands had continually searched for an abundant supply of unskilled plantation and mill workers. In 1906, Albert F. Judd arrived in the Philippines to recruit such laborers. After a six-month campaign, he recruited fifteen male Ilocanos from Northern Luzon—far short of the three hundred families he had hoped to attract. On November 18, 1906, as he led his fifteen aboard the S.S. *Doric,* Judd set the pattern followed by all later recruiters of the Hawaiian Sugar Planters' Association (hereafter cited as HSPA) when he outfitted each man with warm clothing and his first pair of shoes. The fifteen arrived in Honolulu on December 20, 1906, and were assigned to the Olaa Plantation on the island of Hawaii.

When Judd left Manila, he placed the recruiting effort in the hands of George Wagner, a former resident of Hawaii. Wagner sent some one hundred and fifty laborers during 1907, but by November, the president of the sugar association deemed the project a virtual failure and recruiting was halted.[7]

Hawaii's Territorial Board of Immigration, which always responded quickly to the needs of the plantations, determined, however, in 1909 that there was no pool of workers other than in the Philippines. The Chinese, Japanese, and Koreans, recruited heavily in the past, were barred by 1909 from immigrating. Additionally, most of these Asians sought to leave the plantations

as quickly as possible for the towns to become small businessmen, day laborers, or independent farmers, while others returned
to their homelands or moved to the West Coast. Their movement caused the planters to turn to the Philippines.[8]

In April, 1909, Oswald A. Stevens and Lucius E. Pinkham
arrived in Manila to commence large-scale recruiting. Stevens
scouted for workers in the vicinity of Manila and on the island
of Cebu. He sent his recruits to Hong Kong where Pinkham
drew up labor contracts, supplied food and clothing, and
arranged transportation. The first shipload of these workers
arrived in Honolulu on July 20, 1909. By December 31, eight
other groups had arrived, bringing the year's total to 803.[9]

The HSPA had high hopes for the Filipinos. In September,
1909, Richard Ivers, president of Hawaii's Board of Immigration
informed the United States Immigration Commission that the
Philippine Islands had become the only available source of
plantation labor. By that time, some five hundred Filipinos
from the Visayan Islands had arrived. Ivers reported that they
"created a most favorable impression by their cleanliness and
apparent intelligence."[10]

Throughout 1910, the HSPA's intensive program brought 4,173
new Filipinos. One problem was the large imbalance between
men and women which portended difficulties in establishing families. Late in 1910, a wave of hostility against Filipino
immigration spread through Honolulu when it was learned that
several Filipinos on the S.S. *Mongolia* had serious cases of
amoebic dysentery, beri beri, trachoma, and tuberculosis. If
these people had been nationals of a foreign country, immigration
officials would have sent them back to their homeland. But as
wards of the United States, they were allowed to disembark.
This concern about the health hazard was but a momentary
flurry. The territorial legislature was much more concerned
about the presence of Alaska salmon cannery agents and Pacific
Coast agricultural recruiters seeking to entice away their new-
found workers.[11]

In spite of any real or potential problems, the HSPA continued recruiting in the Philippines. From 1909 to 1915, the
association paid a worker's fare to Hawaii, but he had to pay
for his return ticket. The prospect of working in the Hawaiian

Islands continued to be attractive and workers already there
voiced few complaints. But the HSPA, still confronted with
worker turnover, longed for tighter controls. Filipinos who
achieved their financial goal returned home; others migrated to
the Pacific Coast. The American government in the Philippines,
in the face of the continuing recruitment program, became concerned about the possible exploitation of Filipinos by the
planters.[12]

In 1915, a Philippine act regulated the export of workers,
set up a licensing system, charged the Bureau of Labor with
the supervision of contracts, and provided for a resident commissioner in Hawaii. The law required the HSPA's Manila office
to give each laborer a written contract before he left the islands.
The contract was binding upon the association, but not upon
the laborer. If the workers chose not to work on a plantation,
the association had no legal recourse. But the association, in
making its guarantee, fully expected the transported worker
to labor on an assigned plantation, which was what usually
happened.

The 1915 law also required that any person or corporation
doing recruiting had to be licensed. The HSPA quickly paid
six thousand pesos for its national license and secured, at an
additional five hundred pesos each, provincial licenses for Ilocos
Norte, Ilocos Sur, La Union, Manila, and Zambales on Luzon;
Capiz on Panay; and the island provinces of Cebu and
Rambolin.[13]

Prior to 1915, recruiting had centered around Manila with the
result that Tagalogs were among the earliest to emigrate. But
living near Manila gave these people a variety of economic
opportunities not readily available elsewhere in the Philippines.
Most of the Tagalogs who did go to Hawaii returned home at
the end of their contract period. Through the period of HSPA
recruitment, Tagalog emigrants were few in number, compared
to other groups. During these early years, HSPA also sought
men from the Visayan Islands. The people of Cebu, Panay, and
Rambolin who came to Hawaii became closely integrated as
Visayans, regardless of their home provinces. Interestingly,
Hawaiian Filipinos characterized the Visayans as being less

volatile than the Tagalogs, more religious, more indulgent, more outgoing, and friendly than those from Luzon.[14]

At the time of the new recruiting law, Ilocanos, who soon made up the bulk of the immigrants to Hawaii, were actively recruited. Following World War I, HSPA agents concentrated upon the provinces of Ilocos Norte, Ilocos Sur, Pangasinan, La Union, Tarlac, and Abra. Because of economic hardships and scarcity of land in their provinces, the Ilocanos willingly migrated. The Hawaiian plantation owners, by the 1930's, found the Ilocanos to be "stalwart, mild mannered, energetic and saving," and that they were the "best workers."[15]

The HSPA, faced with annual licensing fees and more restrictions, became more selective in its recruiting. Since the planters showed a preference for rural workers over those of the city, a recruiter received seven pesos ($3.50) for an unmarried worker from the provinces and five pesos ($2.50) for a worker from Manila. For every laborer who took his family with him, the recruiter earned twenty pesos ($10). Recruiters did not receive salaries but earned these commissions.[16]

The 1915 contract, developed by HSPA to conform to the recruiting law, guaranteed free subsistence, clothing, and transportation to the laborer (and his family, if any) from his home to one of the Hawaiian plantations. For signing the three-year contract, each unmarried worker was paid a bonus of ten pesos while married workers received twenty pesos. He and his family were given free housing, water, fuel, and medical attention at the plantation. Laborers assigned to the field worked a ten-hour day while those in the mills labored for twelve hours. Each worker was to work twenty-six days a month. Men earned forty pesos ($20) a month; working wives received twenty-eight pesos ($14) per month and children were paid according to the amount of work they did. At the expiration of the contract, and if they had worked a total of 720 days, workers received free transportation to their homes in the Philippines. A worker was not penalized for violating the contract but he forfeited all guarantees, including the return passage.[17]

From 1915 to 1919, recruiters sent two thousand emigrants annually to Hawaii. In 1919, Governor General Harrison sent Prudencio A. Remigio to Hawaii as a commissioner to investigate working conditions. Remigio expressed concern about the large number of Filipinos who had come to Hawaii prior to 1915 without a guaranteed return passage and those who had broken their contracts. He found that many in both groups were frustrated in their efforts to return to the Philippines.

Harrison then sent Francisco Varona in 1920 to see what solutions might be found to the continuing problems. Varona reported that there was growing unrest on the plantations, largely because of the racial intolerance of both Caucasians and Japanese. He recommended that each plantation appoint Filipino interpreters from among recognized Filipino leaders to work out problems between management and labor. Varona also negotiated the "Honolulu Contract," which gave workers who did not have return passage benefits the opportunity to gain this advantage.[18] The official reports of the two commissioners, while noting that problem areas existed, found that the plantations met their contractual obligations. But labor under contract tended to generate economic and social antagonisms.

Substantial numbers of recruits continued flowing to Honolulu through Manila from Ilocos Norte and Ilocos Sur and other rural areas. In 1920, the United States Bureau of the Census reported 21,031 Filipinos residing in Hawaii; by 1930 this number had reached 63,052, an increase of 66 percent.[19] The high point of emigration came in 1925 when 11,621 Filipinos migrated to Hawaii.

After 1925, the HSPA found it no longer necessary to recruit, for Filipinos appeared voluntarily at its Manila office. During the next six years, ending in 1931, several thousand Filipinos migrated each year. Many came with labor contracts; others recruited by private agents were promised jobs in Hawaii. As long as the Philippine Islands remained part of the United States territorial system, sugar planters seemed guaranteed a source of cheap labor. From 1909 through 1931, 112,828 Filipinos arrived in the Hawaiian Islands. Of those, 38,946 returned to their home islands while 18,607 moved to the West Coast.[20]

Filipinos from rural provinces migrated because of growing poverty, lack of available land, and increasing farm tenancy. On Cebu, a future emigrant had first to mortgage his share of his family's land in order to survive. He lamented: "Though I

worked hard daily, half of what I made I gave to my master
as every tenant had to do. Therefore, my financial affairs were
discouraging and most disappointing." Hawaii and the West
Coast offered an economic solution to young men of the
barrios.[21]

The subsequent impact of this migration upon rural villages
was twofold. The first was the actual return of the *Hawaiianos*,
a term applied to an Ilocano, who had lived in Hawaii, or on
the mainland, and had returned with some degree of financial
affluence. He was a good advertisement for Hawaii. He
demonstrated his success by buying land. In one Ilocano *barrio*,

... those Hawaiianos who came back were very showy. They
would walk around with white high-heeled shoes, even in the dust,
and wear those Amerikana suit *[sic]* and stetson hats, even on hot
days in town. They looked so rich and true they had some money
to blow on the outside.[22]

Equally important to the *Hawaiiano* was the fact that he was
back in his own culture—no longer a social outcast.

The second impact was the inflow of dollars sent from Hawaii
and the mainland which either purchased land immediately or
went into savings accounts for eventual land purchase.[23] The
Cebu emigrant who had been forced into tenancy has movingly
described his desire to own land:

My sole ambition was to save enough money to pay back the mortgage on my land. In the Philippines a man is considered independent
and is looked upon with respect by his neighbors if he possesses
land. The amount of land possessed by a person determined his
social status and wealth. My forefathers had always been wealthy
and were respected citizens of the village. Therefore, I was anxious
to uphold our family name and role in the community. To work there
in the fields with common peasants was a great disgrace and disaster to my family.[24]

The actual impulse for migration varied. Some sought, in the
view of Manuel Roxas in 1930, adventure in a land described
in Philippine schools as the place of opportunity; education
merely increased these aspirations. Roxas claimed that the

Filipino "To satisfy his wants, seeks a white collar job. He fails
to get it because of the limited opportunities at home. To him,
America is the land of promise."[25] Additionally, steamship companies, such as the Dollar Line, sent agents into provinces to
advertise the ease of transportation westward across the Pacific.
Letters from those in the United States about the good life, the
enclosure of money orders, and the presence of returned
Hawaiianos all stirred young men to want to escape from
economic difficulties and seek success in the United States.[26]

Whatever the motivation for emigration, the gathering place
was Manila. Most of those who were going to Hawaii checked
into the HSPA Manila office where they received physical examinations and were issued bedding and clothing for the trip. As
the emigrants awaited their sailing, doubts sometimes began
to enter their minds and rumors about the Hawaiian Islands
grew. One such traveler recounted:

At four o'clock the boat sailed from Manila Harbor carrying about
two hundred or perhaps more Filipino emigrants to a new land
which would mould and determine the lives of so many people.
We were all ushered to the very bottom of the boat where several
families slept on the floor on their mats in one big room. The smell
of freight and oil together with Japanese food filled the air as we sat
together like a pack of sardines in our room. Different tales concerning Hawaii were the main topics of conversation among the passengers. Some said that Hawaii had great big eagles which swept away
children from the very cradles of their homes whenever they were
hungry. . . . Some said that women and maidens were often seized
from their homes to be mates of bachelors who captured them. Others
said that some men were going to be forced to join the army.

. . . .

The boat journey was very trying. The smell of machines and food
was enough to make everyone sick. One by one became seasick for
lack of pure air. No one was allowed to go upstairs on deck. Food
was placed and served in a great bucket and the taste was very
oriental. Everyone ate bread instead of the usual rice for breakfast,
food which every hardworking Filipino cannot do without, especially
in the morning.[27]

As the immigrant ships approached Honolulu, people forgot
their sicknesses as they anticipated with some apprehension this

new venture. Upon disembarking, the immigrants were segregated by assignment to the plantations and then transported to their final destination.[28]

For about two decades, these steerage passengers from the Philippines continued to disembark in Honolulu. The last major year of migration was 1931 when 4,768 immigrants arrived. As the depression of the 1930's deepened, and with a surplus of plantation employees, immigration declined sharply. In 1932, new arrivals numbered only 232. For the years 1932–36, the total number of Filipino immigrants was 462. At the same time, as contracts expired, 19,618 Filipinos returned home. By 1940, 52,659 Filipinos lived in Hawaii, 16 percent fewer than in 1930. The bulk of these still resided in rural areas; only 6,800 lived in Honolulu.[29]

In the face of growing West Coast animosity against the Filipinos during the 1930's, the Hawaii Sugar Planters' Association grew uneasy about the permanence of its source of manpower. Even with mounting unemployment in the Hawaiian Islands, the association sought an exemption from any federal legislation which might cut off the supply from the Philippines. The planters lobbied successfully during the 1934 hearings on the Tydings-McDuffie bill. Section 8 of the bill permitted unlimited Filipino immigration to the islands whenever the need could be demonstrated. The determination of any labor shortage and the approval to import workers were vested in the Department of Interior. While this represented a major victory for the Hawaiian planters, they only asked once—in 1945—for the utilization of that section.[30]

As World War II ended, the HSPA and the Pineapple Growers' Association sought permission to bring six thousand male laborers and their families, if any, to Hawaii. On August 11, 1945, Territorial Governor Ingram M. Stainback authorized the importation. During the war, laborers, regulated under martial law, were frozen in their pre-war occupations. Even so, thousands of Filipinos received permission to work at one of the major military installations on Oahu. Few intended to return to the plantations.[31]

The sugar association again sent recruiters to the Philippines. The search centered in Northern Luzon with about 5,800 workers recruited from the provinces of the Ilocanos. Fewer than two hundred came from areas around Manila and only one was recruited from another island—Cebu. Of the six thousand workers, 3,626 were married. But only 452 wives and 909 children came. The total who entered the Territory of Hawaii in 1946, prior to Philippine independence and the end of the existing immigration regulations, was 7,361.[32]

* * * * *

Large-scale emigration of Filipino agricultural workers to the mainland coincided with the influx to Hawaii. The mainland movement, started early in 1920, continued until the depression and the Tydings-McDuffie Act which stopped any significant traffic after 1934.

The first migration of any consequence, as noted earlier, was the arrival of the *Pensionados,* though there were others. In 1903, the first Filipinos coming to the United States encountered discrimination when a group of island carpenters on their way to St. Louis to build a Philippine village at the Exposition was detained on the West Coast by immigration agents. Since workers did not have funds to pay the required head tax, the agents felt they were likely to become public charges. The United States War Department secured their release and the Commissioner General of Immigration ruled that people migrating from the Philippine Islands did not have to pay the head tax. It was as a consequence of the St. Louis Exposition of 1904, where Igorots and other tribes demonstrated village living, that some Americans gained the impression that all inhabitants of the archipelago were not too far removed from a primitive tribal stage. Hostile and prejudicial attitudes against all Filipinos resulted subsequently.[33]

In 1910, 2,767 Filipino immigrants resided in the United States, but only 406 lived outside Hawaii. The state of Washington had seventeen while California had only five. The largest mainland group of 109 was centered around New Orleans. By 1920, 5,603 Filipinos lived either in Alaska or on the mainland as young Filipinos and West Coast agriculture and the northern fisheries discovered each other.[34] Just under four thousand resided on the Pacific Coast—of these, 2,674 lived in California;

958 in Washington. The second largest regional grouping was
in the northeastern states where there were 1,844 Filipinos.

The decade of the 1920's was a period of dramatic increase—
at a time when exclusionists were working to eliminate unassimilable alien elements. During these years, some 45,000
Filipinos arrived on the Pacific coast; about 16,000 of these
came from the Hawaiian Islands. While most immigrants remained on the West Coast, many moved to Chicago, Detroit,
New York, and Philadelphia.[35]

California's Filipino population increased about 91 percent
in the 1920's. In 1930, the California Department of Industrial
Relations, in response to racist pressure, released its findings
on this most recent influx of Asians. For the ten-year period,
1920–29, just over 31,000 disembarked at the ports of San Francisco and Los Angeles. In 1923, 2,426 were admitted; one-third
of these came from Hawaii, where a major sugar strike was in
progress. The failure of the strike and subsequent blacklisting of
strikers accounted for large numbers from Hawaii the next year
as well. The high point was reached in 1929 with 5,795 arrivals.
The California study estimated that 35 percent of the total
number of immigrants arrived directly from Manila, 56 percent
moved from the Hawaiian Islands, and the remaining 9 percent
came from Asian seaports such as Hong Kong, Shanghai, Kobe,
and Yokahama.[36]

Most of those Filipinos who came during the 1920's were
single young males. One-third were between sixteen and twenty-
one years of age while another 48 percent were in the 22–29
year range. In 1930, by comparison, only 23 percent of California's
total population was less than thirty years old. State compilers
also saw the unbalanced sex ratio as a danger—a view endorsed
by white exclusionists. For persons of Filipino descent, the ratio
was fourteen males to one female while for the total population
it was 1.1 male to one female. While about 22 percent of those
Filipino men migrating to California were married, only 12
percent brought their wives. The Department of Industrial Relations observed with some alarm that Filipino and Mexican
immigrants had more single persons in their groups than did
any other contingent of aliens being admitted to the United

States.[37] The department had forgotten earlier charges of a similar nature made against the Chinese and Japanese.

Most of the 1920 immigrants had little formal education and spoke neither English nor Spanish. Upon arrival, these new-comers sought jobs—both in urban and rural areas. They were immediately herded, or manipulated, by others into a variety of occupations. Carey McWilliams estimated that in 1930 about twenty thousand Filipinos worked in West Coast agriculture; some eleven thousand were employed as servants or in hotels and restaurants; and another 4,200 labored in Alaska salmon canneries.[38]

As racial fervor climaxed in the 1930's, Filipino unemploy-ment and the inability of these American nationals to secure federal relief in Pacific Coast states relayed the message to other young men of the Philipines not to come.[39] And many in the United States returned home. By 1940 the Filipino population on the mainland and in Alaska hardly increased over the 1930 census count while in California the number increased by 928, a major slowdown when compared to the 1920's. Hawaii's Filipino population declined significantly—9,725 less than in 1930; most of these returned home at the completion of their labor contracts.[40]

The Tydings-McDuffie Act of 1934 brought immigration to a virtual halt. During the spring of 1934, Filipinos who still hoped to migrate to the mainland bought steerage tickets in the face of the uncertainity of immigration limitation to be imposed by the act. In early April, 160 Filipinos sailed on the S.S. *President Hoover* in an attempt to reach San Francisco and clear im-migration before the 50-per-year quota went into effect. On April 26, 1934, the *San Francisco Chronicle* reported the S.S. *President Grant* left Manila without a single Filipino passenger; the newspaper stated that the Dollar Line was not accepting any reservations until the exact status of immigration was solved.[41] One of the exclusionists' goals was being realized.

By the outbreak of World War II, immigration to the main-land United States had stabilized at a very low level. After the war, immigration resumed and the number of arrivals kept in-creasing from a 1948 level of 1,122 to the early 1960's when the annual rate had reached three thousand.[42] Between 1940 and

1960 the Filipino population in the United States increased by almost 78,000. While Hawaii, the newest state, had the largest number of Filipinos in 1960, the West Coast showed the greatest increase; its number more than doubled in twenty years.[43]

In the 1950's California agriculture sought to reverse the 1930 position of exclusionists by calling for the importation of Filipino and Japanese labor as an alternative to the bracero program—the use of unskilled Mexican labor. In 1956, the California Vegetable Growers Association, Governor Goodwin Knight, and United States Secretary of Labor James Mitchell signed an importation agreement. A year later, fifteen Filipino farm laborers arrived, the vanguard of one thousand, and signed a three-year labor contract, which set the minimum number of days of employment and wage levels. Each worker had to pay his own transportation costs. Plans, calling for assigning the one thousand workers near the California agricultural centers of Santa Maria, Salinas, San Jose, Fresno, and Marysville, were not successful because of American labor union hostility. By 1960 the California Department of Employment reported that there were only twenty Filipino nationals working under contract.[44]

Between 1960 and 1970 Filipino population in the United States again doubled with more than half of the increase occurring in California and Hawaii. For the first time since Filipinos started migrating in 1909, California replaced Hawaii as the state with the largest number in residence. Major American cities such as Honolulu, Los Angeles, San Francisco, San

TABLE II

FILIPINO IMMIGRANTS ADMITTED INTO THE
UNITED STATES, 1965–1974[a]

YEAR	NUMBER	YEAR	NUMBER
1965	3,130	1970	31,203
1966	6,093	1971	28,471
1967	10,865	1972	29,376
1968	16,731	1973	30,799
1969	20,744	1974	32,857

[a]U.S. Department of Justice, Immigration and Naturalization Service, *Annual Report, 1974*, pp. 3 & 59.

Diego, Seattle, Chicago, and New York continued to receive substantial numbers.[45]

The immigrants of the 1960's and 1970's were vastly different from those who had come fifty to sixty years earlier. After 1965, both male and females were attracted to the United States. Many were well educated. The influx consisted of families which contributed large numbers of school age youth and senior citizens.[46]

Hawaii, since 1966, has received more immigrants in proportion to its total population than has any other state. Such an impact made for a greater awareness of resulting problems. Because of their high visibility, Filipinos have received considerable attention from state officials. In December, 1971, the University of Hawaii School of Social Work, in a study for the state immigration service, interviewed a representative sample of five hundred people. Most of the new immigrants, like the earlier ones, were Ilocanos—461. Only twenty were Tagalogs and fourteen were Visayans. Almost all had grown up in either a *barrio* or a town; about two-thirds of the adults had a high school education and a large number had received some form of higher education.[47]

These new arrivals faced problems similar to those which confronted the earlier immigrants to Hawaii and the mainland. The first, and most serious, problem in Honolulu was to find living space in a city where housing was in short supply. A solution, which was not satisfactory, was to move in with relatives or to rent a small apartment. A second concern was locating suitable employment, particularly difficult for the better educated who were unable to find positions comparable to those they had just left. As with every immigrant group, social adjustment was difficult for their culture conflicted with that of Hawaii.[48]

In seventy years of migration to the United States, Filipino immigrants have always been plagued by adjustment problems and have found it difficult to locate and keep suitable employment. As a color-visible minority, they have continually encountered prejudice and discrimination as they pursued their objectives—economic or educational. In the face of these hardships, Filipinos have continued to migrate. Many have achieved their goals; many, many more have been frustrated and embittered by their experiences in the United States.

CHAPTER III

Citizenship for Filipinos

A CONTINUING problem for Filipinos in the United States prior to July 2, 1946, was the issue of citizenship. Filipinos had been classified since 1898 as American nationals and remained in that status until the 1946 act provided for their naturalization.

West Coast exclusionists during the depression years used a campaign of hate and fear to oppose both Filipino immigration and citizenship. In 1929, when the Commonwealth Club of California examined Filipino immigration, its study section reported that the Filipinos' education did not fit them for American society. Admittedly based on incomplete evidence, the study found the Filipinos to be belligerent and a public health liability. Morally and socially, the Filipinos did not improve life in the United States, for the absence of home life and Filipino women led them into undesirable associations with white women. The report further stated that Filipinos did not spend their wages properly, lived extravagantly, and engaged in gambling. The Commonwealth Club thus reinforced complaints of economic competition, improper sexual relationships, and problems of health, crime, and vice.[1]

Carey McWilliams claimed that a Los Angeles Chamber of Commerce official denounced the Filipinos as "the most worthless, unscrupulous, shiftless, diseased, semi-barbarians that ever came to our shores."[2] A viewpoint that gained statewide acceptance was made by Northern Monterey County Justice of the Peace D.W. Rohrback who charged the Filipinos with being disease carriers, destroying the American wage scale, and attempting to allure young American and Mexican girls. The judge asserted that Filipinos, migrating from a very primitive society, were able to live fifteen in one room and to sustain themselves

46

on only rice and fish.³ In short, they corroded American standards of labor and morality.

In January, 1936, San Francisco Municipal Court Judge Sylvain Lazarus commented during a case involving a Filipino: "It is a dreadful thing when these Filipinos, scarcely more than savages, come to San Francisco, work for practically nothing, and obtain the society of these girls. Because they work for nothing, decent white boys cannot get jobs."⁴ Such attitudes by the white Establishment did little toward its understanding adjustment problems facing Filipinos and much toward making the right of citizenship difficult to acquire.

As West Coast exclusionists argued against Filipino immigration and sought ways to exclude this "third Asian invasion," they encountered a unique problem. The 1898 Treaty of Paris made the Philippines part of the United States and all Filipinos were American nationals until the islands gained their independence. Congress appeared to resolve the question of United States citizenship in 1902 when it declared that all residents of the Philippine Islands who were Spanish subjects as of April 11, 1899, and their subsequent children were thereafter citizens of the Philippine Islands.⁵ Congress then confused the issue by passing an act in 1906 which indicated that any person owing allegiance to the United States might, under certain circumstances, apply for citizenship. Additionally, opinions differed over the interpretation of the 1790 statute which had provided that only "free white persons" were eligible for citizenship.⁶

For about a decade, several people sought to prove that the 1906 act repealed Section 2169, *Revised Statutes*, but the courts consistently rejected this view. When a Filipino, who was one-fourth Caucasian and three-fourths Malay, held that Section 2169 did not apply, the court denied his application because he was not a white person. In 1916, a federal court decided that the son of a Filipino mother and a father who was half Filipino and half Spanish was not a white person and therefore not eligible.⁷ But on November 5, 1917, a federal district court judge in California ruled that a Filipino who owed allegiance to the United States was entitled to naturalization.⁸ This favorable decision was offset in May, 1918, when the 1906 act was amended.

While new legislation allowed Filipinos and Puerto Ricans who had enlisted and served three years in the United States Navy, Marine Corps, or the Naval Auxiliary Service, and received an honorable discharge, to petition for citizenship, the amending act especially noted that Section 2169 was in no manner changed.[9] In 1919, a federal district court in New York determined that the 1918 amendment, limited only to those who had served in the armed forces named, excluded all other aliens who did not meet the requirement of Section 2169. Any questions raised by the 1906 and 1918 laws and the *Revised Statutes* were settled by the United States Supreme Court when it declared in *Toyota v. United States* that only whites or persons of African descent were entitled to citizenship. The 1918 amendmen for qualified Filipinos did remain in force.[10]

The 1917 immigration law noted that while most Filipinos could not become citizens, they were not considered aliens. This status of "national" was continued in the 1924 immigration act which specified that they were not aliens and were free to enter the United Sates. This proviso remained in force until May 1, 1934, when the Philippine legislature accepted the Tydings-McDuffie Independence Act's annual quota of fifty immigrants.[11]

Prior to Philippine independence in 1946, Filipinos travelling beyond the territorial limits of the United States or the Philippines had carried United States passports, which gave them the apparent status of citizenship. However, the residents of the Philippines had only the "fundamental rights" of life, liberty, and property as set forth in the Insular Cases.[12] While the question of citizenship rights for Filipinos continued during the 1930's, the courts always held to a strict interpretation of the law.[13]

Without citizenship, Filipinos were closed out of certain professions and had difficulty obtaining marriage licenses. In the early 1930's, the United States Civil Service Commission allowed them to take examinations to qualify for federal jobs but each state had its own rules pertaining to Filipino nationals and their professional licensing. The District of Columbia, Indiana, and Michigan allowed Filipinos to practice law, medicine, and other licensed professions. New York, on the other hand, required that a Filipino be a citizen in order to take the bar examination and that he must have declared an intention of becoming a citizen in order to practice medicine. The Filipinos, for their part, did not have access to any recognized voice of protest against this economic discrimination as did aliens who had foreign offices to back them.[14] Even with the granting of citizenship in 1946, some professions remained closed. While it was possible, for example, through reciprocity for a graduate of the medical school of the University of the Philippines to apply to practice in California, the decision rested solely with the state board of medical examiners.[15]

Filipinos found it difficult early in the New Deal to qualify for federal relief. One Filipino wrote in 1934: "If Filipinos are not considered United States citizens, . . . why does the American government register Filipinos, hire them for city projects and then let CWA [Civil Works Administration] officials fire them?"[16] It was certainly true that, with jobs in short supply, the one important screening which the Filipinos could not pass was eligibility for citizenship. In 1937, Harry Hopkins, head of the Works Progress Administration, indicated that the United States Attorney General had restated in an opinion that Filipinos were nationals. While they were eligible for employment on WPA projects, the ruling stated they could not be given preference since they were not citizens.[17]

Other cases of employment discrimination against Filipino nationals were reported by Joaquin M. Elizalde, Resident Commissioner to the United States. In 1939, Elizalde protested unsuccessfully against the Merchant Marine Act which required that crews on fishirg vessels be 75 percent American. This law increased Filipino unemployment in Baltimore, New Orleans, and New York. Testifying before the Senate Committee on Territories and Insular Possessions in 1939, Elizalde also called attention to the "particular case of Filipino civil service employees who have honestly and loyally given the best of their useful lives to the United States government, but who . . . may find themselves in an undefined and unclarified status, and faced with menacing danger of losing their life-long means of subsistence."[18]

While exclusionists, in and out of Congress, wanted to stop immigration and to repatriate those Filipinos in the United States, other Americans suggested amending the naturalization

laws to include Filipinos. Senator Elbert D. Thomas of Utah
in 1938 and 1939 introduced measures to naturalize them. Before
and during World War II, several bills were introduced by Representative Vito Marcantonio of New York City to grant citizenship to Filipinos who were permanent residents.[19] Sentiment
grew that these American nationals should have equal status
with the Chinese who in 1943 had become eligible for naturalization. But Congress passed no such law for the Filipinos during
the war.[20]

On July 2, 1946, just two days prior to the granting of Philippine independence, Congress enacted legislation making Filipinos
eligible for citizenship. On July 4, President Harry S. Truman
issued a proclamation setting the annual immigration quota at
one hundred. This quota remained in effect for two decades. In
1946 and again by virtue of the 1952 immigration law, all
Filipinos who had come to the United States prior to 1934 and
had resided permanently in the United States were eligible for
naturalization. Also eligible were citizens of the Philippines
who came with a certificate of arrival. With the nullification of
the quota system in 1965, all who entered the United States
legally were eligible for citizenship.[21]

Prior to 1946, Filipinos in the United States encountered some
legal discrimination in areas other than professional licensing
which restricted their activities. The outbreak of World War
II and the struggle for the Philippines made for an unusual
situation. While fighting for freedom across the Pacific, the
United States denied it to Filipinos within its borders. Many
Filipinos attempted to volunteer for military service but the
existing law made no provision for the enlistment of nationals.
They were also denied employment in defense factories.

On March 6, 1942, President Roosevelt opened the way for
Filipinos to work in government and in war industry. Earlier,
on February 19, Secretary of War Henry Stimson announced the
formation of the First Filipino Infantry Regiment.[22] The
President, by proclamation, changed the draft law to include
Filipinos. Classified first as 4-C, they were moved to 1-A and
eligible to be drafted. A subsequent problem developed about
where a Filipino might best serve—in the military or as a civilian.
California agricultural associations, some of which had called

for exclusion, now sought draft deferments for their field laborers. Filipinos were informed that they would be exempt from military service if they remained on the farms. Two associates of President Quezon during visits to the Pacific Coast both recommended that the workers remain on the farms until drafted but the two differed on whether or not to seek exemption. By the winter of 1942, thousands of former farm laborers were working for the war effort in western industry.[23]

While the Filipinos could enlist, be drafted, or work in war industry, entry into the professions and the right to own real estate remained restricted. The evacuation of the Japanese from the West Coast in 1942 made it essential to find people to operate the evacuated property. While farm loans were made available to Mexicans and Filipinos, land laws, California's in particular, prevented the Filipinos from owning or leasing farm land because of their ineligibility for citizenship.[24]

In February, 1941, the Washington state supreme court ruled that Filipinos could own land. But in March, 1943, Alfredo Mendova was told in California, as he applied for citizenship, that he could not own land even if he became a citizen. The Philippine Resident Commissioner worked with California's Attorney General to reinterpret those provisions. The Attorney General held that the Filipinos were not controlled by the alien land laws, making it possible to lease lands, particularly Japanese holdings, but Filipinos still could not purchase land in California. The Filipinos also had difficulty securing bank credit and ran into problems in marketing their produce.[25]

In February, 1943, the First Filipino Regiment, in training at Fort Ord and Camp Roberts, was transferred to Camp Beale, Marysville, California. There, as the United States government prepared to grant citizenship to about one thousand Filipinos, the solidiers' reaction was: "On that Sunday in February in Marysville, we knew we had been looking at another mirage of democracy, that the reality was a gruesome thing." Even as they took the oath on February 20, many wondered, "What good would it do to become citizens of America if we are still brown-skinned inferiors?"[26] Filipinos in military service had the right, after three months, to apply for United States citizenship. If they did not do so then, they had a six months' period follow-

ing the end of the war in which to file. They could also apply
after receiving an honorable discharge during the war.[27]

Four years after it had been organized, the First Filipino
Regiment "came home" to San Francisco. The *San Francisco
Chronicle* reported that 555 men, all Filipino, mostly from
California, had returned. In prestige, the unit closely equalled
the record of the 442nd Regiment, of Nisei fame. But unlike
the 442nd, the role of the Filipinos in the Pacific was not widely
known. The regiment had been organized with one primary
task in mind—pre-invasion intelligence work. Six months before the Leyte Gulf landing on October 20, 1944, the First
Reconnaissance Battalion was ashore gathering information and
organizing the guerrillas. The rest of the regiment participated
in the campaigns for the islands of Samar and Leyte. Following
the war's end, eight hundred of the regiment elected to remain
in the Philippines with the American army while five hundred
of those who returned reenlisted.[28]

Prior to World War II, the Filipinos, subjected to the same
covert economic and social discrimination as other Asians, were
overtly denied fewer civil rights. The only direct legislation
aimed against them involved mixed marriages. As a consequence
of California's laws, many couples who wanted to marry lived
together without benefit of clergy. So reported Iris Buaken of
her marriage to her husband, Manuel. With the awarding of
citizenship to those in the First Filipino Regiment, many thought
they were free to legalize their marriages. This was important
because the army would not give family allowances or designate
any "common law" wife as an insurance beneficiary. The regi-
mental chaplain appealed to Governor Earl Warren and to the
California legislature, but to no avail. Thus the Red Cross
loaned money and the army granted emergency furloughs so
that the men and women could travel to New Mexico to become
legally married before the regiment went overseas.[29]

White Californians had long been opposed to Asian males
marrying their daughters. In 1901, Californians had enacted a
law forbidding whites to marry blacks, Mongolians, or mu-
lattoes.[30] Although California Attorney General U.S. Webb
believed, in the early 1930's, that Filipinos were Mongolians,
his opinion did not have the force of a judicial decision. Each

county clerk could make his own interpretation as to the racial origin of Filipinos.[31] In 1931, the Los Angeles County Clerk, accepting Webb's interpretation, denied a marriage license to Salvador Roldan, who then filed suit against the county. Claiming that the term, Mongolian, did not include Filipinos, Roldan was successful in both superior and appellate courts. In 1933, the county appealed to the California Supreme Court which upheld the decisions of the two lower courts on the grounds that the state legislature had not specifically forbidden marriages between whites and Filiipinos.[32] The California legislature quickly closed this loophole in 1933 by amending the state's civil code to include persons of the Malay race in the list of people whom whites could not marry. This action, which nullified the court decision, was soon imitated by other state legislatures.[33] By 1937, Nevada, Oregon, and Washington had enacted laws prohibiting marriages between Filipinos and whites.[34]

California's miscegenation law was eventually ruled unconstitutional in the 1948 case of *Perez v. Sharp*. The California Supreme Court held that legislation limiting the right of members of one race to marry those of another race was a violation of civil rights. Such laws, the court stated, had to be based upon more than "prejudice and must be free from oppressive discrimination."[35] During the year following the *Perez* decision, some 21,060 marriage license applications were issued in Los Angeles County. Of these, one hundred could be classified as interracial, and Filipinos comprised most of them—forty males and two females.[36]

In addition to legal discrimination, there were, from time to time, incidents of violence against Filipinos. In California and Washington, hostility manifested itself in acts of individual violence and riots. As early as 1926, street fights between whites and Filipinos were reported in Stockton as the New Year celebration got out of hand. A number of white men were stabbed and several Filipinos badly beaten. One year later, two hundred men fought in the streets of Seattle.[37] Vigilante committees, in Washington's Yakima Valley in 1928, grew out of white farm workers' fears that they would be replaced by Filipinos. On September 19, 1928, the white workers forced the Filipinos to leave the valley. Two days later at Wenatchee, Washington, two hundred whites descended upon a camp of twenty Filipinos and forced them to flee.[38]

California's most violent discrimination came through vigilante action. The motives of the whites were based in part upon the fear of economic competition and in part upon concerns about Filipino relationships with white women. The state's first serious riot occurred on October 24, 1929, when a Filipino stabbed a white man at a carnival in the San Joaquin Valley town of Exeter. Prior to the stabbing, white farm workers had molested and shoved Filipinos off the town's sidewalks in an effort to intimidate them into leaving the region. At the carnival, whites threw objects at the Filipinos, particularly those escorting white women. This provoked the knifing. Following the stabbing, a mob, estimated at three hundred, rushed to the nearest ranch employing Filipinos and burned the barn. The Filipinos had fled before the mob arrived.[39]

The most explosive California vigilante incident occurred in January, 1930, near Watsonville. This farm area, with many specialty crops, depended upon large numbers of transient farm workers. By the late 1920's, farmers had come to rely upon Filipino contract labor, which migrated to the region from other parts of the state, to harvest the crops. This dependence upon nonwhite labor sowed the seeds for conflict, for Watsonville was a town not prepared to accommodate such an influx. Soon white inhabitants of the community were voicing a common complaint about Filipino transients who spent their money on flashy clothes and new cars in order to attract white women. The whites' growing resentment was perhaps best expressed by the anti-Filipino resolution adopted by the Northern Monterey County Chamber of Commerce.

Whereas, any foreign people coming to the United States of America whose customs, habits and standards of living prohibit them from assimilating and adopting our standard of living, are detrimental and dangerous to social conditions, and

Whereas, the unrestricted immigration into the state of California of natives of the Philippines is viewed with alarm both from a moral and sanitary standpoint while constituting a menace to white labor, therefore be it

Resolved, That we . . . petition . . . to prevent further immigration.[40]

Judge Rohrback, a leader of the Chamber of Commerce and a respected community leader, added to the growing hostility with his announcement that Filipinos "possessed unhealthy habits and were destructive to the living wage scale" of others. He categorized them as "little brown men attired like 'Solomon in all his glory,' strutting like peacocks and endeavoring to attract the eyes of young American and Mexican girls."[41]

At the same time that Watsonville citizens were becoming highly agitated about the presence of the farm workers, a small Filipino group leased a dance hall in Palm Beach, a few miles west of Watsonville on Monterey Bay. About a dozen white women were engaged as professional dance partners. The thought of white women dancing with Filipinos led to demonstrations by self-appointed white vigilantes—demonstrations which started on January 19 and lasted through January 23. On the 20th, about two hundred armed men searched the streets for Filipinos, and, on the next night, raided the dance hall. On the 22nd, a mob of five hundred went to nearby farms and fired shots into the camp buildings. One Filipino was killed, several were beaten, and much property destroyed. Following this outbreak of violence, community leaders belatedly formed a law-and-order group to put down the vigilantes.[42]

California continued to experience anti-Filipino assaults. In December, 1930, a bomb was thrown into a building in Imperial, killing one Filipino and wounding several others. Two white men were arrested; one was found guilty of manslaughter.[43] At Escalon, in August, 1933, fifty white men drove twenty-one Filipinos out of town. In 1934, following anti-labor strong-arm tactics in Salinas, Filipinos fled to other areas. Many moved to Modesto where, on September 11, night riders gave Filipinos two hours to evacuate because they feared wage cutting among grape pickers. White workers were receiving $1.50 to $1.70 a ton while Filipinos were willing to pick for 90 cents to $1.00.[44]

Legislation and violence had been two weapons often used by exclusionists in the past against Chinese and Japanese. Violence had had only a short-run effect. Now fearing a third flood of Orientals, the whites set out to eliminate Filipino immigration through legislation. Encouraged by organizations such as the American Legion, the California Federation of Labor, the Com-

monwealth Club of California, and the racist California Joint
Immigration Committee, the 1929 California legislature asked
Congress to restrict the immigration of Filipinos because cheap
labor "has had a tendency towards destruction of American
ideals and American racial unity."[45] Unlike other Asians, the
Filipinos, however, enjoyed the unique status of being American
nationals with certain rights that exclusionists found impossible
to deny.

This different status did not daunt the exclusionists, however.
At the federal level, Richard Welch, a San Francisco Congressman, introduced exclusion and repatriation legislation. Nativist
and humanitarian motives were entwined in these proposals.
While there was an outright push to eliminate Filipino immigration, there was some concern about the plight of the immigrant
farm workers in California. During the depression, Filipinos
were among the first workers to be laid off. In 1931, the Philippine Society of California, comprised of recently arrived Filipino
immigrants, urged the federal government to use army trans-
ports to take unemployed Filipinos home. The society found
that thousands of Filipinos wanted to go home, but did not have
funds to purchase a ticket. Members of the society, who wanted
to maintain the option of open access to the mainland for
Filipinos, hoped that this voluntary return of the unemployed
would reduce the clamor for complete exclusion.[46] But this hope
dimmed as white racists continued to push for their goals.

Repatriation, another exclusionist aim, was considered for
several years by the House Committee on Immigration and
Naturalization. Although cleared for House action by the committee in 1933, final passage of a repatriation bill did not come
until 1935. The legislation provided that transportation would be
provided at federal expense for those who wanted to return
to the Philippines. Those who accepted this aid lost any right
of immediate reentry and could return only as part of the annual
quota of fifty immigrants.[47] Repatriation, as an exclusionist tool,
did not work, for only 2,190 of the 45,000 Filipinos resident in
the United States took advantage of the federal legislation.[48]

Actually, the exclusionists' efforts were largely unnecessary
for with the collapse of the American economy in the early
1930's and the creation of a farm labor surplus, Filipinos stopped

migrating in any large numbers. The objective of exclusion was at the same time essentially achieved with the establishment of the small quota by the Tydings-McDuffie Independence Act.

The granting of citizenship in 1946 provided Filipinos with the opportunity to fight the exclusionists and their attempted legal discrimination. The Filipinos' newly acquired status also provided the means by which they could seek economic and social rights.

CHAPTER IV

Problems of Accommodating to Life in America, 1920–1940

FILIPINOS migrating to Hawaii and the mainland United States from 1920 to 1940 were considered "birds of passage." Juan C. Dionisio, a member of President Quezon's government in exile, conveyed the feelings held by California Filipinos he had interviewed during World War II:

> The tragedy of our life in America . . . is that it has been predicated on wishful thinking—"I want to go home." We have been sentimental rather than realistic. "Why should I plan, why should I take life seriously here, when this is only an interlude in my life? I am going home. It is there where I am going to take root."
>
> Birds of passage, Mr. President, do not plan. They drift aimlessly.[1]

Those new arrivals who found ready employment during the late 1920's in unskilled urban or agricultural labor frequently misunderstood the attitude of countrymen who had been in the United States for some time. Newcomers quickly discovered that long and hard hours of work dulled one's outlook and that color and language set them apart from the American majority. Young Filipinos became lonely and began to regret their decision to migrate. Cut off in an alien world, they turned to prostitutes, dance halls, and gambling establishments to offset their isolation. Other Filipinos in these years made a satisfactory adjustment to American life. They earned the needed money, or completed their studies, and returned home. Others became economically successful in skilled labor, the trades, or the professions. Some of these married and made their new homes in the United States.[2] Unhappily, many of the 45,000 Filipinos in America could not easily adjust to their new environment. At the height of the

West Coast immigration in the 1920's, D. F. Gonzalo, after investigating the degree of accommodation made by Filipinos, concluded:

Perhaps the most outstanding characteristic . . . is the lack of any tangible aim in life. . . . The conflicts of adjustment seem to have reduced to ashes the fires of their enthusiasm in the earlier days. . . . They are either bitter or resigned, in their attitude toward life.

Many of the immigrants in this group wish to go home but they have not enough concentration left to earn the money with which to pay their way. Some hesitate to go back as a consequence of their failure to make good their early dreams. Others have lost much of the sense of responsibility even to themselves and have become dependent upon the goodness and hospitality of their countrymen.

. . . .

The simple reason for this is that the Filipino labor immigrant does not have the background which is necessary for a successful adjustment in America where, practically, every wage earner is a specialist in his own trade. There are other factors which bar him from a better contact with real American life. . . . It is true that he feels nearer to the American than any other Oriental does but experience teaches him soon enough that in earning a livelihood and in trying to get ahead those feelings count little, if any.[3]

West Coast and Hawaiian residents reacted to the Filipino influx in various ways. Those who relied upon "cheap" labor saw them as necessary and could abide the resulting problems. Racists, who had long fought Chinese and Japanese immigration, rose to the occasion during the 1920's and 1930's to spread the word about new dangers. By 1930 Californians who came into contact with Filipinos tended to have negative value judgments about them. Some West Coast residents, whose attitudes were largely paternalistic, employed Filipinos as house boys or observed them casually in hotels or restaurants, and tolerated them in these service jobs.

Those Americans, however, who came to know the Filipinos as individuals did not share in racist attitudes but accepted them as equals.[4] A more prevalent white view was that Filipinos were savages, not far removed from the tribal state. Some American missionaries, self-professed friends of the Filipinos, furthered public apprehension as they recounted the primitive conditions of some rural Filipino tribes. A young Japanese woman in Hawaii also viewed the Filipinos with much concern:

When the Filipinos were first brought into the camps, they were thought of as being "cannibalistic" and "savage-like," because of their views of living. This first group of Filipinos were considered "filthy," unapproachable, and had tastes for wild weeds and grass. They smoked a lot of the strong, offensive, nauseating, Filipino "rope" tobacco anywhere with no consideration of others. They would stage "cock fights" during week-ends and end it up either in a fight or stabbing. In general people feared them. Weird tales were told about the head-hunters in the Philippines. Sometimes these Filipinos would proudly flash their small automatic knives on which the blades open with a slight touch of a button on a knife. This display of knives meant a warning to other racial groups. People were afraid to go near them for fear that if one would displease them, his life would be in danger.[5]

Unthinking acceptance of such beliefs made possible the growth of exclusionist propaganda and the fear of workers about loss of their jobs. Similar views led to increased apprehension by farm owners who were afraid of their unskilled laborers becoming militant.[6]

One major economic factor causing hard feelings was the willingness of rural and urban Filipinos to work for wages not acceptable to American workers.[7] Social problems grew out of economic difficulties. Discrimination, arising from "uncritical thinking" and "plain prejudice," frustrated the Filipinos' attempt at social advancement. Their open interest in white women remained an explosive issue for white America. Americans saw in alleged low morals a tendency to a life of crime and a reputation of unreliability. Other reasons also gave them sufficient justification to keep Filipinos at arm's length.[8]

Over the years, certain stereotypes about Filipinos developed both in Hawaii and on the mainland. In some circles, a controversial description, current in Hawaii in the 1930's, of Visayan migrants suggested that they were "decidedly improvident and shiftless." Their ambition was "to live as nearly as possible like the lilies of the field—without toiling or spinning—and yet to be arrayed like Solomon."[9] On the other hand, the Ilocanos at the same time were viewed as "hard-worker[s], thrifty, industrious." While there was common agreement about such characteristics, some regarded the Ilocanos as having shortsighted planning capacities. Opponents also saw them as violent and hot-tempered people, full of "jungle fear," leading frequently to crimes of passion. The claim was also advanced that they were braver and more violent as a mob than as individuals.[10] One stereotypical newspaper account in 1931 reported a tribal fight had broken out in Salinas after ten Visayans entered a pool hall, armed with billiard cues, and started beating thirty Ilocanos. By the time the police arrived, about one hundred Filipinos were fighting in the street. One was killed, four hospitalized, and nineteen arrested, fifteen of whom were quickly released.[11]

White racists found many outlets for their warped perceptions about the newly arrived immigrants. Dr. William C. Hobdy, a long-time public health official in Honolulu, writing in the hostile *Seamen's Journal,* stated in 1928: "The typical Filipino child is short of stature, underweight, malnourished, pot-bellied, bandy-shanked and afflicted with intestinal parasites. I can hardly conceive of my son or daughter or any of my grandchildren intermarrying with these people."[12] The "tragic results" of such marriages were always in the forefront of racist arguments. C. M. Goethe, a prominent Californian and a leader in discrimination against Asians, wrote that: "The Filipino tends to interbreed with near-moron white girls. The resulting hybrid is almost invariably undesirable. The ever increasing brood of children of Filipino coolie fathers and low-grade white mothers may in time constitute a serious social burden."[13]

Filipinos have commented freely about the racial prejudice they encountered in the United States. Those who came during the 1920's were perplexed, as have been other color minorities, about the dichotomy between American democratic philosophy and actual practice. One Filipino, interviewed by the Social Science Institute of Fisk University, demonstrated his confusion and vented his anger by saying:

If I had the one chance of my life to express what I feel deepest about America and Americans, I would say that the white race is supe-

rior in either doing good or bad for others than any of the dark or
colored races. The Americans can be the most generous people on
earth towards other people and at the same time be unkind or un-
christian in their dealings with the same, when they come face to
face with each other.

The Americans are stupid when it comes to understanding foreign
people because they think of themselves at their best and of the
foreigners at their worst. They do not take any time to stop and
think that foreigners, especially my people, have a different psy-
chology and civilization.[14]

Carlos Bulosan in 1937 confirmed this confusion in this
poignant expression about his sad recollection of his experiences
in the United States:

... Western people are brought up to regard Orientals or colored
peoples as inferior, but the mockery of it all is that Filipinos are
taught to regard Americans as our equals. Adhering to American
ideals, living American life, these are contributory to our feeling of
equality. The terrible truth in America shatters the Filipinos' dream
of fraternity.

I was completely disillusioned when I came to know this American
attitude. If I had not been born in a lyrical world, grown up with
honest people and studied about American institutions and racial
equality in the Philippines I should never have minded so much
the horrible impact of white chauvinism. I shall never forget what
I have suffered in this country because of racial prejudice.[15]

In their day-to-day living, Filipinos found their dark skins and
their imperfect English did indeed set them apart. On the
West Coast they were frequently denied service in restaurants
and barberships, barred from swimming pools, movies, and
tennis courts.[16]

The impact of prejudice shook those who had had contact
with the teachings of Christianity in the Philippines. Many
were stunned by the double standards maintained by white
Christians. One Filipino stated:

During my active membership in church, it always puzzled me
to find that many members of the same church would converse with
me congenially in the church but when I met them in the streets or in

school or later on in college they acted as if ashamed to talk to me, even more so when they were with their friends. And when sometimes I would talk with them in spite of their being with their friends, they looked embarrassed and indicated that I should not appear to be knowing them.[17]

Another had this to say:

... in my disgust, we've found even in churches Filipinos are not welcome. If they are welcome they are seated in a corner, and one sees all the pews crowded but those around Filipinos are empty. It's bad enough for theaters to do it, but churches! ... No wonder why so many Filipinos think of American Christians as hypocrites. No wonder the taxi-dance halls exist, for if the Filipinos aren't welcome in Churches and in Christian homes and other so-called decent places, where else could they go?[18]

Most white Californians were unaware of the contradictions that their attitudes created. One segment of white society welcomed Filipinos to the state because they provided cheap labor. But white prejudicial and discriminatory attitudes relegated them to low levels of economic and social existence. As a consequence, many Californians, critical of the Filipino's substandard living conditions, attacked them for creating health problems and lowering the American standard of living.

Californians, in particular, have had a long record of discrimination in real estate, and Filipinos found housing difficult to obtain. In 1930, a joint meeting of the Monterey and Pacific Grove Chambers of Commerce concluded: "Encouragement of Filipinos should be discouraged not only because they deprive permanent residents of positions, but because of other economic aspects. Establishment of Filipino boardinghouses and club-houses in any section of the peninsula will have an immediate effect on property values of the surrounding neighborhood."[19]

Both in Los Angeles and San Francisco, Filipinos were forced into "Little Manilas." Denied access elsewhere, these districts became home bases for young unattached Filipino males, providing housing, food, and recreation. To save money during periods of seasonal unemployment, several men shared one room or rented a house which became little more than a dormitory.[20]

"Little Manilas" existed in other American cities. Chicago had long been the major inland center for Filipinos, many of whom attended the area's outstanding educational institutions. Others, during the 1930's, found civil service employment in the Chicago Post Office while a sizeable number were attached to the Great Lakes Naval Training Station. Most Filipinos, with service jobs similar to those held by their West Coast compatriots, encountered in Chicago the same social and economic roadblocks. To meet their social needs, they too organized clubs which vied for members, causing further divisiveness—a perennial problem.[21]

The "Little Manilas" of New York City and Washington, D. C., sheltered composite groups of drifters. Washington, with a steady flow of dignitaries from the Philippines, had a more organized social life. New York had a range from "well-to-do [to] penniless bums." New Orleans had a prospering community, for Filipinos had lived there from Reconstruction days. In 1931, the Crescent City had more than one hundred Filipino families. The first Filipinos, mostly merchant marine sailors who had left their ships, married local girls, found work in various trades, sailed on fishing boats, or rejoined the merchant marine. This well organized community thrived within its own sphere in this southern city.[22]

All Filipinos in America sought a variety of leisure-time entertainments to relieve the monotony of their daily work. They enjoyed, and attended frequently, spectator sports. They joined together for national celebrations, such as Rizal Day on December 30, honoring Dr. Jose Rizal. A commonly held view saw Flipinos as "easy marks" for gambling. They held cockfights, bet on prize fights and wrestling matches, and played cards and dice for money. Pool halls in the "Little Manilas" provided both recreational and gambling outlets.[23]

The Filipinos brought cockfighting with them. A major form of entertainment and gambling in the agricultural camps of California and Hawaii, it has remained both a pastime and a legal controversy. Cockfighting, a remunerative enterprise for older Filipinos in the past, remained an important, although illegal, recreation in the 1960's and 1970's.[24]

Filipino agricultural workers in California acknowledged that their long hours under the hot sun had often been spent working for the "Chinaman" since they regularly lost their wages at Chinese-owned gambling houses. With a wry sense of humor about receiving an education, several commented that they had completed a comprehensive gaming course at the local "Chinese university."[25] During the 1930's, Filipinos contributed around two million dollars annually to Stockton's gamblers and prostitutes. The *Philippine Free Press* of Manila saw in 1929, as had many other observers, that young Filipinos with time on their hands became ensnared by gambling:

Those Filipinos who send money home are the "blanket boys." These have steady jobs on the farm. . . . The pastime of the "blanket boys" is playing cards. After a day's work they assemble around the improvised table and play cards till late at night. Poker and black jack are the popular games. Their hard-earned money is easily lost. In the town or city the *Pinoys* [Filipinos] may be found in the billiard rooms and pool-halls from after breakfast till late at night.

There are many gambling houses, mostly managed and controlled by Chinese. They are popularly known as "sikoy-sikoys". . . . In Stockton there is one gambling house managed and controlled by white men. It is for Filipinos. It is one mile south from the heart of the city. Anyone who wants to go there gets a free ride back and forth. These hired automobiles are owned by Filipinos.

In Walnut Grove there are six "sikoy-sikoys"; in Isleton there are four; in Dinuba one; in Reedley four, and so on. All these gambling houses are patronized by Filipinos and a few Mexicans.

The gambling houses in Walnut Grove and Isleton serve free meals: breakfast at eight o'clock; dinner at twelve; supper at five; coffee and bread at ten in the evening.[26]

Filipino gambling, although tolerated by native Americans, seemed to indicate to them that the young immigrants lacked seriousness of purpose. Gambling, dance halls, and prostitution, all marketable varieties of vice, gave credence to the charge that Filipinos were immoral and lawless.

At the height of animosity against Filipinos, the United States Commission on Law Observance and Enforcement reported in 1931 the views of San Francisco authorities:

The Filipino is our greatest menace. They are all criminally
minded. . . .

. . . .

The Filipino, with a comparatively small number in the population, give a great deal of trouble. They commit acts of violence, being
untamed. They slash, cut or stab at the least provocation. Their natty
appearance is an added incentive in attracting women of various
low types with whom they continually travel. These Filipinos are
undesirable nationals because there is not one of them but who is
not a potential criminal.[27]

Yet a survey of crime in Seattle from 1928 through 1932 showed
that the Filipino male arrest rate (11.8 percent) compared favorably with that of Caucasian males (11.1 percent). Most arrests
of Filipinos, stemming in part from the prejudice of arresting
officers, were for disorderly conduct, gambling, and minor violations which were resolved in police courts. The survey concluded
that between 1919 and 1935 the Filipino crime profile was the
same as that of whites and blacks.[28]

These Filipinos were no different than other immigrant minority groups composed mostly of young males. All have been
charged with immorality and with trafficking with white girls
of low virtue.[29] Dr. David T. Barrows, President of the University
of California, testifying before the House Committee on Immigration and Naturalization in 1930, claimed that the Filipino
problems were:

almost entirely based upon sexual passion. . . . The evidence is very
clear that, having no wholesome society of his own, he is drawn into
the lowest and least fortunate association. He usually frequents the
poorer quarters of our towns and spends the residues of his savings
in brothels and dance halls, which in spite of our laws exist to
minister to his lower nature. Everything in our rapid, pleasure-
seeking life, and the more or less shameless exhibitionism which
accompanies it, contributes to overwhelm these young men who
come, in most cases, only a few years removed from the even, placid
life of a primitive native of a barrio.[30]

Both friend and foe of the Filipino have agreed that the young
men who sought the company of white girls were lonely and

isolated. Many girls, concerned about the opinion of their peers, would not associate with the young men, while those girls who did were viewed by the white majority as having low morals or being prostitutes. The situation was fraught with conflict whenever Filipinos approached white girls. A Filipino who succeeded in breaking down barriers not only experienced ego satisfaction, but gained prestige among his fellow immigrants. But these successes stirred animosity in the minds of white men, who professed not to understand how any white woman could mingle with these people. Fred J. Hart of Salinas during his appearance before the 1930 House Committee on Immigration and Naturalization explained his apprehension:

The Filipinos are poor labor and a social menace as they will not leave our white girls alone and frequently intermarry. I might say I saw a sight the other day I never expected to see in Washington, D. C. I went to the automobile show and lo and behold on the second floor as we were looking at some of the nicer cars along comes a Filipino and a nice looking white girl. We followed them around to be sure we were not mistaken. And that was in this city. I don't know what she saw in him.[31]

The fact that prostitution flourished in "Little Manilas" and in agricultural camps caused harsh words. In Stockton, Charles Crook, deputy labor commissioner of San Joaquin County, reflected:

The Filipino never has a dime.... His money goes for cards, women, clothes and the like. The Filipino contractor furnishes some of these things. He brings women (white women) into the camp as well as booze and gives each laborer who cares to indulge a ticket. That is, he takes it out of wages.

I know of one taxi company in this city that makes $500 per month running prostitutes into the islands [the San Joaquin River Delta area]. These women must be white, weigh not over one hundred pounds, and be comparatively young—not over 24 or 25 years old.... They are worked through the islands and back down the coast toward the city. Then, they are worked back again.[32]

Manuel Buaken agreed that prostitution was a major enterprise but felt that it was based upon the seduction of the Filipinos

by white women. "Women professionals," he insisted, "fleeced
the innocent Filipino of his money by pretending they love their
Filipino victim and so manage to cheat and deceive him."[33]

All observers have commented about the unbalanced Filipino
sex ratio during the 1920's and 1930's, and the commercialization
of one of the Filipinos' pastimes—dancing—through the taxi-
dance halls.[34] Great crowds of Filipinos subsidized these taxi-
dance halls, defined as "dingy institutions for the public entertainment, which cater solely to male customers."[35] The halls
were staffed with hostesses who, paid by the dance, were
obligated to accompany any man who so requested and for as
long as he paid. To meet the Filipino trade in Los Angeles
during the 1930's, six taxi-dance halls employed several hundred
women. McWilliams opined that they provided the most costly
entertainment in the state for each dance, lasting one minute,
cost ten cents.[36]

In addition to permanent dance halls in California's urban
centers, a series of "floating" taxi-dance halls followed the
migratory workers. Starting in El Centro, during the early months
of the year, these groups accompanied the workers through the
California valleys as they moved to the next crops.[37]

Honolulu in 1935 had seven taxi-dance halls. One, viewed as
a "high-class joint," excluded Filipinos. Those that accepted
Filipinos

waste no money on overhead. The Filipinos have a need for feminine
companionship, and accept it under any conditions. They are offered
partners, room to dance, and exceedingly "hot" music. The police
listed about 350 taxi dancers, with an age range of eighteen to thirty-
eight. Most were eighteen years old. The largest national group represented were Portuguese followed by Filipinos. The older dancers were
Caucasians from the mainland—old hands in the taxi-dance business.[38]

White Americans expressed considerable concern because Filipinos patronized taxi-dance girls. Yet the girls were generally
treated with consideration and kindnesses. In a dispute involving
a Los Angeles dance hall, one of the lawyers discovered that
the Filipinos had gained the girls' high regard:

The proprietor and others swore that the general behavior of the young men was more polite than that of other races frequenting similar places. The American female instructors unanimously agreed that the Filipino boys are invariably gentle, polite and entirely devoid of immoral suggestions by speech or gesture. Such a statement can hardly be made of other races of similar age and under similar circumstances.[39]

From these relationships, nevertheless, sharp conflicts frequently led to "fights, shootings and stabbings." These were the "results of (1) the jealousies between Filipino factions, (2) the resentment on the part of the white men in seeing white women associating with Filipinos, and (3) the Latin attitude of Filipinos toward the opposite sex; he is assertive and possessive; she is his and his alone."[40]

A long bitter opponent of Filipinos, Judge Lazarus of San Francisco denounced taxi-dance hall operators "who make white girls dance with Filipinos." The judge had just held a Filipino for assault and attempted murder of a taxi-dancer after he had pursued her to her apartment and stabbed her twenty-two times. The taxi-dancer assured the judge that she was like any other girl caught in the depression; with no job, she was forced to the hall and the Filipinos. Stated Judge Lazarus:

I have become nationally known as commenting on conditions that bring about these circumstances. . . . I once referred to Filipinos as savages. There was never a more typical case to justify my statement. The Filipinos are not at fault. They are vainly attempting to adjust themselves to civilization, but haven't the training or education. They are only one jump from the jungle. It is our fault for bringing them here.

And what about operators of dance halls that compel white girls to dance with Filipinos? Nearly all the robbery, shooting and theft involving Filipinos is directly attributable to their association with white girls.[41]

About four months earlier, Judge Lazarus gained that national prominence of which he spoke as he professed shock that white girls attended parties given by Filipinos: ". . . it is apparent that girls of tender years are being ruined and led astray by the strange influence these men seem to have on women of a certain type. . . . It's enough to make a man's blood boil and mine is boiling at this minute."[42]

Thus did the Filipino immigrants of the 1920's and 1930's encounter racial prejudice and discrimination as they sought to accommodate to life in the United States. These young immigrants, firmly believing that they would be in the country a short time, did not think seriously about making a permanent home. They remained a vibrant group of men with energy, enthusiasm, and exuberance that bubbled openly. Without the restraint of parents or elders, they frequently became excessive in their love for clothing and new cars, in their attention to white girls, and in their recreational habits that ran counter to the norm established by white America.

CHAPTER V

Filipino Encounters in the American Job Market

THOSE Filipinos, East Indians, and Koreans who migrated to the United States prior to World War II, came primarily, as have other immigrants before and since, "to get rich quick"—at least by homeland standards—and to return home to a life of affluence. With jobs as their goal, most did not think too seriously about adjusting to their new environment. Motivated by the desire to make money, they sought work that would provide high returns. But Asian immigrants were restricted in what they could do because of their limited qualifications—little education, inadequate communication skills in English, no skilled vocational experience—and because of racial prejudice. Unfortunately, the dreams and hopes that motivated their ambitions more often than not never materialized. Those seeking education frequently encountered unexpected difficulties.

Until the depression of the 1930's, Filipinos on the West Coast were highly mobile, moving between major urban areas and rural regions to provide needed migratory farm labor. Some found employment in the merchant marine, the United States Navy, and the Alaska salmon canneries.[1] The lure of high wages proved to be a delusion as earnings, which seemed abundant when viewed from the Philippines, evaporated in the face of higher living costs in the United States. These young men, with a high sense of pride, would not return home in defeat; large numbers found that they had to remain longer than they planned in order to return as rich *barrio* heroes.[2]

In their search for high paying jobs, young Filipinos gravitated to the West Coast's large cities. By 1930 Los Angeles, San Francisco, and Seattle each had sizeable "Little Manilas." Fili-

pinos preferred jobs in these cities, but usually had to go to
the agricultural districts for seasonal work which was unpleasant
and very hard. Wages were always lower; and opportunities for
job advancement were lacking.[3] California's specialized crops,
particularly in the San Joaquin Valley around Stockton, the
Coachella, Imperial, and Salinas Valleys, and the Santa Maria-
Guadalupe coastal area all provided Filipinos with ready employment.[4]

The number of Filipinos residing in a "Little Manila" rose
and fell, depending upon the time of year. In 1931, Seattle's
summer population was only a few hundred while in the winter
some 3,500 filled its ghetto. Stockton, in the midst of the asparagus fields, had a crowded summer population of over six
thousand and only about one thousand winter residents. In San
Francisco, the Filipinos crammed into the Kearney Street area,
along the northern limits of Chinatown during the winter. Los
Angeles' "Little Manila" residents, located first adjacent to "Little
Tokyo," later moved from their First Street area to the neighborhood of Figueroa and Temple Streets, where Koreans had earlier
settled. In these districts, a few Filipinos catered year round
to their countrymen's needs—barber shops, fruit and grocery
stores, restaurants, pool and dance halls, and garages to service
the migrant workers' cars.[5]

"Birds of passage," just arriving from Manila or returning
from a stint in the fields or the canneries, found only service
trade jobs available in hotels and restaurants. Employers considered the Filipinos to be good workers and many preferred
them to Caucasians because they were "considered steadier, more
tractable, and more willing to put up with longer hours, poorer
board, and worse lodging facilities. Where a white worker may
feel restive and disgruntled because of bad working conditions,
the Filipino newcomer is satisfied to stay on the job 'without
kicking.'"[6] Needing both a job and money, the young men accepted these conditions. Manuel Buaken, in writing of his first
job, saw an opportunity to advance by working hard as a dish-
washer in Pasadena's Huntington Hotel. His energy paid off; he
was transferred to the pantry department to learn the funda-
mentals of cooking, "one of the two [trades] open to Filipinos
in the United States that pay an adequate wage."[7]

In 1929, Paul Scharrenberg, an American Federation of Labor leader who opposed Asian immigration, charged that Filipinos, with lower standards of living and a willingness to work for lower wages, "have taken the place of white workers in the culinary trades; they have displaced white bell boys and elevator operators and made it more difficult for white hotel maids to find employment."[8] Bruno Lasker's study found them to be serious competitors to white women in hotel and domestic service, but, generally, proved no threat to white males. The California Department of Industrial Relations also concluded that Filipinos took jobs from white workers, particularly in the service trades. But "the exact extent to which Filipinos have displaced white labor cannot be readily established but it is not unreasonable to suppose that with the increase of Filipinos in the states the further substitution of Filipino laborers for white and other groups will take place."[9]

Buaken contended that most white workers did not really want the unskilled jobs of dishwashers, porters, or elevator operators. They accepted "such work only as a last resort, but the Filipino knows he must take these for keeps, because this is the only type of work open to him in the United States." Buaken countered Scharrenberg's argument by citing his personal experience. In 1930, many white workers haunted Los Angeles employment agencies, saying they were desperate for "any honest work." As Buaken sat in these offices, he saw that unskilled service jobs which paid about $18 a week were left for the Filipinos as white workers were interested only in jobs that averaged $50.[10]

In 1929, Filipinos working in hotels and restaurants, or as domestic servants, received about $67 a month with room and board or $74 without room and board. Nationally, in 1929, service trade employees averaged a monthly wage of $104.[11] At a time when California employers were strongly anti-union, wages were uniformly low, but the availability of people willing to work for even less made those workers desirable.

While a small percentage of the Filipinos remained in service jobs all year, the cities felt an additional surge in September as unemployed farm workers streamed back from the valleys. The cyclical nature of farm employment posed a serious problem to migratory workers. Farm work, begun in March, extended through the fall harvest months. During August and September, the workers drifted to a "Little Manila," looking for urban employment. While some found jobs with the salmon canneries that kept them busy until December, for many, the fall and winter months were periods of no work.[12]

California agriculture, by the time of the 1920 Filipino influx, had established itself as the producer of specialty crops that kept several large canning companies operating and sent long strings of refrigerated freight cars eastward. From the Imperial Valley to the Sacramento Valley, farmers constantly sought an adequate labor supply to tend and to harvest crops. White workers stayed in the fields only briefly, leaving when opportunities for better jobs arose. Farmers had earlier turned to Asia for inexpensive labor. Those Chinese already in California were first utilized; after replacements from China were stopped, the Japanese were encouraged to migrate. The Gentlemen's Agreement of 1907 stopped Japanese and Korean immigration. Filipinos and Mexicans were next urged to come to the fields. Filipinos soon dominated asparagus cutting; thinning and picking lettuce, strawberries, and sugar beets; and potato harvesting. In the 1950's, Filipinos still comprised most of the work force in these crops.[13]

In the early 1900's, the Imperial Valley was reclaimed from the Colorado Desert by irrigation. At first the tendency was to raise midwestern field crops such as alfalfa, barley, corn, and wheat. Then came specialty crops of cantaloupes and cotton. Filipinos first came to the valley in 1916 as cotton pickers. By the 1920's, cultivators of citrus fruits, asparagus, lettuce, peas, and tomatoes relied upon Filipinos and other migrant workers to harvest their crops. They returned annually to work under contract as organized work gangs. Few settled in the valley permanently.[14]

In Stockton, the northern San Joaquin Valley's agricultural center, the Filipino was characterized as "an ideal worker... ably suited for stoop labor." Stockton edged the great marshy delta of the Sacramento and San Joaquin Rivers. By the 1930's most of the world's supply of asparagus came from the delta as did large quantities of strawberries, potatoes, and other truck vegetables. Stockton has remained the agricultural headquarters for Filipino workers since the 1920's.[15]

Filipinos were sought as asparagus harvesters, claimed Buaken from his own ethnic view, because "the agile, medium and low built Filipino can move faster than the clumsy, stocky-built Mexican, the lanky Hindu or the indolent Negro." Filipinos, accustomed to working in large groups in the Philippines, adapted well to the asparagus "cutter crews" of up to three hundred men. They demonstrated the ability to work in weather conditions ranging from heavy winter rains to summer temperatures of over 100 degrees. "Under these adverse conditions in the asparagus fields Mexican or Portugese [sic] are reluctant to do the job, and white workers won't even try," Buaken stated. "The Filipinos are the only ones who are not afraid to work because the alternate extremes of the dry and wet season in the Philippines have hardened them physically to take any kind of outdoor work." He added: "The soil in the asparagus fields is cultivated very finely so that as the workers trudge along the rows the dust is blown in clouds to settle in the ears, nose, around the neck and in the eyes of the cutters. I know from personal experience that when the sun beats down on the backs of the workers, the perspiration combined with the dust becomes almost unbearably itchy."[16]

The legend persisted that Filipinos were not bothered by long hours of bending over in the fields or inhaling peat dust. Carey McWilliams contended that this belief continued because farmers sought a rationalization for using these young men, but it was agricultural economics, not mythology, that tied these workers to the soil. They were considered outstanding migratory agricultural laborers because they worked rapidly and endured the dust and heat. They remained in high demand until the depression years, following the ripening crops from the Imperial Valley to the valleys of Idaho. Western specialty agriculture needed crop specialists and the farmers considered the Filipinos to be professional harvest workers.[17] Finding other work difficult to obtain because of prejudice in the cities and often faced with heavy gambling debts, the Filipino worker returned, season after season.

Many Filipinos were drawn immediately into this migratory

stream as they disembarked in San Francisco, easy prey for farm labor agents, contractors, and others anxious to live off their earnings. Taxi drivers would herd together four or five arrivals and drive them directly to Stockton for a fare of $65 to $75; the usual train or bus ticket cost about $2 a person. Once engaged as migratory farm laborers, the Filipinos moved in groups of five to fifty from job to job in battered cars or trucks. Each contingent worked under the padrone, or boss, system, headed by a contractor, usually a Filipino.[18]

The labor contractor has played a significant role in Western agriculture as the middle man between farmer and worker. The contractor, knowing where jobs were available, directed his crews to these locations, and it was his responsibility to obtain satisfactory arrangements regarding hours and wages. Growers depended upon the contractors because of the clear benefits of divesting themselves of responsibilities for recruitment, supervision, living conditions, transportation, or keeping any books related to hours and wages. Growers additionally appreciated the padrone system for it led to competition between contractors who frequently accepted lower wage rates in order to secure jobs. The contractors then had to pressure their gangs to accept less money. The contractor was responsible to the grower for providing the workers and supervising their work. Additionally, he supplied his crew with food and all other necessities of life. For every service, a fee was charged against their wages.[19]

Salinas Valley contractors during the 1930's organized themselves as the Labor Supply Association. They received sixty cents a day from each worker for room, board, and baths in the camps or "clubs." Each contractor might have from thirty to 120 men working at different locations. When the work was completed, the men moved to the next location. In 1930, labor gangs worked in lettuce or sugar beets from five to ten hours a day for forty cents an hour. When the rate dropped to fifteen cents in 1933, labor disturbances and strikes resulted.[20]

The daily agricultural wage rate in 1929 throughout California ranged from $2.50 to $5. The Department of Industrial Relations reported that the lower figure was more common for Filipino labor. From 1922 to 1926 asparagus workers' average daily earnings exceeded $5 but the influx of additional workers reduced the pay. By 1929 it was $4.14; five years later workers averaged $3.30 a day.[21]

As the number of Filipinos increased in Western agriculture at a time of rising national unemployment, the merits and benefits of their labor were debated. The fact remained that stoop labor was still required to keep vegetable and fruit production high, and Filipinos filled this need; farm operators in the 1920's judged them to be more efficient than Mexicans and more dependable than itinerant white workers, but by 1930, some growers had different views. All still employed Filipinos because there was no other alternative, but attitudes ranged from one of high appreciation to the view that the Filipino was irresponsible and unreliable.[22] Paul Lewis, San Joaquin County Horticulture Commissioner, claimed in February, 1930, that Filipinos had forced down wage rates for white workers to about three dollars a day. Lewis found that a Filipino arrived "green but after he has been here a while he becomes educated and sophisticated. Hence he becomes increasingly hard to manage."[23]

Charles Crook was more emphatic in his opinion that San Joaquin farm conditions suffered greatly because of Filipino labor. The farmer who thought he was receiving cheap labor, said Crook, had not calculated the inefficiency that characterized these people and most owners after several seasons had second thoughts about utilizing Filipinos. He claimed that:

Some of the employers have sat right here in my office and told me they wouldn't have another God damn Filipino on their place. Some of the grape growers have told me that they don't know a grape from a brick, that they don't know how to cut them, pack them or nothing else, and that their work has made their crop, when marketed, fall below standard. But you see, here's one man paying 50¢ an hour for whites and here's another paying 40¢ or less for Filipinos and he figures that he can either lower the wages of whites or else employ Filipinos.[24]

The matter of discontent over farm labor, however, was a two-way street. During the 1920's, unscrupulous labor contractors, both Filipino and white, took advantage of their workers

by overcharging for services, absconding with wages at the end
of the harvest, or arguing that the workers had misunderstood
the terms of the contract.[25] Dr. M. A. Rader, former Methodist
missionary in the Philippines, declared that the Filipinos around
Stockton encountered three major problems: "exploitation, gambling and overcrowding. . . . he is exploited by the white man
who hires him at low wages, and holds out on him by charging
big bills for board and room and also fines for not showing up.
They are even exploited by labor contractors of their own
race."[26] McWilliams in his study has concurred that it was
impossible to know how much field workers lost to the
contractors.[27]

As noted, the first Filipinos received very low wages. A study
by Harry Schwartz revealed that farmers employing both whites
and nonwhites prior to 1928 normally paid higher wages to
whites. Among nonwhites, only Mexicans and blacks earned less
than Filipinos.[28]

Before long, the Filipinos demanded higher wages. Labor was
the one commodity that they had to offer and they willingly
used the principle of supply and demand to their own advantage. Filipinos learned early that one way to change conditions
was not to work at the critical times of harvest. They adopted
techniques used earlier by the Japanese field workers—threats
of strikes and boycotts of hostile farmers.[29]

Central Valley Filipino laborers during the 1920's organized
collectively, struck at inopportune moments, or ran off to the
cities. Reported one dissatisfied San Joaquin Valley fruit grower
and employer of Filipino labor:

In 1924 there were many Filipino laborers sent to the Valley. During
the grape season we employed a crew of about fifty Filipinos. However, they proved to be the most unsatisfactory of any unskilled
laborers we had ever hired. They were the very essence of independence, taking every advantage to cause the employer trouble, quar-
relsome over contract prices, and very intolerant toward workers of
other races in the same field.

During the peak of the season of 1927, I was forced to hire a
crew of Filipino laborers to pick the crop of grapes. . . . These two
weeks of harvest were the most bitter I have ever spent. I was constantly forced to warn them and tell them over and over again

concerning the methods to use which they knew perfectly well. About the third day when we were in a great rush, the Filipinos evidently thinking we were in a tight place, struck for higher wages. We refused to meet their exorbitant demands whereupon general rioting ensued. The Filipinos became enraged and began to destroy everything they could lay their hands on. A neighbor, having finished picking his grapes, sent over a crew of Mexicans to finish our harvest which was consummated without any more difficulty and at a lower price.[30]

There were more and more such confrontations. Farmers saw market prices continue to decline; workers saw their seasonal earnings tumbling downward. Unemployed whites blamed the Filipinos and Mexicans for the economic squeeze on jobs. Filipinos, seeing owners hiring larger numbers of workers which greatly reduced individual earnings, felt compelled to counter this by protests and by unionization.[31]

The American Federation of Labor in these years made only halfhearted attempts to organize migratory farm labor, and the California state federation did not pursue the matter with any enthusiasm. Both Mexicans and Filipinos, who were repugnant to men like Paul Scharrenberg and other exclusionists, received little union support. But the idea of a union remained alive. In February, 1928, when asparagus growers cut wages, Filipino labor contractors and laborers, with the backing of the Stockton AFL Central Labor Council, drew up a protest petition signed by two thousand harvesters. In April, Mexican workers in the Imperial Valley organized an ethnic union which excluded the Filipinos in part because the latter group was already working for lower wages than the Mexicans were asking. When the AFL started to organize white workers at the same time in the Imperial Valley lettuce packing sheds, Filipinos eagerly sought to have the union organize all lettuce workers.[32]

The 1930's saw Filipino workers seeking some organization that would keep wages high. Yet in the face of rapidly declining agricultural prices and the reduction of available work, they willingly undercut other groups to get or keep jobs.[33] In 1934, the *San Francisco Chronicle* reported that Filipinos were accused of working for lower wages than whites. But once successful in cornering jobs, claimed the paper, Filipinos banded together to raise wages. Frequently, this led to white retaliation in the form of vigilante groups. An Imperial Valley newspaper reported in 1935 that Filipinos undercut Mexican lettuce workers anywhere from fifty cents to $1.25 per acre and, faced with declining market prices, farmers chose the cheaper labor. Filipinos had the additional advantage of working for a contractor while Mexicans still hired out to growers as individual workers.[34]

The efforts of growers to reduce wages brought a wave of strikes and the genesis of many new agricultural unions. In 1930, in the Imperial Valley, Filipino and Mexican field workers and white packing-shed workers struck separately. Both groups protested wage reductions and called for better living conditions and settlement of existing grievances. The Trade Union Unity League attempted to organize all agricultural workers into a single union, the Agricultural Workers Industrial League.[35] Although the strikes failed, the union sought to build for the future. Authorities in the valley quashed the effort by arresting over one hundred workers with individual bail set at $40,000. Although the union failed, the lessons of disunity and the need for a common front were understood by the agricultural workers.[36]

They utilized tactics developed in the 1920's as they continued to strike in an effort to improve their lot. Sometimes they won; more often they lost. In 1933, major unrest swept through California agriculture as strike after strike protested the new fifteen-cents-an-hour wage rate. Some strikes were led by radicals, others by ethnic unions. In Salinas, the labor contractors, through their recently organized Filipino Labor Supply Association, struck, but the growers stood firm.[37]

Early in 1934, utilizing the collective bargaining clause in the National Industrial Recovery Act, the newly formed Filipino Labor Union called upon growers to recognize it as the collective bargaining agent for Salinas agricultural workers. That union and the shed workers' union both recruited members during the spring and summer. In August, 1934, three thousand Filipino field workers and Caucasian shed workers struck, tying up the industry for several days. The field workers wanted increased wages, clarification of working time, and improved living conditions. Confusion resulted from a vote by both unions on tentative agreements and arbitration with shed workers returning to work. The Filipinos, thinking they had voted approval of a forty-cents-an-hour wage rate and not arbitration of the issues, voted again and continued the strike until September 25.[38]

Most Filipino labor contractors, members of the rival Filipino Labor Supply Association, joined the growers to defeat their opponents. State highway patrolmen were sent to assist the growers. Vigilante groups, comprised of patrolmen, local special deputies, and interested citizens, went into the fields and advised striking Filipinos to leave the valley. Some seven hundred who refused to return to work were driven from the area.

On September 21, vigilantes raided the camp of Rufo C. Canete, president of the Filipino Labor Union. The *Philippine Mail*, a Salinas newspaper, reported that as Canete's camp was being burned to the ground and residents forced to flee at gunpoint, the police raided the union headquarters in Salinas and arrested forty-eight men as mass pickets. The next day an additional twenty-one were arrested and Canete was apprehended when he went to the sheriff's office to pick up his truck which the vigilantes had seized. He was charged with aiding and abetting a riot. The following Monday, September 24, the captain of the state highway patrol telegraphed Sacramento: "Everything is very quiet, I think strike is over. Have leader in jail." The assessment was correct—the strike was broken with the growers firmly in control.[39]

Two years later, when Salinas shed workers led in another major strike, growers offered to increase wages to forty cents an hour to keep Filipinos in the fields. Additionally, armed deputy sheriffs patrolled the fields. Whenever pickets appeared, they were arrested and removed. The growers again defeated the strikers by mobilizing citizen forces into vigilante activities which took over from legal authorities.[40] The repression of agricultural labor set a pattern that lasted until the 1960's, with workers forced to acquiesce to the growers.

A major option to working in West Coast agriculture was to spend a season in the salmon canneries of Alaska and the Pacific Northwest which by 1900 were major industries. Chinese labor was first used but exclusion laws turned the companies to Japanese, Koreans, and Filipinos as replacements. In 1909, five recruiting firms in San Francisco sent 2,766 workers to Alaska and Puget Sound. Of these, 1,235 were Japanese, 1,166 Chinese, 362 Filipinos, and 53 Koreans. The United States Immigration Commission reported that companies held Koreans and Filipinos in higher regard than Japanese.[41] The recruitment of Filipinos continued at a low level for another decade. Canneries arranged with Chinese contractors to provide labor necessary to clean, pack, cook, label, and box all the fish delivered. In turn, the contractors received a fixed sum for each case of packed salmon with a minimum number of cases guaranteed. They agreed to furnish a specified number of men and were subject to a penalty for every man short of this number. They in turn subcontracted to various ethnic contractors, such as Japanese and Filipinos, who recruited workers for a guaranteed seasonal earning. In the late 1920's, this was $250 to $300 for six months' work, usually the full amount the Chinese contractor allowed per man since a subcontractor made his money from so-called fringes.[42] When a worker signed his contract, he received a forty-dollar advance. One interesting charge made against earnings was the fee paid for watchmen and detectives who saw that no one deserted prior to transit north. At the cannery, the subcontractors ran gambling games; men had to supplement their diet with purchases from the "slop chest," and to make other purchases at the store of the Chinese contractor. A later technique for separating Filipinos from their wages was the shipping of minor white male homosexuals to Alaska since unattached women were not allowed in the cannery districts. The earnings of these men were divided between themselves and the subcontractors.[43]

Upon return to Pacific Coast ports, workers and contractors made a final settlement. When deductions were assessed for gambling debts, liquor, food, etc., arguments frequently resulted. In 1912, for example, the average wages for a crew member of a subcontractor was $163. But he also had $128.42 in deductible expenses, leaving a final payment of $34.58. Even this amount was not always certain for often a subcontractor would disappear taking the payroll with him.[44] That the workers were being maltreated was borne out by an investigation following a protest about the contractors from Manuel Quezon in 1914 to General Frank McIntyre, chief of the Bureau of Insular

Affairs. Quezon claimed that twenty Filipinos were dying of famine. Secretary of War Lindley M. Garrison asked Attorney General James C. McReynolds to investigate this complaint and others which "are too numerous and insistent."[45] Unfortunately nothing came from the inquiry.

During the 1920's and 1930's, as California's Filipino manpower pool expanded so did the number of Filipino cannery workers. Thirteen percent of the Alaska cannery workers in the 1920's were Filipinos; this level increased to 15 percent in the 1930's.[46]

Other young Filipinos joined the United States Merchant Marine. From 1925 through 1932, the number ranged between 5,500 and 5,800. The high point was 7,869 in 1930. The owners, for their part, found the Filipinos to be excellent seamen. More importantly, during the 1930's, they were willing to work for lower wages.[47] Their success led to hostile words by the International Seamen's Union which saw its members' jobs being threatened. Union President Andrew Furuseth, an early West Coast agitator against the Japanese, claimed that the Filipinos were not good sailors. Protesting vehemently about their use in the coastal trade, which was not regulated by shipping commissioners, he argued: "I have sailed with Filipinos. I know from personal knowledge and experience that they are difficult to live with on board a ship. The reputation of the Manila man, as we seamen call the Filipino, is that of being treacherous, swift with the use of the knife, and always in the back."[48] Furuseth's hostility was not unexpected.

Filipino merchant marine employment disappeared with the passage of the 1936 Merchant Marine Act. One important provision mandated that 90 percent of the crews on American flag ships must be United States citizens. By 1938, large numbers of Filipinos, American nationals but not citizens, found themselves on the beach.[49]

The United States Navy actively recruited Filipinos in the Philippine Islands, Hawaii, and the mainland. The number in the navy during the 1920's and 1930's ranged around four thousand. It turned out, however, that the only billet open was mess steward. During World War I, the navy decided this was an appropriate assignment for Filipinos. In 1932, the Communist newspaper, the *Western Worker,* reported that the Filipinos, once recruited, were surprised at the sharp discrimination they encountered relative to promotions, ship duty, and shore leave. They were disgruntled to find that, as mess stewards, they were merely flunkies to white officers. Those who asked to be transferred to other ratings "always tested out as unsatisfactory."[50]

During World War II, the United States Navy continued its policy of mess boys only, which made Filipinos unhappy. The Coast Guard Reserve, on the other hand, accepted them for equal duty. The patrol boat, *Bataan,* was staffed with an all-Filipino crew. The navy's long stand on this issue subjected it to vocal criticism about a remnant of "white-gloved days of U.S. colonialism."[51]

After three decades in the United States, at the outbreak of World War II, Filipinos remained confined largely to unskilled or semi-skilled jobs, but they had demonstrated their ability and willingness to do hard work. Their search for financial success—their prime motive for emigrating—however, continued to elude them.

CHAPTER VI

Filipino Labor Problems
in the Hawaiian Islands, 1907–1941

THE practices and attitudes of Hawaiian Island agriculture paralleled developments on the West Coast in the years prior to World War II. The one major difference was that Hawaiian contract workers had few economic choices. The Hawaiian Sugar Planters' Association imported Filipino labor to produce sugar or to work for its sister association, the Pineapple Growers Association of Hawaii. As newly arrived workers cleared immigration in Honolulu and received HSPA plantation identification tags, they were transported to one of forty-four plantations on the four major islands: Hawaii (twenty plantations), Maui (six), Oahu (nine), and Kauai (nine).[1]

Each plantation had a variety of jobs. In 1925, day work—cutting weeds and grass, cleaning gardens, picking up field rubbish, or sweeping out the mills—paid a daily wage of one dollar. To encourage laborers to work a monthly minimum number of days, a 10 percent bonus, the turn-out bonus, was added to the wages of those who met or exceeded this minimum. "Short contract" workers carried out specific tasks such as irrigating, plowing, and cutting and loading cane. Cane cutting was done by a contract crew with each member sharing equally in the total earnings. These workers earned in 1925, exclusive of any bonus, from $2.25 to $2.50 a day; in 1933, their average earnings had dropped to $1.39.[2]

Wages for loading cane in the 1920's were about $2.38 for ten hours. One man, recalling his early plantation days, noted that the worst and hardest job he had ever had was loading wagons with cane on hot and humid tropical days.[3]

Long-term contract workers were organized into gangs selected and supervised by a *luna*, or foreman, who had contracted to

cultivate and irrigate the cane until harvest time. The crew
was paid for the amount of clean cane delivered to the mill,
with the pay rate determined by the current world price of
sugar. Prior to harvest, each worker was advanced one dollar a
day for subsistence. He was entitled to the 10 percent bonus
if he worked the minimum twenty-three days a month. He collected the remainder of the "big pay" after the cane was harvested
and the total earnings calculated. In 1925, the average daily
wage for long-term contract workers was $2.40 a day; this had
been reduced to $1.88 by 1933.[4]

Sugar mill workers were also organized into gangs that contracted to handle a particular mill operation, such as moving
the cane to the crushing mills, operating the mills or the cen-
trifugals, or bagging and warehousing the sugar. Their daily
wages in 1925 ranged from $2.20 to $3.27.[5]

Plantation and mill jobs were routinized so that each worker
carried out a limited specialized assignment under close supervision of the *luna*. One former worker explained that the normal
work order of the day for his eight-man crew was to weed and
chop cane fields.

So hoe hoe hoe is what we did for four hours in a straight line and
no talking, resting only to sharpen the blade and then walk to the
next lot. Hoe every weed along the way to your three rows. Hoe—
chop chop chop, one chop for one small weed, two for all big
ones.... So, hoe hoe hoe is what we did until the siren blew at
11:00 sharp for lunch.

. . . .

... It was December ... and the weather was cool but when you
work out there in the sunlight hoeing like that—you burn up.

. . . .

After one week of hoe hana [work], I felt as if I had been kicked
and beaten all over. My body was tight and my back ached like
it does now that I'm old and weak with a broken body. I got used
to the pains of work after awhile but that was the first time in
my life that I had stooped and worked at one thing for so long
without a say and without fun mixed in.[6]

Following the lunch break, the workers continued at their
jobs until 3:30 or 4:30 P.M. depending upon the task. The mills

ran until 6 P.M. Not until passage of the Sugar Act of 1937 was the work day shortened to eight hours.[7]

Single workers lived in barracks or cottages that housed seven to eight people. Those who were married received separate housing. At the Nealehu plantation on Hawaii's south shore, the field hands were assigned four to a room. The crew also had its own kitchen in which to cook breakfast and pack lunches. Food, clothes, and lunch boxes purchased at the plantation store were charged to the worker's account and deducted later from wages.[8] Workers could shop also in private stores.

Hawaiian plantation settlements were relatively self-sufficient and isolated. Each company provided medical and hospital service, a recreation center for billiards, athletic fields, and once a month many plantations admitted an orchestra and dancers.[9]

In a way, the plantation was complete to live on, if you liked it. And there were hardly any cars then so we didn't go very far. There were activities all year around sponsored by the plantation so there was always something to occupy your time if you liked it. There was a plantation chapel with the Pilipino priest. . . .

Only a few went, except when there was a wedding, baptism or funeral—then you can see all the Pinoys go to church. And there was a clubhouse for everyone to use and was convenient. In that clubhouse, we had social-box dances and that's how the Queen Contests began.

The plantation also sponsored baseball teams and boxing and weight-lifting teams. Each race had a team and the plantation manager never missed a baseball game on Sundays. . . . But Sunday when the Lord rested, we Pilipinos mostly gambled on cocks, dice, and cards, liquor and women, but not necessarily in that order.[10]

To outsiders, particularly labor organizers, the plantations were closed. This closed world was clearly demonstrated by a 1929 announcement in the *Filipino Nation* that the Filipino Federation of America had been granted free access to the Maui Agricultural Company camps:

TO WHOM IT MAY CONCERN:

This will introduce Mr. Isidor E. Edillo, Secretary of the Honolulu Branch of the Filipino Federation of America.

Mr. Edillo has my full permission to enter any and all of our camps
to talk with his countrymen, both individually and collectively at
meetings for which he may make arrangements.

> Very truly yours,
> H.A. Baldwin, Manager
> Maui Agricultural Co., Ltd.[11]

Isolation was held to be necessary to keep the workers under
control of company management.

Pay days came on Saturdays twice a month. Each worker had
a *bango*, a copper disc, with his identification number stamped
on it. Plantation police checked the *bango* to make certain
that each worker received the right envelope. On the face of
each envelope was an accounting of deductions made for purchases at the plantation store. Pay day also brought an
assemblage of outside creditors: private store owners, fish-
mongers, vegetable vendors, and merchants seeking monthly in-
stallment payments on time purchases for phonographs, radios,
cars, and tailor-made suits. Others on hand were wives of
Filipinos collecting from single men for laundry and taxi drivers
seeking partial payment on bills. By the time a worker settled
with the last of his creditors, he had little left.[12]

A long-standing dictum of Hawaiian planters seemed to be:
locate cheap labor and then keep that labor on the plantations.
In 1882, the *Planters Monthly* had enunciated this view: "The
experience of sugar growing the world over goes to prove that
cheap labor, which means in plain words servile labor, must be
employed to render this enterprise successful."[13] The demand for
higher wages and improved working conditions led to union
organizations and strikes; all ran counter to the plantation
objective of cheap docile labor.

The first major sugar plantation strike, in 1909, met with
complete disaster as far as realizing immediate goals.[14] The
strike firmed up the planters' resolve not to recognize any union
as a bargaining agent—a position maintained until the mid-1930's.
But the workers received certain long-range gains, mostly
paternalistic in nature. The plantations provided better housing,
installed water and sewage systems, and enlarged medical
services. Wages were increased and the 10 percent monthly

bonus incentive system was installed. Early HSPA contracts set this minimum at twenty days. This was raised to twenty-three days in 1921.[15] The incentive system remained unpopular with the workers. In October, 1919, the Japanese Association of Hawaii met in Honolulu to discuss hours, wages, and the bonus incentive. The acting president of the recently organized Filipino Federation of Labor, Pablo Manlapit, and two other Filipinos attended this meeting.[16]

Pablo Manlapit, a key figure in the Filipino labor movement, was born in the province of Batangas in Southwest Luzon. After completing intermediate school, he worked on a number of government projects in the Manila area and was soon dismissed for being a labor organizer. In 1910, he went to Hawaii as a HSPA contract worker. An intelligent individual, promoted quickly to foreman and then to timekeeper, he was discharged following a plantation strike. Manlapit then moved to Hilo where in 1913–14 he organzed the Filipino Unemployment Association, but the outbreak of World War I soon provided ample employment opportunities in Hawaii. He worked next in William J. Sheldon's Hilo law office and began to study law. In December, 1919, he was licensed as a lawyer, the first Filipino in the territory to pass the bar examination. In November, 1918, he started to organize Filipino labor and by August, 1919, launched a statewide drive for his union. During September and October the Filipino Labor Union made vigorous recruitment drives on Oahu, Maui, and Kauai.[17]

Both the Filipino and Japanese unions in 1919 demanded an eight-hour day, a minimum daily wage of $2.50, abolition of the bonus, and improved working conditions. Manlapit, trying to advance his union as the sole spokesman for Filipino workers, pushed for and received a strike vote, but the Japanese Association of Hawaii had not yet moved as far as had Manlapit's organization in calling for a strike.

On January 3, 1920, Manlapit's union issued a strike notice and asked the Japanese to do likewise. On January 19, over three thousand Filipino workers struck four Oahu plantations. On February 1, with the Japanese federation calling for a general strike, Filipino and Japanese workers joined forces. After February 9, there was considerable confusion; Manlapit, for his part, appeared to be dealing behind the scenes with both the Japanese union and the planters' association. By mid-February, with a majority of Oahu's Japanese and Filipino laborers on strike, the planters began evicting strikers from their homes. Strikebreakers were brought in and orders were issued by the territorial schools' central administration not to enroll children of strikers in school. Under these desperate conditions, coupled with the 1919 influenza epidemic, strikers were pushed to the breaking point. But many persisted and the strike lasted 165 days, ending on July 1, 1920, with five hundred Filipinos still on strike; by the end of July most of the strikers were back at work.[18]

But labor unrest continued. From 1920 to 1924, Manlapit organized incoming Filipino immigrants into the Filipino Higher Wage Movement. On May 28, 1922, one of the movement's leaders, in a memorial to Manuel Quezon and Sergio Osmeña, urged that a resident commissioner be stationed in Hawaii as an advocate for the workers about their working and living conditions, wages, and equality with other races. The writer also charged that the sugar plantations had violated many contracts when they raised the minimum number of days required for the monthly bonus from twenty to twenty-three. He finally noted that the plantations did not adhere to the compensation laws for injured workers. In August, Manlapit's followers sent an additional petition to the Philippines calling for a resident commissioner.[19]

Subsequently Governor General Leonard Wood sent a special investigator to Hawaii. In advance of that inspection, Quezon received a confidential letter from the HSPA's Manila office providing information about the recruiting process and the association's view that workers received fair treatment.[20] The report of Cayetano Ligot, the special investigator, about conditions in the islands was released in March, 1924. His findings, sympathetic to the HSPA, blamed troubles confronting the Filipinos upon themselves and their ways. In short, he told the workers to reform and engage in their work enthusiastically. Many Filipinos concluded that Ligot had fallen under the control of the HSPA.[21]

In April, 1924, Manlapit called a Filipino strike which spread from one plantation to another; soon twenty-three of Hawaii's sugar plantations were struck. The strike lasted eight months and involved about three thousand Filipino workers. The plantations, having learned from prior strikes, brought in new workers; harassed and jailed the leaders; and evicted strikers from plantation housing. On the island of Kauai, strikers captured two Filipino strikebreakers and a sheriff's posse invaded the strikers' camp. A riot of several days' duration ensued. At its conclusion, sixteen Filipinos and four policemen were dead. Governor Wallace R. Farrington sent the National Guard which arrested 101 strikers. Sixty of these were sentenced to jail. Manlapit, indicted for subornation of perjury, was sentenced to serve two to ten years.[22]

Protesting in Manlapit's behalf, the Honolulu Japanese language newspaper, *Hawaii Hochi,* addressed an open letter to Quezon, Manuel Roxas, and other Philippine legislators. The paper claimed that the HSPA:

. . . set detectives to dog his steps and employed spies and stoolpigeons to undermine his prestige and discredit him. . . .
Then he was indicted by what was known locally as the "millionaire grand jury." He was tried before a jury in an atmosphere of hostility, race prejudice and hatred. The testimony against him was discredited by competent witnesses, and the implication of a frame-up against him [was] so strong that all impartial witnesses expected an acquittal.
Immediately after the trial, the witnesses against Manlapit were hurried out of the territory and sent back to the Philippines.

The newspaper then cited the fact that the chief witness against Manlapit had prepared an affidavit indicating that witnesses were "paid $10.00 in Honolulu, their transportation furnished to the Philippines by the Hawaiian Sugar Planters' Association, and they were given $100.00 each on their arrival in Manila as 'compensation for our testimony and declarations we made . . . against Pablo Manlapit, Labor Leader.' "[23] All claims of facts were to no avail. The association emerged from this and all other strikes of the 1920's victorious and strengthened.

Pablo Manlapit's career continued to be turbulent. In early 1928, he was arrested in Los Angeles for being a Communist agitator as he was about to speak to the All-America Anti-

Imperialist League. The charges against him were that he was engaged in recruiting the seven thousand Filipinos in the United States Navy for the Communist Party and that he had been instrumental in the recent asparagus workers' strike in Stockton.[24] He returned for a time to Hawaii in the 1930's.

In his later career, during World War II, Manlapit served on various labor advisory boards for the Philippine government; after liberation of the islands, he worked briefly as a labor advisor for the United States Navy in the Philippines. Active in the political campaign of Manuel Roxas in 1946 and 1947, he returned to government service with the election of Roxas in 1948.

In June, 1949, he returned to the Hawaiian Islands to see his grandchildren. However, he was detained at the docks by immigration officials until the Philippine Consul guaranteed his return to the Philippines. Manlapit claimed he then had to sign a statement that he would not address any meeting, speak on any radio station, attend church, mass, or write in any newspaper. He retorted that such treatment was "worse than communist rule."[25]

During the 1930's, workers continued to strike for improvements but planters countered their moves. In March, 1932, almost one thousand Filipinos held a mass meeting at Aala Park, Honolulu, to protest growing unemployment. Cayetano Ligot, now resident commissioner, continued to urge discretion upon the Filipinos. Ligot was recalled to the Philippine Islands after Roosevelt's administration appointed Frank Murphy as governor general. Behind the scenes politics in the Philippines involved Francisco Varona in Manila and Pablo Manlapit who was back in Hawaii. Varona wired Manlapit and Epifanio Toak, another labor leader, that the new Hawaiian commissioner, Jose Figueras, was on his way and urged the two to support him. In an interesting letter from J.K. Butler to Quezon on December 2, 1933, the secretary-treasurer of the HSPA protested these political undercurrents. "Dear Casey," wrote Butler, "I am worried about this situation. Manlapit and Toak are issuing circulars now and demanding 'memberships' in the various Filipino Labor Unions of which they are the sole organization." He concluded: "I hope you have given Figueras a little picture of the situation here so that he will make no mistakes that will cause him and us and all the Filipinos a lot of trouble."[26] Figueras, however, asked that Manlapit be recognized as the Filipino labor leader for collective bargaining and that other Filipinos be appointed as camp bosses and to other positions in order to improve everyone's working conditions. Figueras' requests so angered the Hawaiian economic and political establishment that Governor Lawrence Judd asked that the new commissioner be recalled.[27]

During 1933, two hundred workers rioted on Oahu when a worker was discharged but the police quashed the effort. In 1937, on Maui, the Filipino union, *Vibora Luviminda*, led one of the territory's last ethnic strikes against three plantations as about 3,500 workers struck. In face of the usual management tactics, the workers held on with aid from the CIO and gained a 15 percent wage increase, the first direct plantation victory resulting from a strike.[28]

The long struggle of the workers in their fight against the plantation owners climaxed when a CIO union at the McBryde Sugar Company on Kauai called for and won a collective bargaining election. In 1940 that union signed the first contract for sugar workers. From this beginning, unionization of the field and mill workers proceeded, with the International Longshoremen's & Warehousemen's Union moving to the dominant position.[29]

Hawaii's second most important agricultural product during the twentieth century was pineapple. James Dole started growing pineapple in 1900 and the next year formed the Hawaiian Pineapple Company. In 1903, utilizing a primitive cannery, the first pineapples were packed and the industry's growth assured. Its development followed the path of the sugar industry. By 1907 the Pineapple Growers Association of Hawaii had been formed. In the early years of operation, the growers and canneries relied upon surplus labor from the sugar industry. But by the 1920's, the pineapple industry paid the HSPA an annual stipend to recruit Filipino labor.[30] During the 1930 depression, the market for pineapples virtually disappeared and crops rotted in the fields. Only through reorganization and retrenchment did the industry survive.

By the late 1930's, Filipinos constituted the largest ethnic group working in the pineapple fields, comprising 57 percent of all plantation labor. They earned 41.7¢ an hour or $3.34 a day. In the canneries, Japanese men and women formed 78 percent of the work force; only 15 percent were Filipino men.[31]

Other employment opportunities in Hawaii prior to World War II were limited to a few town and city jobs. By 1926, five thousand Filipinos had gravitated to Honolulu from the plantations. Hilo had four hundred while Wailuku on Maui and Lihue on Kauai had 150 and 100 respectively. They worked in the pineapple canneries, as stevedores, in hotel and home service trades, and as telephone and street workers. Some met the cultural needs of their fellow immigrants, working as barbers and musicians, or operating pool halls, restaurants, and stores.[32]

Life for the Filipinos in these Hawaiian cities was "difficult and miserable because of their irregular periods of employment. ... The dwelling houses of those who live in community [sic] can not be said to be comfortable. They rent houses from $13 to $20 a month, capable of accommodating from four to eight persons."[33] Even so, city life seemed more attractive than camp life as there was a consistent drift from rural plantations to Honolulu. Throughout the twentieth century, it has had the largest Filipino population of any city in the United States.[34]

In Hawaii and on the West Coast, the Filipinos proved to be willing workers both in their agricultural and urban jobs as they strove to meet their fundamental goal of acquiring money in order to return home. At the same time, the Filipinos proved that they would not be used, cheated, or forced into serfdom for long. They fought hard for equality in labor's struggle over wages, hours, and working conditions.

CHAPTER VII

Filipino Economic and Social
Adjustments since World War II

DURING and after World War II, as the West Coast industrial base expanded, Filipinos increasingly found employment in factories, in some trades, and in wholesale and retail businesses. The gaining of citizenship in 1946 enabled those properly qualified to secure professional licenses. Those recent arrivals, part of the post-1965 influx, found employment mostly in unskilled jobs although some entered skilled and semi-professional occupations. Slowly changing union regulations throughout the United States in the 1950's and 1960's, spearheaded by the CIO, made it possible for Asian minorities to join various unions. But, other than the CIO, unions were notoriously slow in providing equal access for all, regardless of race.[1]

Hawaiian unions, however, were in the forefront in providing equal opportunity. The imposition of territorial martial law after the Pearl Harbor attack suppressed the Hawaiian union movement until 1944 when the International Longshoremen's and Warehousemen's Union's organizational efforts met with phenomenal success. In elections held in 1945 on nineteen sugar plantations, the ILWU received 5,568 votes, with only 222 negative votes, in support of its bid to be the bargaining agent. By 1947, the ILWU had a reported membership of thirty thousand on the docks and at the sugar and pineapple plantations.[2]

A 1948 study demonstrated that Seattle's racial minorities were at a substantial disadvantage in competing with Caucasians for jobs. The consequences of such discrimination, said the report, had to be borne by employers, unions, co-workers, and the general public who shared common prejudices about minority groups. The labor situation in Seattle was fairly representative of the West Coast. Two-thirds of those Filipinos surveyed were in the "now traditional" hotel and restaurant service trade. About 18 percent were classified as factory operatives while about 14 percent were unskilled laborers. Some 4 percent worked in retail sales. No Filipino was employed in the building trades, in any managerial position, or as a professional.[3]

In California, even with the move from rural to urban areas, agriculture in 1960 remained the largest employer of Filipinos, providing jobs to 31 percent of those in the work force. In 1950 that percentage had been 55.[4] In Hawaii, Filipinos in 1960 still provided the bulk of plantation labor—40 percent of the gainfully employed males. This represented a decline of 12.5 percent since 1950 as they found employment as craftsmen and factory workers.[5] As the "latest arrivals and least fortunately situated" of the immigrant groups, Filipinos comprised most of the unskilled plantation labor and remained at the bottom of the wage scale. However, Hawaiian Filipinos fared better in the post-World War II years than those in California, largely because the ILWU gained substantial wage increases for its members. The union boasted that the sugar industry "pays the highest year-round agricultural wages in the world."[6]

One occupational career, which remained economically attractive to residents of the Philippines, was that of mess steward in the United States Navy. In 1970, in large part due to conditions in the Philippines, more Filipino volunteers served in the United States Navy than there were sailors in the entire Philippine Navy. The recruitment program of the late 1960's stemmed from the 1947 military bases agreement which allowed Filipinos to join the United States armed forces. In 1970, over fourteen thousand served in the navy. Most of these were at sea, working as personal valets, cabin boys, and dishwashers—admirals and captains had Filipino stewards assigned directly to them. Others had shore duty—at the White House, the Pentagon, the United States Naval Academy, and at various naval bases.

During the 1960's, some 100,000 tried to enlist each year, but the slots were few in number because of a 94 percent reenlistment rate. In 1969, the navy accepted 1,284; in 1970, only 420 new men were enrolled. During the 1950's and 1960's, the navy found that its ships' galleys had turned into "Filipino ghettos." To redress this and to provide for other opportunities, some 1,600 Filipinos were transferred to other ratings. But in the Philippine Islands the recruiting was still aimed at securing mess stewards. Those Filipinos in the navy did not complain about their job as much as did those on the outside. The base pay for a new recruit was $1,500, a high economic level in a land of considerable unemployment. That income equalled the salary of a lieutenant colonel in the Philippine Army. Additionally, many served in the navy as a means of gaining American citizenship.[7]

By 1969, 78,680 Filipino males and 52,875 females, all over the age of sixteen, were gainfully employed in the United States with the Bureau of Census reporting that they had entered all levels of employment. In California some 5,100 men worked in service trades, the largest employment category. But the next largest number were professionals—2,963. Some 2,600 were laborers and only 1,899 were classified as farm laborers. In Hawaii, with its more liberal union policies, 3,800 men worked in the building trades and three thousand were listed as operatives. The service trades and agriculture each employed a little over 1,800. There were 788 classified as professionals.[8] Substantial progress had been made in securing equal opportunity for employment in all fields.

According to a socioeconomic study by the California Department of Industrial Relations, California's Filipinos had not improved their earning power relative to other groups between 1934 and 1959. Their median annual income for 1959 remained the lowest of three Asian groups: Chinese, Filipino, and Japanese. Those in Hawaii shared with other Pacific Island people the dubious distinction of having the lowest earnings of all ethnic groups. Hawaiian Filipino males in 1969 still had the lowest median income.[9] In 1972, as a result of the large influx into California, that state's annual income average for Filipino men had declined to $2,925.[10]

The Los Angeles area and the San Francisco Bay region continued to attract large numbers of Filipinos.[11] By 1973 the Filipinos, the fastest growing minority in the bay area, openly expressed their ethnic consciousness. Early that year Sid Valledor,

TABLE III

COMPARATIVE MEDIAN
INCOME FOR EMPLOYED MALES IN
CALIFORNIA AND HAWAII, 1959 & 1969[a]

Group	California		Hawaii	
	1959	1969	1959	1969
Caucasian	$5,109	$7,471	$7,649	$8,699
Japanese	4,388	7,746	4,302	7,839
Filipino	2,925	4,698	3,071	5,252

[a]California Dept. of Industrial Relations, *Californians of Japanese, Chinese and Filipino Ancestry* (San Francisco, 1965), p. 14; U.S. Bureau of Census, *General Characteristics, of the Population, California, 1970*, I, pt. 6, 2259; ibid., *Hawaii*, I, pt. 13, 96.

representing San Francisco's Filipino community, told that city's Human Rights Commission about the plight of the some 34,000 Filipino residents. A survey of racial and ethnic employment showed that Filipinos comprised 5 percent of the city's population but only 1.5 percent were employed. Valledor, in calling for Filipino representation on every city board and commission, stated: "We are Americans who are neither white, black, Chicano, native American, Japanese or Chinese in ancestry, but we are always lumped as Asian, Spanish-speaking or whatever seems politically expedient."[12]

San Francisco Filipinos lived in clusters in the city's Mission District and Bernal Heights. "Little Manila" of the 1930's still existed next to Chinatown where elderly Filipino men were living out their days. Some young men lived temporarily in the old settlement as they sought employment elsewhere.[13] The plight of the elderly men, long away from their Philippine homes, led other Filipinos to unify for a time in a common cause. In November, 1968, it was revealed that the residents of the International Hotel, mostly Filipinos, were to be evicted from that "Little Manila" building so it could be torn down and replaced by a modern structure. The elderly Filipinos depended entirely upon their monthly Social Security checks of $120 to meet their needs. Almost all had lived in the hotel for several years, paying $30–38 a month, and could not afford the rent being charged elsewhere in the city.[14]

Filipino groups appeared before city agencies to protest the eviction and succeeded in securing an indefinite postponement until a satisfactory alternative for the residents could be developed. Many of these aged men had sufficient money to return to the Philippines, for their $120 monthly pension would have provided adequate living but, tragically, time had passed them by. Having lost touch with the Philippine culture, these old-timers had become men without a country, captive in what was to have been their temporary home.[15]

Many who had migrated in the 1920's still worked in agriculture nearly fifty years later. In 1970, two students of Filipino ancestry, seeking to increase their understanding of their own heritage, interviewed Filipino residents of a Salinas farm labor camp. Those interviewed portray vividly the hopes and frustrations of men who had become a permanent part of California's agricultural labor force. Even though their average age was sixty-five, the men still dreamed of returning to the Philippines. Some were semi-retired, working only long enough to pay for their board and room at the camp. Others, too young to retire, worked daily in the fields.[16]

The sadness of it all was that while these Filipino agricultural workers still had great optimism, many had come to rely upon an external factor—a big win in gambling—to bring reality to their dream. The experiences of three camp residents underscore the difficulties they and other aging Filipinos, who had come to California in the 1920's, encountered.

Manong had migrated in 1924 to Hawaii where he had spent three years on sugar and pineapple plantations. Securing financial support from a relative in Stockton, he then moved to California where he had worked in the potato and asparagus fields of the San Joaquin Delta. In 1938, he arrived in Salinas which became his permanent residence. Like many of his compatriots Manong did not seek citizenship because he always planned to return to his homeland. Given an opportunity to return in 1938, he indicated that he could not pay for the ticket. Since that time, though he had made no effort to return to the Philippines, he maintained family ties. He customarily sent money home, but that practice had become more difficult as retirement age approached.[17]

Nanding, another of the camp residents, came to San Francisco in 1925 to study engineering. But his future was more or less determined at dockside when he and others were "greeted ...by a man from an employment office in Stockton whose job was to pick up a truckload of men and transport them to Stockton." The driver, Nanding reported, made five dollars' profit on each passenger by charging more than the normal fare. After his arrival, Nanding worked in the fields. Once the harvest season ended, he and several friends enrolled in the seventh grade, but he soon dropped out because he was nineteen and the white students were thirteen; he never went back to school. Nanding subsequently became a migrant worker, settling finally in the Salinas camp. Like Manong, he never applied for United States citizenship. He viewed that step as unnecessary for he planned to return to the Philippines "as soon as he makes it in Reno." Although he had never won enough money to cover his transportation costs, he had sent money home to support his relatives, several of whom had gained an education because of his financial aid.[18]

Benigno, a third Salinas camp resident, arrived in California in 1924. He, too, began as a field laborer in the Delta region before moving to Salinas in 1935. There he worked in the lettuce fields until the start of World War II. Drafted into the army, he became an American citizen. He was soon discharged because the Salinas agriculturalists needed his labor—the same reason that caused many other drafted Filipino farm workers to be released from military service. Though he was now a citizen, Benigno still wanted to return to the Philippines. Like so many others, he was still "waiting for his big win in Reno" so he could buy his ticket. Although he had never had much luck, his hopes remained high.[19]

California's agribusiness successfully resisted unionization of field workers until the 1960's. During most of the 1930's, the powerful Associated Farmers of California stayed all efforts to organize migratory farm workers, although by 1940 the Filipino Agricultural Laborers Association had achieved limited success. Created initially in response to a threatened wage cut

in asparagus, the union had, by 1941, won several strikes and
secured wage increases and improved working conditions. The
union ceased to be an effective force during World War II
when most of its members joined the armed forces. The economic
motivation for unionism also dissipated as farm wages increased
during the war years.[20] Following the war, agricultural workers
called for better working conditions and higher wages to counter
inflation. California agriculturalists met this challenge during
the 1940's and 1950's by utilizing strikebreakers and court in-
junctions to hold union activities at bay.[21]

The situation changed dramatically during the 1960's. In 1959,
the AFL-CIO formed the Agricultural Workers Organizing Committee (AWOC), and, at about the same time, Cesar Chavez
founded the National Farm Workers Association (NFWA). While
both unions were racially integrated, the AWOC local, led by
Larry Itliong, was predominantly Filipino. These unions spent
several years recruiting members. The climax to these activities
came in 1965 over the pay scale of grape pickers in the lower
San Joaquin Valley. On September 8, 1965, AWOC struck against
thirty-three grape growers near Delano in northern Kern County.
Domestic grape pickers were being paid about $1.20 an hour,
while braceros, under a United States Department of Labor
ruling, received $1.40. Domestic workers, including Filipino
Americans and Mexican Americans, demanded $1.40 an hour
plus 20 cents a box.[22] Chavez's NFWA joined AWOC's effort
eight days later. After a seven-month strike, which generated
much public sympathy, Schenley Industries, owner of the largest
vineyards, recognized NFWA as the sole bargaining agent.
NFWA and AWOC continued to organize workers and to
pressure other growers for recognition. Chavez's union became
the stronger of the two. To end unnecessary conflict between
themselves, the unions in August, 1966, merged as the United
Farm Workers Organizing Committee (UFWOC) and soon
became the bargaining agent for the workers of the Di Giorgio
Corporation, another large Kern County vineyard owner.[23]

The naming of a bargaining agent for these farm workers
marked a turning point in California agriculture's labor relations.
The Filipinos and Chicanos, working together, improved wages

and working conditions. Through UFWOC, they have continued to pressure big agriculture.[24]

While Filipinos in California recognized that power through political unification would provide equality in social and economic areas, it proved difficult to achieve. At the state level, as an outgrowth of common urban and rural problems, the Filipino-American Political Association, with delegates from San Diego to the Bay Area, met in a "first annual convention" in 1969 to organize with other groups to work on human rights issues. The association was the brainchild of UFWOC. Cesar Chavez was one of the major convention speakers and Larry Itliong was elected president of the new organization.[25]

In 1970, the Filipino-American Coordinating Committee, a coalition of thirty Filipino American groups, sought federal funds to create ten centers in California to counsel the poor, the disadvantaged, and the elderly. M. H. Iacaban, publisher of Sacramento's *Bataan News*, and chairman of the conference, speaking for equality for California's Filipinos, claimed that "Our people are highly educated and competitively ambitious, and once equality for these people is attained, they will assume a very important role in making America a better place to live in." Iacaban identified a long-standing problem for Filipinos in the United States. So many organizations had their own agenda that there was no common front and little public visibility for any one group to attack problems confronting the Filipinos. As late as 1973, some fifty San Francisco Filipino groups were working for similar goals, but their very numbers caused a lack of harmony.[26] Others did not see this as a reason to be discouraged. Jose Alba, president of the Filipino Club of Stockton, observed: "The same social and economic processes that have worked on other groups will affect the Filipino minority and with similar results." He concluded that Americans of Filipino extraction would keep an interest in the Philippine Islands but that "they will supply their share of poor and rich, Democrats and Republicans, laborers and merchants, doctors and lawyers and clergymen."[27] In California only a few have achieved success in politics. Maria Lacadia Obrea was a Los Angeles municipal judge in the early 1970's while Glenn Olea served as a councilman in the Monterey Bay community of Seaside.[28]

Filipinos also encountered difficulty in the business community. From time to time they organized to help each other face their competitors. In Hawaii after World War II, the Filipino Businessmen's Association of Hawaii, under the leadership of V. S. Galang, sought to provide such assistance for Filipinos seeking independent business opportunities.[29]

While the 1950's brought change for Filipinos in California, Hawaii's Filipinos did not experience any substantial change in their mode of living until the 1960's. As late as 1958, Philippine ethnic identity remained an important divisive factor in the territory. Juan Dionisio, Philippine consul general, attempted to harmonize these groups as had Francisco Varona earlier in Hawaii and on the mainland. In 1959, on the eve of statehood, the Filipinos held a statewide convention to plan the role they would play in the new state. They had strength in the ILWU where they held key leadership posts. They were all outspokenly proud of the community leaders—the names of those few lawyers, doctors, engineers, and teachers who had entered the dominant culture were well known.[30]

At the time of Hawaiian statehood, Filipinos found the political climate much more favorable than had been the case on the mainland. During the last years of the territory, three Filipinos had served in the legislature.

Peter Adúja was the first to be elected. Successful in his bid for a seat in the lower house in 1955, he served only one term. Born in the province of Ilocos Sur, he came with his parents to Hawaii when he was eight years old. Following graduation from Hilo High School, he received his bachelor's degree from the University of Hawaii. During World War II he served with the First Filipino Regiment. After the war he graduated from Boston University School of Law and then returned to Hilo to practice. Defeated for reelection, he was appointed by Governor Samuel W. King to be a deputy attorney general. After statehood, he was elected three times, first in 1966, from Windward Oahu to the Hawaii House of Representatives.[31]

In 1958, Bernaldo D. Bicoy, one of only five Filipino lawyers practicing in the territory, and the only one in Honolulu, was elected to the House of Representatives, representing West Oahu. A graduate of Waipahu High School, he received degrees from the University of Hawaii and the University of Missouri Law School. In 1959, he was defeated in his bid for a seat in the territorial senate.[32] In 1968, he was successful in being elected to the state's lower house and served one term.

The third pioneer Filipino territorial legislator was Pedro dela Cruz, long-time representative from the island of Lanai. Born in Mindanao's northern Cagayan Province, dela Cruz came to the Hawaiian Islands as an independent immigrant. After working on a sugar plantation on the island of Hawaii, he secured a job on Lanai as a truck driver. He became a foreman and served for ten years until the Dole Pineapple Company discharged him in 1947. The company charged incompetence, but he and the ILWU claimed it was due to his union activities. He opened a store in Lanai City and remained an important ILWU spokesman on Lanai. Unsuccessful twice in being elected to the lower house, dela Cruz won in 1958. That victory started a sixteen-year career in the territorial and state legislatures which lasted until his defeat in 1974. During his later years in the state legislature, he served as Vice Speaker of the house.[33] In 1975, Eduardo E. Malapit of Kauai became the first Filipino in the United States to be elected mayor. Malapit had already served several terms on the Kauai County Council.[34]

When Governor George Ariyoshi, Hawaii's third governor, took office in 1975, he appointed Joshua C. Agsalud as Director of the Department of Labor and Industrial Relations. The son of Filipino immigrants, Agsalud was a University of Hawaii graduate, a newspaper reporter, and later a teacher and school administrator.[35]

But Agsalud was not the first Filipino to hold this position. That honor went to Alfred Lareta who served from 1962 to 1967 under Governor John A. Burns. The first Filipino in the United States to hold a state cabinet post, Lareta, born on Oahu, grew up on Maui. He worked his way through the University of Hawaii and then gained a scholarship to Fordham University School of Law. He returned to Honolulu and formed law partnerships, first with George Ariyoshi and then with Bernaldo D. Bicoy. In 1969, Governor Burns appointed him to be judge of the fifth judicial circuit which encompassed the County of Kauai.[36]

In April, 1974, Benjamin Menor became the first Filipino to be appointed to the Hawaii State Supreme Court. Menor, his mother, and sister arrived on the island of Hawaii in 1930 to join his father who had come in 1925. After graduating from Hilo High School, he served with the First Filipino Infantry during World War II. He graduated from the University of Hawaii and earned a law degree at Boston University. He then returned to Hilo to work in the Hawaii County Attorney's office. In 1962, in his first bid for public office, he successfully ran for the state senate, becoming the first Filipino state senator in the United States. In 1968, Governor Burns appointed him to the third judicial circuit in the County of Hawaii and later appointed him to the State Supreme Court.[37]

By 1975, the Filipinos' increasing numbers made them very much aware of their latent political strength. The ILWU estimated that they comprised 50 percent of that union's membership. Carl Damaso, president of the Hawaii ILWU local, was Filipino. Forty percent of the AFL-CIO Hotel and Restaurant Workers membership were Filipino; in the Teamsters Union, they comprised 25 percent of the membership. But the Filipinos still were not able to organize a cohesive voting bloc. As in California, the Filipino community remained disorganized. In 1974, the United Filipino Council of Hawaii was formed to develop a coalition working for common interests.[38] For most Filipinos, the desire to improve their economic status was more important than political control. But one leader suggested the easiest road to economic success was:

to make their mark in the community and be recognized . . . through politics. We are not sophisticated businesswise like the Chinese. Economically, we are at the bottom level. The only way we are going to make it is through education and to enter professions, and with that, gain respect in the total community.

Just walk into the state tax .office or the department of labor and see who is behind the counter. . . . Accidentally, you might see a Filipino carrying a bucket of water. But, we can correct this: we can get our children highly educated.[39]

The new immigrants of the 1960's brought the same economic goals but more abilities to Hawaii. Those who had arrived prior to World War II found themselves still pushed to one side. According to one of the old-timers, the only certainty in the 1970's was his social security check. He added:

I get $119 something and that is more than what some of the other retired men here receive. That amount affords less than my lowest pay of a dollar a day when I first came here. My rent is $25 a month with everything included.
But this retirement money is starvation pension! . . . Anyway, the Security pension still is not enough. So I gamble for a dollar here and there betting on the cockfights, and dimes and quarters playing card games of payot and hearts. Sometimes, I go pick flowers for my Japanese friend there on his farm if there is no other way of getting money.[40]

The plight of these old plantation workers exploded upon the consciousness of Hawaii in 1972 when 109 residents of Ota Camp of the former Waipahu Plantation were ordered to leave the camp because the land was needed for development purposes. Three-fourths of them had lived most of their Hawaiian years there. Younger Filipinos rallied to the support of the old-timers; both were joined by other concerned citizen groups to protect the housing rights of these people. The Ota Camp controversy was only resolved when the State of Hawaii built a new community, Makibaka Village, for these residents which permitted them to follow their own life style.[41]

As indicated earlier, Hawaii's larger number of recent Filipino immigrants in the 1960's and 1970's caused social and economic problems. A most difficult task has been to match the skills of the new arrivals with available jobs. In both California and Hawaii, a basic problem was the ability to communicate in English. Unskilled workers, who sought jobs unsuccessfully, ended on welfare rolls.[42] Substantial numbers of professionals in a time of labor shortage in 1969 in Hawaii had trouble finding suitable employment. Some had difficulty in validating their professional credentials since there had been cases of fraudulent credentialing in the Philippines. College graduates often found their college degrees were equal to only two years of university work in California.[43]

By 1970 significant numbers of professionally trained Filipinos, many educated in the United States, had become part of the "brain drain" from the Philippines. Teachers and accountants comprised two large groups of such specialists. About 11 percent of the professional immigrants were engineers. The medical sciences, as a combined group, provided significant numbers: 983 physicians, 796 nurses, 294 pharmacists, and 198 dentists.[44] While most Filipino medical practitioners have located in California and Hawaii, another major concentration has been in Chicago where more than five hundred Filipino physicians and surgeons have their practices. There is a sufficient number of nurses in that area to make the Philippine Nurses Association of Chicago an active organization.[45]

Professionals found, however, that their degrees were not recognized and that they had to study for medical and dental examinations. Many worked as technicians until they passed these. Dr. Antonio Degadio, a nurse at San Francisco General Hospital, was a dentist who had led a three-year fight to change the law regarding the practice of dentistry. He had come from Guam where he had been a dentist for the United States Navy for eight years.[46] Identical difficulties were encountered in Hawaii. One physician, licensed in the Philippines in 1954, had served in various medical positions in Southeast Asia. Then he moved to Hawaii. With sixteen years of medical experience, he found employment as a janitor in a drive-in restaurant. Emotionally unsatisfying, the job lasted three months. He reminisced: "They didn't know I was a doctor. They might not let me have the job if they had known. Too many places had turned me away saying I was 'overqualified.' Then I went to work as a meat cutter. They thought I was very good at separating the meat from the bone."[47]

Other professionals had similar experiences—pharmacists, teachers, optometrists, lawyers, and dentists. All ran into notoriously protective bureaucratic screens erected and enforced by state functionaries. A woman pharmacist was not allowed in 1971 the opportunity even to take an examination to see if she was qualified because she was not a graduate of an American school of pharmacy.[48]

In spite of such setbacks, the Filipino people continued to flow to Hawaii and California in large numbers, seeking a better life for themselves and particularly for their children. They were willing to undergo discomfort and cultural alienation so that their children might improve their economic status.[49] A tragic flaw in this scheme was the language barrier that their children encountered. The public schools were not able to cope with the problem and many school age immigrants did not receive the hoped-for education. Additionally, in Hawaii, racial conflicts developed with other ethnic groups. Particularly disheartening were the fights between the Filipino youth of the older immigrant families and the newer ones.[50]

In the decade since the signing of the immigration law in 1965, the number and the character of Filipino immigrants have changed dramatically. The story of how these recent arrivals have adjusted to the United States and how citizens of the United States have adjusted to them is still unfolding.

PART II

KOREAN-AMERICANS

CHAPTER VIII

Korea, a Troubled Land

KOREAN immigration to the United States has only assumed major proportions in recent years. Until World War II, emigrants from that land were excluded because the United States considered Korea part of the Japanese Empire. All Americans became conscious of Korea, the Land of Morning Calm, during the summer of 1950 when President Harry S. Truman set in motion the establishment of a United Nations force to oppose the movement of North Koreans southward across the thirty-eighth parallel. Since the Korean War, the United States continues to be involved in varying degrees in Korea's internal affairs. And with the change in the 1965 immigration law, many Americans have been aware that increasing numbers of Koreans have been arriving at United States ports of entry.

Korea's position as an exposed East Asian peninsula has had a significant impact upon its inhabitants. The 600-mile-long peninsula, pointing southeastward from the Manchurian border toward the island empire of Japan, divides the Yellow Sea and the Sea of Japan. Honshu, Japan's major island, lies only 120 miles away. Siberia is only a few miles along the coast from Korea's northeastern corner. Over the centuries Korea has felt the surge and ebb of various peoples as they moved through the peninsula. All discovered that Korea presented in actuality a difficult invasion route.[1]

Not a large country, Korea, counting its numerous islands, comprises 85,285 square miles—just a bit larger than the state of Minnesota. Its eastern part is marked by high ranges of mountains which become extensive in the North. The geographical features of the country are diverse but the mountains, steep, abrupt, and stony, predominate. These continue to be important sources of coal, gold, iron, graphite, and tungsten.[2] Southern

111

Korea, less rocky, has more river plains. There is more arable flat land along the western slope which drains into the Yellow Sea than there is along the rocky and rugged east coast. But only 20 percent of the total land mass can be easily utilized for farming.

Korea's Manchurian border measures about 450 miles. The peninsula narrows to 120 miles between Wonsan and Pyongyang and then widens at the thirty-eighth parallel to about 160 miles.[3] The east coast provides few good harbors—the best ones are in the North at Wonsan and Chongjin—and has a tidal range between one and two feet. The less indented west coast is characterized by extensive mud flats and large tidal movements. Inchon, the west coast's major harbor, has the second highest tidal movement in the world with a variation of twenty-seven feet. Korea has about 3,300 offshore islands, but only about two hundred of these are populated.[4]

In a country where people depend upon the land for their livelihood, climatic conditions, such as rainfall and temperature, play an important role. During the winter months, cold, dry air, sweeping out of Siberia, brings varying amounts of rain and snow. The blowing winds drop temperatures below freezing and create a very high chill factor. During May and June, the weather pattern shifts and warm humid air moves in from the Pacific Ocean. As temperatures rise, the days become hot and sticky in the lowlands. The warm air brings a heavy rainy season during July and August.[5]

Climate and geography have dictated the direction of Korea's economy. In the North where it is colder and more mountainous, hydroelectric power, industry, and mining have been important developments, particularly under Japanese control. In the South, over 75 percent of the people tilled the soil, working the basic crops of rice, barley, and vegetables.[6]

Koreans have evolved a distinctive society through an amalgamation of several different ancient Asian tribal groups. Living between China and Japan, they have absorbed much from their two neighbors but have maintained a culture that is clearly their own.[7] The fundamental units in this culture were elder male dominated families which clustered together in villages and were organized as clans. This concept was based upon the Confucian view of proper relationships between people in which the ruler of the family group was always the oldest male member. This Confucian obedience and reverence to one's elders continued after death in the form of ancestor worship. The family unit grew as sons married and brought their wives to join the household or to live in nearby houses. Holding each extended family together was the clan which might occupy an entire village or share villages with other clans. During the twentieth century, family ties have been broken as younger sons moved away from the villages.

Koreans usually have names consisting of three syllables. One represents the family name; another, the generation name, indicates a person's place within the total family; and the third is the personal name. Shannon McCune has estimated that there are over one thousand clans in Korea but only 326 surnames. The most common family name is Kim; 20 to 25 percent of all Koreans bear that name. Other common family names are Ahn, Cho, Choi, Chong, Han, Kang, Lee, Lim, and Yu.[8]

Villages abound throughout Korea's countryside. These mud-walled and thatched-roofed settlements stand in the midst of cultivated land. Each house has a vegetable garden. Farm workers trudge daily from their homes a mile or so out to the fields to work. The village also provides opportunities for sharing certain work. Grist mills, wells, laundries, and markets are all communal attractions holding the people together. At the end of each day general socializing occurs and all villagers look forward to holiday festivals.[9]

Korean culture manifested itself through distinct language, dress, and foods. Although there have been heavy borrowings from China and Japan, the Korean language remains unique and serves as a bond of unity. During Korea's formative years, the influence of Confucian classics was strong; Chinese was the language of scholars and governmental officials. A major language change came during the reign of King Sejong (1418–1450) when a royal commission developed a phonetic alphabet. This alphabet, known as *Han'gul*, is the oldest known alphabet of its kind still in use. Considered an inferior system by inflexible and conservative Confucian scholar-officials, *Han'gul* consequently was used little until revived by missionaries in the nineteenth century. Suppressed by the Japanese during their years of occupation, *Han'gul* was adopted in 1945 as the official written language. Both South and North Korea have endorsed *Han'gul* to symbolize their new nationalism. The invention of this alphabet has been held in such high regard that a national holiday celebrates this event.[10]

Korea's geography and its economy have dictated the people's dietary habits. Rice is basic. White rice, served at each meal, is supplemented by meat or fish soups, seasoned meats and chicken, and vegetables. In North Korea, where rice is scarce, people substitute cereals such as barley, grain sorghum, millet, and wheat. To give variety to this bland diet, kim chee, pickled vegetables which are highly spiced, fermented, and laced with red peppers, is an important part of each meal. Kim chee pots are visible everywhere—in village and in city. The vegetables, peppers, and spices are stored in these pots to ferment throughout the winter.[11]

In Korea, as in other agricultural societies, the harvesting of food crops is a time for high celebration. Special events honoring one's family are equally significant. New Year's Day, celebrated according to the lunar calendar, is an occasion for paying homage to parents and grandparents and for reaffirming family ties. On *Dongsin-jae*, the fifteenth day of the first month, villagers pray together for a season of good crops. The harvest festival, *Chusok*, on the day of the full moon of the eighth month is the gayest celebration. The day begins with visits to ancestors' graves and the presentation of food. Dances, much eating and drinking follow.[12]

Two major occasions in the lives of every Korean family are the first and sixty-first birthdays. Both are, in a sense, reflective of the hard existence of people dependent upon subsistence agriculture. Infant mortality was a hard fact of life. Children who survived their first year were honored at a family party. The highlight of the celebration came when the child, dressed in traditional costume, was placed on a table upon which rested several objects, such as a pencil, money, ruler, or a Bible. Tradition had it that those the child touched would have impact upon his future. Touching money might mean a business career and/or riches; the pencil could symbolize scholarship or writing. A spool of thread indicated long life while the Bible suggested qualities of fearlessness and honesty. The adults eagerly watched the child and applauded his actions.[13]

Since life expectancy is not very long in Korea, anyone who attained a sixty-first birthday was indeed special. Such an event called for the clan to hold a large party in the person's honor. A man was expected to retire and be supported in as much comfort as his sons could provide. When a woman attained her sixty-first birthday in this patriarchal society, she wore brilliant garments, as did her husband. If she were a widow, she wore a traditional white costume.[14]

Korean life has been significantly shaped by various religions. As with many other civilizations, the earliest Korean religious expression was Shamanism, or animistic nature worship, which venerated objects not understood or controlled. The sun, the moon, high mountains, great rivers, and rocks were such objects. There still remains an awareness of good and evil spirits. Carved "devil-posts" stand guard at the edge of the village against evil spirits.[15] In times of illness, pieces of clothing from the sick are tied to tree branches at some distance from the village so that the evil spirits will remain with the clothing and not abide with the ill. As a result of Shamanism, present-day Koreans continue the long-time practice of locating lovely hillside burial sites, which usually command panoramic views of the plains below. The site was selected, in all probability, by a fortune teller as an auspicious location for the family's future luck.[16] The graves themselves are distinguished as domes of earth. It is to these attractive locations that families go to honor their ancestors and to hold their picnics.

While the teachings of Confucius do not constitute a religion, their importance in developing a philosophy and a set of ethical standards for Koreans has been monumental. These ideas first appeared in Korea about 108 B.C. Confucius held that the goal of man was to live in peaceful coexistence and harmony with the universe. This, he said, was best achieved by loving and obeying one's parents. Such teachings in China and in Korea led to patrilineal societies where family responsibilities and leadership passed from father to eldest son. Confucianism gave impetus and strength to Korea's male-dominated culture, where women were relegated to hard chores and only men could pursue intellectual careers.

As had been the case in China, Korean scholars used Confucianism to maintain their hold upon education and civil authority. The country moved easily into a class system dominated by scholar-politicans, many of whom also became in time wealthy landlords. Between this class and the rest of the people existed a wide social and economic gulf.[17]

Another cultural influence, Buddhism, came from China in A.D. 372; it spread through the peninsula and across the sea to Japan. Buddhism reached its greatest power during the Koryo dynasty (936–1392), the dynasty from which the name Korea was derived. After 1400, during the Yi dynasty, Confucianism became strong again, replacing Buddhism as a national creed and the Buddhists retreated into mountain monasteries. Buddhism has remained an important religion for many Koreans.

Ideas from Western cultures began to infiltrate when Korean diplomats to China first came in contact with Christian documents in the seventeenth century. While some Koreans expressed interest, the government's policy of isolation led to the persecution of early Christians. After the Hermit Kingdom signed a commercial and friendship treaty with the United States in 1882, Christianity quickly flowered. By 1885 Methodist and Presbyterian missionaries arrived to complement Catholic priests already there. Many Western ideas, other than religion, were adopted. The missionaries built an excellent system of schools and medical facilities and gained, at the same time, large numbers of converts, particularly from the upper classes.[18]

In the mid-1800's, during the last decades of the Yi dynasty, a new religion, Ch'ondo-gyo, sought to provide an alternative. First known as Tonghak, this religion, founded by Ch'oe Che-u, was a composite of what he viewed to be the best aspects of Buddhism, Christianity, Confucianism, and Taoism. The fundamental premise was that each man, already potentially immortal, was linked to God through his soul. Ch'ondo-gyo gained favor during periods of high nationalism because it was a Korean religion. At the time of early revolts against the Japanese and after the Korean War, Koreans endorsed Ch'ondo-gyo as another means of expressing support of their country.[19]

Cultural influences, then, played an important part in developing the Korean nation. Tradition has it that Korean civilization began with the descent of Tan'gun-wanggom, a spirit king of divine origin, who ruled for a thousand years. The Korean calendar starts counting time from the end of Tan'gun's reign. Archeological evidence shows that a neolithic people had settled by the tenth century B.C. By the fifth century B.C., with the start of Korea's Bronze Age, tribal nations began to emerge. One legend holds that several thousand Chinese founded the ancient kingdom of Chosen during the fourth century B.C. In any case, Chinese influence manifested itself from the earliest times.[20]

From the first century B.C. until A.D. 668, Korea was divided into the Three Kingdoms. The largest, Koguryo, in the North, reflected the greatest Chinese impact of the three. The southern part of the peninsula was divided between Paekje and Silla. These two maintained contacts with Japan, and served in effect as a funnel through which Buddhism, Chinese writing, and other aspects of Chinese culture were introduced into Japan. Silla, with the help of China's T'ang emperors, defeated Paekje in 661 and then in 669 unified Korea through the conquest of Koguryo. The Silla dynasty ended in 936 as Wang Kon, known in Korean history as T'aejo, launched the Koryo dynasty which lasted until 1392. Actually after 1270, Korea was a virtual vassal of the Mongol emperors and the Koryo rulers had little say.[21]

In 1392 General Yi Song-gye attacked and overthrew the weakened Koryo government. Like the founder of the Koryo dynasty, Yi became known posthumously as T'aejo, the first of the Yi dynasty. The old national name, Chosen, was reassigned, and Seoul became the capital. In the early 1600's, the Manchus successfully invaded Korea, and over the next two and one-half centuries forced the Yis to maintain close ties. Korea then retreated into isolation, earning the appellation the "Hermit Kingdom."

Korea, in its isolation, became extremely vulnerable during the nineteenth century when Western powers, joined by Japan, sought territorial expansion in the Far East. Clinging to the hope that its elder brother, China, would provide a buffer against the outside world, Korea was ill prepared for events during the last twenty-five years of the nineteenth century. In the process of becoming an Asian power, Japan effected major changes in Korea. In 1876, Japan forced Korea into a treaty which opened it to Japanese trade. By 1882, Korea signed a similar treaty with the United States. Soon European nations also entered into diplomatic relations. By 1894, Japan felt strong enough to force a showdown with China. One of Japan's goals was to separate Korea from any semblance of Chinese vassalage. In this, she was successful.

By 1904, Japan had become deeply involved in Korea's internal affairs. A year earlier Japan had suggested to Russia that each country recognize the other's Far Eastern position—Japan's "preponderant interests" in Korea and Russia's "special interests" in Manchuria. In the Russo-Japanese War of 1904, Japan used the Korean peninsula to channel its armies into Siberia and Manchuria. The Japanese also wrested additional concessions from the now weakened Korean emperor. Japan established a protectorate over Korea in 1905 and forced the emperor to abdicate in favor of his son who was even weaker. In 1909, after Japanese Resident General Hirobumi Ito was assassinated, Japan instituted tighter controls. On August 29, 1910, Korea was annexed and, until 1945, was used for the economic benefit of the empire of the Rising Sun. Under Japanese rule, Korea moved away from a subsistence economy as raw materials were developed for export. There consequently arose an unskilled labor force which the Japanese managed.

Japanese political and educational institutions were forced upon the people but, internally and externally, the desire for an independent Korea remained strong. Indeed, much of the story of the early Korean immigrants in the United States is entwined with the struggle for a free Korea.[22]

A major demonstration of this hope occurred in 1919 at the time of the death of King Kojong, the last of the Yi dynasty. The national day of mourning launched countrywide demonstrations for independence. Thirty-three leaders had agreed to sign a Declaration of Independence to be proclaimed on March 1, 1919. It was secretly agreed that people would celebrate by waving Korean flags and shouting *Man Sei* (long live). The *Man Sei* independence movement completely surprised Japanese officials who reacted harshly and cruelly to this outpouring which involved peasants throughout the country. Following the repression of this movement, various Koreans organized provisional governments. These factions met in Shanghai and on September 6, 1919, established the Provisional Government of the Republic of Korea.[23]

Following the end of World War II in 1945, the United States Army established a military government in South Korea while the Russians occupied the northern part. In the stalemate that followed, a United Nations commission attempted to hold national elections. It proved impossible to conduct these elections, but in 1948 South Korea approved a national constitution and elected the now old man of Korean overseas politics, Syngman Rhee, as the first president of the Republic of Korea. By January, 1949, the United States, Nationalist China, and other nations recognized the Republic of Korea. In the North, meanwhile, the Communists had established the People's Republic of Korea. When growing friction along the border at the thirty-eighth parallel led to an outbreak of hostilities on June 25, 1950, launching the Korean War, the United States called upon the United Nations to protect South Korea. Technically a United Nations action, the major support came from the United States. After three years of fighting, hostilities ended with the status quo of 1950 reestablished along the thirty-eighth parallel.[24]

After the war, Rhee called for and received United States aid to rebuild South Korea. Economic diversification was stressed as efforts were made to move from exportation of ores and agricultural products. Since 1960, South Korea has developed textile and plywood mills; it has produced wigs, electronic goods, and processed food for oversea markets. For his part, Rhee, the old fighter throughout the years for an independent Korea, became more and more certain that only he had the answers to Korea's political problems. During the twilight of his life, he became more dictatorial. In 1960, in an effort to maintain power, Rhee and his Liberal Party resorted to fraud, military and police force, and illegal ballot counting. On April 19, 1960, college and high school students started street demonstrations protesting these election frauds. Seven days later, when other citizens joined in, Rhee resigned his presidency. The first National Assembly revised the constitution, aimed at diminishing the president's autocratic powers.[25] Yun Po-Sun was elected to the presidency of the Second Republic with Dr. John M. Chang serving as premier of the new cabinet. Chang's Democratic Party soon fractured and political stability proved impossible. Coupled with this was a period of continued unrest and uncertainty.

Into this chaos marched General Park Chung Hee on May 16, 1961. General Park declared that the army acted to end national corruption and to expedite the formation of an efficient government. The army's Supreme Council for National Reconstruction operated all phases of the government for over two years. Park then withdrew from this military junta to be elected president on October 15, 1963. The army's reworked constitution provided for a one-house assembly which Park's Democratic Republican Party controlled as a result of the 1963 election. Sweeping changes were carried out in the name of social and economic reform.

Park, reelected in 1967, gained despotic control of his country, as had Rhee earlier. In 1969, he received through a referendum the right to run for a third term in 1971. After this successful exercise, Park and his followers strengthened their tight control by making the presidency a lifetime job. Repression in Korea became common. By 1974, large numbers of dissidents were jailed for holding opposing views. During this year, an assassin, trying for Park's life, fatally wounded Mrs. Park.[26]

Against uncertain conditions such as a divided North and South Korea and South Korea's repressive police state, many Koreans took advantage of the United States' more liberal immigration laws. In the late 1960's and the 1970's, Koreans began to move to the United States for political as well as economic reasons.

CHAPTER IX

Korean Immigration to the United States

KOREAN immigration to the mainland United States and to Hawaii took place in several distinct waves since 1885. The Koreans left their homeland because of a mixture of motives.

The first Koreans, only three in number, to reach the United States arrived in 1885 following an abortive attempt by pro-Japanese liberals to overthrow the Korean monarchy. Two remained briefly but the third, Philip Jaisohn, attended the American College for Medicine and spent most of his life in the United States. He remained active in the drive for a free Korea.[1] From about 1890 until 1905, the time of the establishment of Japan's protectorate, some sixty-four students trained in Christian mission schools were encouraged to migrate to the United States to acquire an education. Among these students were future leaders who devoted their lives to fostering Korean independence. One such student was Chang-ho Ahn, founder of the People's Society, an underground group in Korea. He became one of the first California leaders in the Korean National Association and the organizer of the Corps for the Advancement of Individuals. Two other students who became leaders of Koreans in America were Yong-man Pak and Syngman Rhee.[2] After graduation from college, most students returned to Korea and became involved in the struggle against Japan. Others emerged as spokesmen and leaders in Korean-American communities.

It was not until 1903 that any sizeable number of Koreans left the Hermit Kingdom. The stimulus came from Hawaiian sugar plantations in their continuing search for sources of cheap labor. As early as 1896, Hackfeld & Company, a German-owned concern, suggested that Koreans be imported into Hawaii. The

Republic of Hawaii's administration rejected this proposal after several months' study.[3]

In 1902, Horace Allen, United States Minister to Korea, met with the representatives of the Hawaiian Sugar Planters' Association (HSPA) to discuss the importation of Koreans to Hawaii.[4] Upon his return to Korea, Allen contacted David W. Deshler and asked if he would be the HSPA's recruiting agent. Deshler already had several economic interests in Korea, including a steamship line that operated between Inchon and Kobe, Japan. Any migration to Hawaii could be routed on this line, redounding to Deshler's advantage. The HSPA, at the same time, dispatched E. Faxon Bishop with $25,000 to Japan and Korea to recruit workers. Allen, a confidant of Emperor Konjong, meanwhile met with the ruler and discussed the advantages of royal concurrence. The timing could not have been more propitious. In 1902, a cholera epidemic had added to the burdens of recent drought, flood disasters, and a plague of locusts. Allen indicated to the emperor that Koreans would be welcome in Hawaii, a place from which, incidentally the Chinese had been excluded; that the Korean economy could benefit from earnings returned from the islands; and that such an enterprise might involve the United States more closely in the internal affairs of Korea.[5]

Emperor Konjong, in November, 1902, established a department of immigration. The department required that emigrants be in good health and of high repute. Additionally, no passport would be issued to anyone who wished to emigrate as a contract laborer.[6]

Deshler, after receiving royal assent, organized the Korean Development Company to manage the recruitment program for the HSPA. The company's advertisements proclaimed that Hawaii had a mild climate in which to work, that workers would be paid sixteen dollars a month, and that they were to work ten hours a day, six days a week. The plantations would provide free medical care, housing, fuel, and water to all workers, married and single. The development company took care to suggest that those who migrated did so on their own and not as contract laborers. Recruiting centers were established in Seoul, Inchon, Pusan, and Wonsan, but few Koreans came forward to make the trip. For most, there was a basic cultural problem related to the abandonment of their ancestors' graves. There was also the matter of financing one's passage. Most Koreans simply did not have funds to pay for the trip and to have the needed "show money" to demonstrate to United State immigration officials in Honolulu that they were not paupers. The Korean Development Company paid the emigrants' passport fees, loaned each individual his passage fare and "show money." The loans, negotiated by the newly created Deshler Bank in Inchon, were repayable ten months from the time of the emigrants' arrival at one of the sugar plantations. Records show that this bank had only one depositor, the HSPA.[7]

Through Allen's urging, several American Protestant ministers influenced members of their congregations to emigrate. George Heber Jones, one of the missionary preachers in Inchon, was particularly persuasive. On December 22, 1902, 121 emigrants boarded the S.S. *Gaelic* for Kobe. Most came from the Inchon area; almost half were members of Jones's church.[8] At Kobe, the HSPA had the prospective workers examined. Nineteen failed the physical examination. The *Gaelic* continued its voyage, arriving in Honolulu on January 13, 1903. On board were the first Korean immigrants—fifty-six men, twenty-one women, and twenty-five children. Two of the men came as interpreters for the group. These first pioneers were sent to Kahuku plantation along the northern Oahu coast.[9]

While these Koreans were planning to emigrate, Horace Allen on December 10, 1902, communicated with Secretary of State John Hay and with Hawaii's Territorial Governor Sanford Dole essentially in order to prepare the way for the *Gaelic's* human cargo and for subsequent shiploads of Koreans. In his letter to Hay, Allen restated arguments and conditions he had discussed earlier with the emperor. He wrote, in part:

There are quite a number of Koreans now residing in the United States, whither they have gone chiefly in quest of an education, the desire for which is so strong that genteel Koreans have taken up menial callings to that end. Other Koreans wish to get to the United States but it is not always easy for them to leave their country, since if they steal away without proper papers they are liable to suspicion on the charge of treason, which would make it dangerous for them to return. Passports have not been easy to obtain, chiefly since a native having sufficient funds on which to emigrate would be liable to such a system of "squeezing" that before he could obtain the necessary documents providing for his departure he would probably have exhausted his small capital.

Lately Koreans have become interested in the Hawaiian Islands where large numbers of Chinese and Japanese reside, and considerable numbers have desired to go to the islands with the hope of bettering their condition and escaping the persistent oppression of their tax collectors. The idea of obtaining an education for their children seems to be an incentive as well.

The severe famine of last winter seems to have brought this matter to a head, while the difficulty of feeding the large numbers of famished people probably induced the Government to look favorably upon the project. At any rate there has been talk of organizing an emigration bureau, ever since last winter. The Emperor seems to feel considerable pride in the fact that while Chinese may not enter the United States, Koreans will be allowed to do so.

. . . .

I hear that a number of Koreans have banded themselves together with the intention of going to Honolulu during the coming winter. Some of them will take their families, it is said. If they make a favorable report on conditions in Hawaii it is quite probable a considerable number of Koreans may follow them or go to the Philippines. Though the number can never be very great I fancy since the Korean Government would probably take alarm at anthing [sic] like a great exodus and withhold the necessary passports, for it seems that the population of Korea has been greatly exaggerated [sic]. . . .

The Korean people are a docile, good-natured, patient and hard working race. They differ from the Chinese in being able to take on our ways rather easily. Koreans have become naturalized American citizens and are a credit to us. There are quite a number of Koreans here in office and in public life who have been educated in the United States and who are conducting themselves excellently. One being a practising physician.

Ages of subjugation to their superiors make them law abiding and easy to govern, at the same time they seem able to absorb ideas of liberty and equality very redily [sic].

It would seem that if these people actually go to our islands and make a report that will lead others to follow; and if the Korean Government allows them to go, they may help to solve the labor question in these islands.

I am satisfied that the Korean Government is not engaged in assisting these people to emigrate by advancing them funds. Rather do they probably hope to gain from them on their return. Most of these people will undoubtedly be too poor to be able to raise the necessary funds for emigrating to any distance, especially with their families, unless their neighbors and friends contribute to assist them with the hope of being able to follow later on with funds sent by these pioneers. . . .[10]

The Korean workers, who came during the first six months of 1903, fulfilled Allen's expectations. They made a favorable impression and word was sent back to Korea to continue recruiting. Agents remained active until April 1, 1905, when the Korean Foreign Office prohibited all overseas immigration. Allen assured the HSPA that suspension was temporary but as Japan assumed control under the protectorate, the department of immigration was closed in November, 1905.[11]

After Allen was replaced as United States minister, Japanese control tightened, and immigration closed to a trickle. But during the years of open migration, 7,226 immigrants, consisting of 6,048 men, 637 women, and 541 children left for Hawaii. The HSPA had arranged sixty-five crossings. The ages of the men ranged from twenty to thirty years. Few of them migrated directly from rural regions; most were unemployed laborers from seaport towns. Others were soldiers, house servants, miners, woodcutters, or policemen. Some 60 percent of the immigrants were illiterate.[12]

TABLE IV
KOREAN IMMIGRATION TO HAWAII, 1901–1911

Fiscal Year	Number	Fiscal Year	Number
1901	4[a]	1905	2,659
1902	12	1906	8[b]
1903	1,133	1910	27[c]
1904	3,434	1911	9

[a]Houchins, p. 553; W. Kim, p. 10.
[b]Territory of Hawaii, Board of Immigration, *Report, 1907.*
[c]Territory of Hawaii Legislature, House Committee on Agriculture and Immigration, *Report, 1911.*

Other immigrants left Korea in 1905 under inducement of an English recruiter who had a contract with Mexican plantations. About one thousand were transported to Vera Cruz and then dispatched to several locations where they were virtually enslaved. Several Korean associations in the United States attempted to aid them. A 1911 plan sought unsuccessfully to transport them to Hawaii. The Korean National Association in San Francisco continued to provide relief for many years to their countrymen isolated in Mexico.[13]

Hawaii was the destination of most Korean immigrants during these first years. According to the 1910 census, there were 4,533 Koreans in the islands. About one thousand of the early immigrants had returned to Korea while another thousand had moved on to the West Coast. Many of this latter group returned home later. The 1930 census, which identified many Koreans as Japanese, reported 461 Koreans residing on the mainland in 1910. Only thirty-one of these lived east of the Rocky Mountains. The largest number, 406, had made California their home, settling in and around Los Angeles, the San Francisco Bay Area, and the Central Valley towns of Delano, Dinuba, Reedley, and Sacramento. Los Angeles in 1906 had only sixty Koreans. Four years later it had only fourteen Korean residents and San Francisco had thirty-nine.[14]

The first Korean immigration to Hawaii and the mainland consisted of only a few people. One reason was that growing Japanese control in Korea after 1905 served as a brake on movement from Korea. The first exodus also coincided with large-scale Japanese immigration to the West Coast which resulted in growing white hostility.

This first Korean immigration to Hawaii and the mainland con- about Korean immigration came during the crisis regarding Japanese in San Francisco schools. President Theodore Roosevelt and Secretary of State Elihu Root early in 1907 negotiated the Gentlemen's Agreement with the Japanese government to settle this international controversy. That government agreed not to issue any more passports to skilled or unskilled laborers, but would continue to do so for "laborers who have already been to America and to the parents, wives, and children of laborers already resident there."[15] On March 14, 1907, Roosevelt issued a proclamation excluding any Japanese and Korean laborers who tried to enter the United States by way of Canada, Hawaii, or Mexico.

The Korean government, even though the Japanese administrators of the protectorate sought to control emigration, kept issuing passports. In November, 1907, Root decreed that the United States would not recognize them. To enter the United States thereafter, Koreans had to have passports issued by the Japanese Foreign Office.[16] Root's action stopped Korean immigration and recognized Japan's presence in Korea.

One Korean group that continued to arrive were picture brides. Following the 1907 Gentlemen's Agreement, they emigrated to Hawaii and the mainland until the passage of the 1924 immigration act which made subjects of Japan, including Koreans, aliens ineligible for citizenship and barred as immigrants to the United States.[17] As early as 1908 when the specific problem of Japanese picture brides had come to the attention of United States authorities, the Japanese Consul-General in San Francisco stated what was common practice in the Japanese Empire. A man sent a photograph of himself to the woman he wished to marry. She in return sent a photograph of herself; if both parties agreed to the union, the marriage was registered in Japan.

The United States Attorney General's staff expressed concern as to the marriage's legality if one of the two parties was a resident in the United States prior to the marriage. The staff concluded that an exchange of pictures constituted a marriage, but it was recommended that any women claiming admission on the basis of having "been married by the photography method . . . shall before being permitted to land, evidence their good faith by being married to the alleged husband under a ceremony whose legality is recognized in the state in which the port of entry is located."[18] The Japanese government permitted Korean men to seek picture brides since there were few Korean women in the United States. The first wave to Hawaii brought 637 women. Between 1910 and 1924, about one thousand picture brides came to the islands while another 115 arrived on the West Coast.[19] From the beginning, both men and women had to make accommodations to their own cultural differences as they started their marriages in Hawaii. The men, in letters to Korea, had depicted life in the islands in rosy colors while statements about their own economic condition were inaccurate.

A groom, for his part, had to locate financial backers who would be willing to contribute to the bride's passage money since few men had adequate resources of their own. After the marriage ceremony, many Korean husbands settled in Honolulu or a rural town since plantation life was both difficult and primitive. The arrival of the brides provided a major incentive for Korean men to leave the fields and seek urban employment.[20]

As already indicated, students formed an important early group of Korean immigrants. But the protectorate's 1905 restrictions on emigration also eliminated them. The Japanese saw in the students an anti-Japanese element which would provide leaders and agitators. In this, their perception proved correct. Besides, the Japanese thought the Koreans should be educated in Japan, not in Europe or the United States.[21]

One of the last students to leave before the 1905 edict was Syngman Rhee, who helped bear out the Japanese suspicion. Born March 26, 1875 in Hwanghai Province, he received his first formal education at the Paichai Mission School. At the age of twenty, he joined the independence club founded by Philip Jaisohn. When Jaisohn returned to the United States in 1896, Rhee became leader. The next year, following a mass demonstration in Seoul which he led, Rhee was arrested and sentenced to life imprisonment. While in prison, he was converted to Christianity. A 1904 general amnesty released all prisoners and Rhee left for the United States. He received his A.B. degree in 1907 from George Washington University and his M.A. from Harvard in 1908. Next he attended Princeton University. His biographers state that he was the first Korean to receive a Ph.D. from an American university, which occurred in 1910—the last year of Woodrow Wilson's presidency at Princeton. Wilson and Rhee became friends during Rhee's graduate days at the university.[22] Rhee was the most highly educated of the Korean independence leaders, one factor that set him apart.

Rhee's university career bridges the first period of student migration, its suspension, and the resumption four years later. In 1909, the Japanese government indicated that student passports would be issued for travel to the United States if there was evidence of endorsement by the United States government and sufficient funds available for support. American Consul-General Thomas Sammons indicated that students could go provided that American nationals sponsored them. The Taft administration, 1909–1913, continued this friendly and encouraging attitude.[23]

Between 1910 and 1918, 541 young Korean political activists in the struggle against Japan fled Japanese oppression. Coming to the United States via Manchuria or Shanghai, they arrived with neither passport nor student visa. Since Japanese documents were not available to them, they claimed exemption. Following Taft policy, the Commissioner Generals of Immigration categorized these immigrants as "working students."[24] Because they were really political refugees and not students, most were not qualified to enroll in schools or colleges. About one hundred did graduate from college. From these activists came the American Korean communities' anti-Japanese leaders of the 1930's.[25]

Following World War I, the Japanese government kept firm control over Korea's internal affairs. While students continued to arrive in the United States between 1921 and 1940, the 289 who came during those years had been carefully screened and they were forced to return home when they stopped or completed their studies. They contributed little to the Korean communities in the United States and they remained apart from any move for independence. As friendly relations between Japan and the United States broke down in 1940, the flow of students stopped. Several Korean students, studying in the United States in 1940 and 1941, became government translators and interpreters when hostilities started. Others joined the United States Army.[26]

The number of Koreans living in the United States reflected the restrictive immigration policies of both Japan and the United States over three decades, from 1910 to 1940. In 1920, there were 1,677 Koreans on the mainland. By 1930 this number had increased to a total of 1,860 and then decreased in 1940 to 1,711. Most lived in the West with the largest concentration still in California. Hawaii's Korean population grew following the arrival of the picture brides. In 1920, the territory had 4,950

Koreans. The total for 1930 and 1940 reflected the substantial birthrate of the 1920's—6,461 in 1930 and 6,851 in 1940.[27]

While World War II was in progress, Asian immigration came to a virtual standstill. Following Korean independence in 1945, an estimated six thousand students came to the United States to continue their education. With the tremendous internal dislocation caused by the Korean War, large numbers of Koreans began in 1950 to enter American ports, mostly as non-quota immigrants. In 1958, for example, 1,604 Koreans were admitted; 1,387 were non-quota entries.[28] The number of arrivals increased gradually each year. By 1965 the number had risen to 2,165. The first major increase occurred in 1969, the year General Park entrenched himself in the presidency. From that time on, the number of Korean immigrants dramatically increased each year. They clearly left their homeland for both economic and political reasons. During the decade 1965–1974, Korean immigration, as shown in the following table, increased 1,194.6 percent as 111,914 Koreans entered the United States.[29]

TABLE V

KOREAN IMMIGRANTS ADMITTED INTO THE
UNITED STATES, 1965–1974[a]

Year	Number	Year	Number
1965	2,165	1970	9,314
1966	2,492	1971	14,297
1967	3,956	1972	18,876
1968	3,811	1973	22,930
1969	6,045	1974	28,028

[a]U.S. Immigration and Naturalization Service, *Annual Report, 1974*, p. 59.

In 1972 and 1973, Korea ranked fifth behind Mexico, Philippines, Cuba, and Ireland in the number of immigrants sent to the United States. By 1974 Korea was a close third to the Philippies.[30]

By 1970 Koreans, having settled throughout the United States, numbered 70,598. For the first time, California had the largest number. Hawaii was second and New York had become a close third.[31] Los Angeles had the largest Korean community. New York City had slightly more Koreans than did Honolulu while Chicago showed a population in excess of one thousand.[32] These recent Korean arrivals, while creating socioeconomic problems for themselves and those communities in which they lived, sought to adapt to the different cultures that surrounded them.

CHAPTER X

The Korean Struggle
for American Citizenship

KOREANS who came to Hawaii and to the mainland United States prior to 1924, and those who arrived after the Korean War, sought to establish new homes and maintain their old life styles. They encountered, like other Asians, racial prejudice and discrimination. They also modified the culture they brought as they adapted to their new surroundings.

In the first years of the twentieth century, as noted earlier, Californians coupled the arrival of Koreans with Japanese immigration. In February, 1905, the *San Francisco Chronicle*, without warning, launched a racist attack against Japanese and Koreans. Within the month, anti-Asian organizations were being formed.

On May 14, 1905, a mass meeting, supported by San Francisco labor union locals and other organizations, was held to organize the Japanese and Korean Exclusion League. From its inception, the league, renamed the Asiatic Exclusion League in December, 1907, maintained that both Koreans and Japanese were undesirable alien elements.[1] The league, and its cohort in the movement, the San Francisco Building Trades Council, enlarged upon an earlier resolution of the American Federation of Labor which had been adopted at its 1904 annual convention in San Francisco: "Resolved, That the terms of the Chinese Exclusion Act be enlarged and extended so as to permanently exclude from the United States and its insular territories all classes of Japanese and Coreans other than those exempted by the present terms of that act...."[2]

In December, 1905, two California members of the House of Representatives, Duncan E. McKinlay of San Francisco and Everis A. Hayes of San Jose, introduced separate measures

132

aimed at prohibiting Japanese and Koreans from entering the United States.[3] The Japanese and Korean Exclusion League claimed the Hayes bill as its own. A form letter, printed in 1906 for distribution to California labor unions, urged:

Pledge the candidates for Congress in your district and the United States Senators to work and vote for our bill, No. H.R. 8975, which extends the Chinese Exclusion Act to all Japanese and Koreans. If your representatives try to evade or straddle this question, or if they are hostile to labor's cause and the people's interest you must, if you are true to yourselves, VOTE THEM DOWN AND OUT AT THE POLLS.[4]

On October 11, 1906, the San Francisco Board of Education issued its directive that all principals were to send "all Chinese, Japanese, and Korean children to the Oriental Public School. . . ."[5] Existing California school law proved ambiguous in the ensuing argument between President Roosevelt and the city of San Francisco and the state of California. The California State Senate hastened to adopt a resolution excluding Indians, Chinese, Malays, Japanese, and all Mongolians from public elementary and secondary schools whenever separate schools for these minority groups had been provided.[6] Such a blanket resolution covered all Asian groups.

During February and March, 1907, as President Roosevelt and Japanese representatives worked out the terms of the Gentlemen's Agreement, racists in California held steady to their course. On February 14, 1907, Olaf Tveitmoe, President of the Japanese and Korean Exclusion League, sent identical telegrams to Representative Hayes and to Mayor Eugene Schmitz, who led the San Francisco delegation to its Washington meeting with the President. Tveitmoe maintained there could be no change in the immigration law and that both the Japanese and Koreans had to be bracketed with Chinese. Total exclusion, he concluded, was the "only solution to the problem."[7]

By the end of 1907, the Japanese had clearly become the real target of the exclusionists for the simple reason that there were many more of them on the West Coast compared to Koreans or East Indians. In January, 1908, the league, as it reported

exaggerated population figures for the Japanese, noted that the
figures did "not include Koreans and Hindus, of whom we have
a great many." But by May, 1908, the league had dismissed
the Koreans: "Nor do the Koreans as yet constitute an important
factor in this problem because with a probable total of 12,000
there are not more than 1,000 women among them. The addition
to the Korean population through native births will probably
be unnoticed for many years."[8] Some indication of how the
league inflated its numbers of Asian immigrants can be seen
by comparing its 1908 figure with the 1910 census headcount
which reported only 304 Koreans in California. It was not until
1960 that the Bureau of Census reported that the Korean population in the United States exceeded twelve thousand.

In 1910, the *San Francisco Chronicle*, while concerned at the
moment about the influx of East Indians, gave brief attention
to what it still saw as a potential Korean immigration problem:
"If Japan formally annexes Corea, the Japanese government
can keep Coreans away as it does Japanese, but in the meantime
their immigration should be forbidden."[9] From 1911 through
1916, as anti-Asian sentiment grew nationally, Western Congressmen developed a list of Asian nationalities to be excluded. In
1911, Hayes introduced an omnibus bill in the House to regulate the immigration of nine specific Asian groups—"Chinese,
Japanese, Koreans, Tartars, Malays, Afghans, East Indians, Las-
cars, Hindoos, and other persons of the Mongolian or Asiatic
race. . . ." He reintroduced the same measure in 1913. Representative Edwin Roberts of Nevada introduced a similar measure
in 1911, and tried again with the same bill in 1915.[10] These
proposals indicate concern that Asians from small countries
migrating to the United States would increase the dangers of
the "Yellow Peril." Such fear was expressed by California's
Democratic Party in 1912 as it called for "immediate federal
legislation for the exclusion of Japanese, Korean and Hindoo
laborers. . . ."[11]

From the time of the Japanese protectorate in Korea in 1905,
most Americans lumped Koreans with what was known as the
Japanese problem. An event illustrating this occurred on June 27,
1913, shortly after the conclusion of the major anti-alien land
law debate between California officials and President Woodrow

Wilson, Secretary of State William Jennings Bryan and the Empire of Japan. Eleven Korean field workers arrived in the Hemet agricultural area, south of Riverside, California, to pick apricots. Residents of the region, mistaking the Koreans for Japanese, drove the eleven away. A representative of the Japanese Consulate in Los Angeles came at once to Hemet to offer assistance, but the nationalistic Koreans refused his aid. The Korean National Association of America, with headquarters then in San Francisco, resolved the matter to its satisfaction.[12]

On June 30, David Lee, president of the association, telegraphed Bryan that all was under control. He added: "Please regard us not as Japanese in the time of peace and war. We Koreans came to America before Japan's annexation of Korea and will never submit to her so long as the sun remains in heaven. We will stay here peaceful under American jurisdiction."[13] Meanwhile, the American consul in Seoul, George H. Leidmore, reported mixed reaction to the incident in the Korean capital. The *Seoul Press* reported that Tokyo's *Japan Mail* found great interest in high Japanese circles in regard to the Hemet affair. An unnamed Japanese official, while announcing that his government was obligated to protect Korean immigrants in every instance, used the incident to launch a diatribe against American missionaries in Korea who had been vocally anti-Japanese in their attitudes against recent government policies. He chided the missionaries for posing as protectors in the Land of the Morning Calm while anti-Korean incidents in California showed the true American attitude.[14]

Bryan's reply to Lee on the Hemet matter became a significant milestone for Koreans residing in the United States. In a statement made public by the Department of State, Bryan, noting receipt of the association's telegram about the Koreans' position regarding Japanese help, indicated that he had decided that any matter dealing with Koreans living in the United States would be addressed to the Korean National Association.[15] This naturally strengthened the association's status. But, the Koreans, relatively few in number and well scattered throughout the Western states, never posed any major problem for the exclusionists who devoted more attention to the Japanese and Filipinos.

The question of citizenship rights for Korean immigrants materialized after World War I. Several court cases involving Asians revolved around the interpretation of Section 2169, *Revised Statutes* and later statutes granting citizenship for military service to certain ethnic groups.[16] In 1918, Easurk Emsen Charr was drafted into the United States Army. He served until December 28, 1918, when he was honorably discharged. Charr, a student at Park College in Kansas City, Missouri, petitioned for citizenship in a federal district court in 1921. The court ruled against Charr for Koreans were "admittedly of the Mongol family" and the 1906 act excluded them from citizenship. As for the 1918 statute relative to military service, the court held that the law clearly indicated that of all ethnic groups previously ineligible for citizenship, only Filipinos and Puerto Ricans who had served during the war were now eligible for naturalization. The court also claimed: "the provisions of the draft law clearly did not contemplate the incorporation of those not eligible to citizenship" into the armed forces. The judge stated "that such [aliens] may have been inducted into the service through voluntary enlistment or inadvertence of draft boards cannot affect the purpose of Congress."

Charr subsequently asked for a rehearing, holding that a 1919 statute stated that "any person of foreign birth who served in the military or naval forces of the United States during the present war . . . and shall have been honorably discharged" could be naturalized. The judge reported that a thorough investigation of the new statute, an undebated rider to a Congressional appropriations bill, showed that the time was simply extended during which eligible aliens leaving military service could apply for naturalization. The rider in no way changed the concept of the word *alien* and only those previously eligible could apply. Thus he denied Charr's petition in the rehearing.[17] En Sk Song had petitioned at the same time in California for citizenship because of his military service. The federal district court there, ruling on the same statutes, came to the same decisions as had the Missouri court.[18]

As the judge in the Charr case had held, the question of Korean citizenship remained tied to any claims made by the Japanese as long as Koreans were considered subjects of Japan.

But with the surrender of Japan on August 15, 1945, Korea became a free nation again and her people, after forty years, regained their status of independence. The result for the United States was questions about renewed immigration and citizenship for alien Koreans resident in the United States. In 1944, Joseph R. Farrington, Territorial Delegate from Hawaii, introduced the first Korean immigration and naturalization bill in Congress. A year later, Senator Claude Pepper of Florida and Representative Adam Clayton Powell, Jr., of New York City submitted similar measures which were shelved by committees. In 1947, as Senator Pepper reintroduced his bill, Representative Emanuel Celler of Brooklyn prepared an identical version for the House. Farrington again presented his measure which called for an immigration quota of one hundred Koreans a year, seventy-five from Korea itself, with the right of naturalization for all.[19] Throughout both sessions of the Eightieth Congress, the Korean Immigration and Naturalization Committee lobbied in behalf of these measures. Speaking for the committee, Walter Jhung, a Hawaiian Korean, called particular attention to the large number of his compatriots in the islands, many of whom had arrived as children. Wholly Americanized, they had never had the opportunity to become citizens.[20]

During the 1949 session, Senator William Langer of North Dakota sponsored a Korean citizenship bill while Farrington and Representative Herman Eberharter of Pittsburgh, Pennsylvania, introduced similar measures in the House. In July, 1950, as the fury of the Korean War raged, Langer scored the Democratic administration for having defeated his measure in the previous session. He reported that after the introduction of his measure in February, 1949, he received a letter from Jhung indicating that the granting of citizenship to Koreans would offset the work of Communists in Korea. Koreans from Hawaii also wrote Langer expressing their continued hope that they would finally become American citizens. However, the decision in the Democratic-controlled Senate committee had been to postpone his bill indefinitely.[21]

In the years following World War II, Congress amended the old immigration laws several times to meet changing circumstances and pressures. The codification of these amendments together with the further liberalization of immigration regulations, at least for Asians, occurred in 1952 with the McCarran-Walter Immigration Act. Korea, as part of the Asia-Pacific Triangle, received an annual immigration quota of one hundred. The act also provided that citizenship could not be abridged or denied because of race, sex, or marriage.[22] Thus, Koreans, and all other Asians, admitted as legal aliens could qualify as applicants for citizenship.

As had been the case for all Asians, prior to citizenship, Koreans were legally restricted in much that they could do. In eleven states, they could not buy, own, or lease land. Twenty-six states refused them old age pensions. New York's laws excluded them from twenty-seven different occupations.[23] Fifteen states refused as late as 1950 to sanction marriages between Koreans and white persons. In California and several other states, Koreans had been classified as Mongolians, which prohibited them from securing marriage licenses. In California, however, after 1948 marriage was possible as a consequence of the Perez-Sharp decision.[24]

From 1952 there was no longer any question about citizenship for Koreans residing in the United States. The only continuing legal bar that hampered their economic freedom was the restriction of professional licensing.

CHAPTER XI

Korean Communities
in the United States

FOR most of the twentieth century, Korean immigrants were not able to return to their ancestral home. The Japanese occupation, war, and internal and external political upheavals caused them to be isolated in various parts of the world. From the outset, Korean communities in the United States centered around churches, schools, and cultural organizations.

The fact that almost all who went to Hawaii between 1903 and 1905 were Christians made the Korean settlement in the islands unlike that of any other Asian group. Both in Hawaii and on the mainland, the Koreans were predominantly Protestants; only a few attended the Catholic Church. In Hawaii, they sought out Christian denominations for help in adjusting to their new environment. The Methodist Church undertook a Hawaiian Korean mission when that denomination and the Congregational Church's Hawaiian Mission Board agreed that the Methodists would be responsible for the Koreans while the Congregationalists would continue their work with the Chinese.[1]

On July 5, 1903, the first Korean Christian service in Hawaii was held at the Wailua sugar plantation on Oahu as the Koreans, without waiting for the missionary board, sought to organize a church. By November, 1903, the American superintendent, assigned by the Methodist board, had overseen the opening of a mission on River Street in downtown Honolulu. Through the dedication and efforts of its Korean minister, C. P. Hong, the mission flourished. On April 1, 1905, the mission was designated the Korean Methodist Church and continued to gain communicants. A year later, the church had purchased a building on Punchbowl Street to accommodate its membership and to provide space for its planned dormitory school for Korean boys.

139

Dr. John Wadman, Superintendent of the Methodist Korean Mission, reported in 1906 that there were from 1,600 to 2,000 professing members in the territory. The church supervised thirty mission stations, staffed by ten evangelists and four teachers, on Hawaii, Kauai, Maui, and in the plantation communities of Wailua and Ewa on Oahu.[2]

In 1916, a dispute divided the Korean Methodist Church membership, which resulted in Syngman Rhee and his followers leaving the church. At that time, the Korean Methodists reported twenty-four missions and a membership of 1,150. After World War II, a new building was erected in one of Honolulu's residential sections on Keeaumoku Street. In 1949, the church had 496 members and supervised two missions—in Wahiawa and Hilo.[3] This pioneer church still flourished in the 1970's as the Christ United Methodist Church.

Episcopal services first became available to Honolulu's Koreans in 1905. Two years later, the diocese regularly scheduled a Korean service at St. Elizabeth's, a church close to the city's Korean community. In 1952, St. Luke's Church was erected on Judd Street to continue meeting the needs of the Koreans.[4]

On December 23, 1918, two years after they left the Methodist Church, Rhee and some thirty followers organized the Korean Christian Church of Hawaii. Meeting first in temporary facilities, the members built their first sanctuary on North School Street. In 1938, the congregation built a new structure on Liliha Street modelled after Seoul's South Gate. The church leadership reported in 1953 a membership of twelve hundred which included Honolulu's communicants and those of the branches at Wahiawa, Hilo, Paia, and Los Angeles.[5]

These churches were important to the early Korean immigrants. Plantation missionaries would hold services in the boardinghouse kitchen, usually the only large room available. At first, the age-old Korean custom of separation of the sexes constrained women from attending but as time passed, they joined the camp congregations, sitting as a group either in front, at the back, or along one side of the room. The older generation, in 1937, still followed this custom in the Honolulu churches, men sitting on one side and women on the other. The second generation sat together.[6]

Almost all of these immigrants were illiterate but they knew that education provided a road to economic independence. The quest for education for their children had been one of the motives for leaving Korea. The success of their children both in education and in the world of work in Hawaii and on the West Coast attests to the dedication of the parents. At the same time, the adults wanted to make certain that their Korean culture was inculcated in their children.

The Honolulu Korean Methodist Church started its educational enterprise in September, 1906, with the opening of its boarding school for Korean boys. From its inception until June, 1913, Mrs. J. M. Wadman, wife of the superintendent of the Methodist Korean Mission, was the school's principal. Boys from rural Oahu and from the neighboring islands attended as well as some day students from Honolulu. Four or five American teachers and two Korean instructors formed the staff. The curriculum was aimed at preparing students for Hawaii's secondary schools and offering Korean language instruction. After one year's operation, the school was recognized by the Territorial Board of Education as a licensed private school which became known as the Korean Compound. In 1913, Dr. Rhee was appointed principal. Under his direction, the curriculum placed greater emphasis upon knowledge about Korea. Within the year, a major dispute broke out regarding the future direction of the education of Hawaii's young Koreans. The church's plan had called for amalgamation of the young into the dominant culture and for high school preparation. But Rhee believed in a basic Korean education with indoctrination in the concept of an independent Korea. In the struggle that followed, Wadman resigned his superintendency in 1914. His successor, however, continued the policies of complete integration which would mean an eventual end to the Compound.[7]

Rhee, during his first year as principal, toured the islands and found several girls who were not attending school for a variety of reasons. The Methodist Korean Mission had already established the Susannah Wesley Home in Honolulu and operated it as a separate enterprise, apart from the boys' boarding school. Twenty Korean girls, living at the home, attended a nearby public school. Rhee arranged for another twenty girls from the Neighbor Islands to move to Honolulu. His plan was to educate them at the Compound with boys. While the argument over curriculum continued, the mission board in 1915 ruled that girls could not attend the Compound school. Rhee had already secured funds from the Korean National Association of Hawaii, which he then dominated, and purchased a three-acre lot in the Liliha-Puunui area of Honolulu. There he built the Korean Girls' Home for the Neighbor Island girls. In 1915, it became the Korean Girls' Seminary which offered a regular preparatory curriculum and the Korean language.[8]

After Rhee and his followers broke with the Methodist Church, he resigned his principalship of the Compound and directed only the girls' seminary. The rupture was finalized with the creation in September, 1918, of the Korean Christian Institute and the formation of the Korean Christian Church later that year. Rhee sold the Puunui property and built a co-educational boarding school in Honolulu's Kaimuki District to carry out the institute's elementary school program. The institute's success led to the demise of the Korean Compound. Rhee's school soon had an enrollment of about 140 pupils. All went well until 1920 when the Territorial Board of Education required a special examination of all private school students who sought to enroll in any public high school. Many parents, feeling it better to have their children start their education in public elementary schools in order to assure admission into high school, shunned private schools.[9]

In 1921, the institute sold its Kaimuki property and purchased four thousand acres in the Kalihi area where most Koreans lived. The institute was converted by the early 1930's into an orphanage but this effort, too, was unsuccessful. In 1947, the land was sold. Rhee, while president of the Republic of Korea, still had considerable power over this Hawaiian enterprise. He let it be known in 1953 from Seoul, at the time of the fiftieth anniversary of the arrival of the first Koreans in Hawaii, that the proceeds from the land sale were to be used to build a technical college at Inchon—the In-Ha College of Technology. The name came from the first letters of Inchon and Hawaii. He also announced that additional funding would be forthcoming from Koreans in Hawaii.[10]

The option of sending their children to a Korean school was never possible for all first-generation Koreans because of cost. While the Korean schools helped set a cultural tone for the community, most children attended public schools. During the 1930's, as the institute continued to decline, 31 percent of the total Korean population attended school, the highest percentage of any Asian group. In 1935, 2,216 Koreans were enrolled in public schools. Most were in intermediate grades, an indication of the general age level of the children. The Korean Christian Institute that year listed only two graduates.[11]

But while parents sent their children to public schools, they patronized the Korean language schools. Between 1907 and 1940 there were eighteen different language schools throughout the islands. In 1924, the total enrollment was 241; by 1931 ten schools had an enrollment of 520 students. On the mainland, too, Korean communities established language schools. Prior to World War II, schools were located in California at Los Angeles, Sacramento, San Francisco, and the San Joaquin Valley towns of Delano, Dinuba, and Reedley.

These schools were sponsored by Korean churches with the teachers' salaries paid from tuition. As was the case with other ethnic language schools, most children were unwilling pupils who were adept at English and inadequate in Korean. The teachers, all Korean-born, on the other hand, were unable to communicate clearly in English. As second- and third-generation Koreans assumed leadership in their communities, they saw no need for language schools, which then disappeared.[12]

The Koreans' devotion to Christianity has made it easier to identify the location of their early communities, for where they settled a Korean church could usually be found. While Los Angeles has had the largest number of Koreans, cities such as San Francisco, Seattle, Chicago, and New York have sustained small Korean centers.[13] San Francisco's community has remained small—under one thousand. As Koreans arrived in the bay city, the Korean Methodist Church was launched in October, 1905. In 1958, Korean Methodists worshiped in the Bishop Yang Memorial Church.[14]

Other Korean Christian endeavors were started in Oakland, Chicago, and New York. In 1924, the Methodist Mission Board established a Chicago mission. The Presbyterians established a New York City mission in 1922 but most of the Koreans were Methodists and they asked to be supervised by the Methodist Board. Both missions served small, changing memberships.[15]

The first Koreans in Los Angeles lived in an area bounded by Vermont and Western Avenues and by Adams Boulevard and Slauson Avenue, just southwest of the present-day Los Angeles Coliseum. A few lived near the Temple and Figueroa Streets area while others were scattered throughout Los Angeles County where they had their businesses. However, they returned to the Korean community for social and religious affairs.[16] Early in the life of the Los Angeles community, Presbyterians and Methodists established missions. The Korean Presbyterian Church of Los Angeles has remained active since its inception in 1906. The Methodist mission, dormant for a time, has thrived since the 1930's. The large number of Koreans in that city made the founding of other denominational churches possible. All these churches, as well as those in Honolulu and other American cities, had Korean ministers who delivered their services in Korean.[17]

Education for the Korean children in California had as high a priority as it had in Hawaii. In the 1930's, about half of the Koreans in Los Angeles were of school age and attending school. They achieved fine academic records.[18]

In June, 1913, Korean students at Hastings College, a Presbyterian college in Nebraska, organized a Korean student association. By 1919 ten different student associations from New York City to Honolulu were meeting to discuss their educational goals and to provide social functions for students far from home. In 1919, the San Francisco association called a national student conference to see if unification was possible and desirable. The meeting, held under the shadow of recent Japanese repressions in Korea, led to the formation of the Korean Student Federation of North America. The federation, first housed in New York, and then relocated in 1923 to Chicago, kept its membership posted about Korean matters through the *Korean Student Bulletin*.[19]

Second-generation Koreans, born in the United States, posed cultural problems for their parents and themselves. In 1927, a young Korean indicated: "So far I have read very little about my parents' native land. I have never felt a sense of pride in knowing about my parents' native land but I have pity and sympathy for them."[20] Young Kang of Honolulu in May, 1930, pointed out the dilemma facing the two generations. The elders' common complaint was that young people were not interested in studying the Korean language. Kang also felt that the youngsters, with little concern about their Korean heritage, had rushed headlong into Americanization. They were not interested, it appeared to him, in becoming part of a Korean community, but wanted their independence. He was concerned, too, about their morals since those who had left the churches seemed bent upon becoming atheists. Kang's views expressed clearly the worries of the older generation—an age-gap problem common to groups which also experienced the shock of cultural adjustment in a new land.[21]

As seen through the eyes of a second-generation Korean, Bernice Kim, the two generations had four areas of conflict. Major problems were that the young Koreans' search for freedom expressed itself in a seeming lack of respect for parents and that the girls demanded equal rights. The youth also broke away from closely knit family circles to start friendships with other people, many from different ethnic groups. Kim agreed with the elders' complaint—young people lacked any motivation to study the Korean language. She also related that young people found the common food of the Korean home, kim chee, made their breath too highly spiced and garlic-flavored for many of their new friends.[22]

As late as 1956, the elders in Honolulu made another attempt to further appreciation of Korean culture and language by publishing a mimeographed newsletter.[23] In one of these, Professor Claude A. Buss of Stanford University discussed the continuing lack of proficiency by the young in the language of their parents. In reporting that few of second-generation Korean Americans had command of the language, he maintained this had occurred because of a false value judgment of the sole importance of English. Buss noted that a Korean American student had been offered a position in the State Department at a salary of $12,000. One job requirement was proficiency in Korean, which the scholar did not have. Unable to qualify, he was presently employed in Honolulu at a salary of $5,000.[24]

Following World War II, the population of Korean American communities, even with a growing social distance between the generations, started to increase gradually. During the war, Korean students could not return home then and many settled permanently in the United States. Los Angeles continued to be the focal point for Korean newcomers. Large numbers of immigrants started arriving in that city in 1968. Estimates in 1974 suggested that Los Angeles County might have a Korean population ranging from sixty to seventy thousand which was dispersed throughout the metropolitan area. The largest concentration was no longer in the old Korean neighborhood but was located several miles to the north along Olympic Boulevard. About one-third of the new arrivals, mostly young families, had moved into this newer area. The average age of the fathers was about thirty years. The extended family frequently came along from Korea—grandparents, father, mother, and one to three young children. About half of the Korean preschool population in 1974 spoke no English. These families experienced their first culture shock when their children entered American schools and learned different traditions and another language.

The immigration to Los Angeles and other cities was predicated on about four reasons. One was a concern for the children's future. With educational opportunities in Korea limited and expensive, children there, as elsewhere, who did not gain a basic education had greater difficulty in facing economic competition. A second reason for migration was the political unrest caused by President Park's assumption of power. Thirdly, in Korea's society of extended families, a rising young employee was apt to be squeezed out of a company or business to make room for a relative of the owner. Many well trained young Koreans migrated because there was no future in working for another family's business. Finally, the lure of American life attracted many. Although daily living was indeed difficult for the new Korean immigrant family in an American city, it appeared to be easier than in Korea and the opportunities were greater.

As Korean immigrants sought employment, the problem of communication was tantamount. Language was actually a total problem in general day-to-day living. At a 1973 civil rights hearing in Los Angeles, it was estimated that 40 percent of the immigrants spoke no English. At the other end of the scale, only 10 percent spoke English fluently. Koreans have generally reported that acculturation in Los Angeles has been easy, but assimilation has been difficult for two reasons. First, the Koreans had trouble with white racism and with the general American culture pattern which attacked problems common to both groups from strange perspectives and usually arrived at different solutions. The second reason was withdrawal from the dominant society. As a consequence of their daily encounters, Koreans settled in "Little Seoul" in the Olympic section of Los Angeles, a base from which to venture forth and, when rebuffed, a place to which to retreat. Here in "Little Seoul" they found friends, could communicate in Korean, and touch the familiar culture and traditions.

One of the great frustrations of these new immigrants, as it had been for the earlier ones, was the break-up of the extended family. The Korean youth of high school age developed a different subculture, involving gang activities, drugs, juvenile delinquency, and sex. As with recently arrived Chinese and Filipino youths, the language barrier set them apart from the American world. But even with these difficulties, the youth adjusted more quickly than the adults and a return to Korea for them was out of the question.[25]

These Koreans in Los Angeles and in the other American cities faced what immigrants before had confronted. Strange customs, unfamiliar economic demands, and the change in their children all exerted strain on old traditions and family ties. Each Korean family agonized, argued, and came out of the test changed in many ways.

CHAPTER XII

The Korean Independence Movement in the United States

KOREANS in the United States passionately hoped for the freedom of their homeland from the time of the Japanese protectorate in 1905 and held firm to the dream of independence from Japan until it was achieved in 1945. Unfortunately, the freedom movement badly divided Korean Americans.

Between 1903 and 1907, Koreans in Hawaii organized several political groups whose objectives were anti-Japanese. In August, 1907, representatives from twenty-four of these met in Honolulu and formed the Korean Consolidated Association with head-quarters on Liliha Street. Within a year's time, the association had forty-seven affiliates throughout the islands.[1]

Koreans in San Francisco in 1905 organized the Korean Mutual Assistance Association with offices on Pacific Street, adjacent to Chinatown. The 1906 earthquake and fire forced a move to Oakland but by 1908 the association was back in San Francisco. The Korean Restorative Association, founded in 1905 in Pasadena, California, had moved to San Francisco in 1907.[2]

What these groups had in common was a hatred of the Japanese protectorate. Violent opposition occurred in San Francisco in 1908 when two Koreans assaulted and shot Durham S. Stevens, a pro-Japanese American. American business interests had suffered under Japanese control in Korea. The Japanese Resident-General in Seoul asked Stevens to go to Washington to explain the situation and to see what accommodations to American business might be made.[3]

Stevens arrived in San Francisco on March 20, 1908. In an interview, he indicated to local newspapers that Korea was benefitting from Japanese rule and that American business would, in the long run, also gain. But his unflattering remarks about corrupt Korean officials and subservient peasants angered the San Francisco Korean community, which held a mass meeting two days later. Interestingly, Stevens' remarks were an echo of views held by Horace Allen in 1902. A delegation of four Koreans went to the Fairmont Hotel to demand that Stevens retract his statement. When he refused, one Korean knocked him down and the other three hit him with chairs. Hotel guests broke up the fracas.[4]

The next morning, as Stevens, accompanied by the Japanese Consul, approached the San Francisco Ferry Building, Myeng-woon Jen, a member of the Korean Mutual Assistance Association, confronted Stevens with a revolver which failed to fire. Jen rushed Stevens and hit him in the face. As Stevens fought back, he was shot twice in the back while Jen was wounded in the chest. In-Whang Jang of the Korean Restorative Association, who was there independently, had fired the shots. On March 25, Stevens died.[5]

While there was some concern that this was a political assassination, the San Francisco police decided the shooting was the work of two individuals who had no such motive. Both Koreans were arraigned for murder. Legal proceedings lasted the rest of the year. On December 22, 1908, the jury acquitted Jen for lack of evidence and found Jang guilty of murder. Early in 1909, Jang was sentenced to twenty years in prison. He was paroled in 1919. When Jang died in 1930, various Korean organizations in the United States accorded him high honors as a great patriot.[6]

The Stevens incident became the catalyst which brought together the diverse units. In October, 1908, seven representatives from the Korean Consolidated Association of Hawaii and six from various mainland organizations met in San Francisco to plan the Korean National Association in America which was officially launched on February 1, 1909. Its goal was to support freedom for Korea and to support all overseas Koreans. The association's headquarters was in San Francisco and there were four regional headquarters in Honolulu, San Francisco, Manchuria, and Siberia. The parent association occupied the offices of the old Korean Mutual Assistance Association and remained

in San Francisco until 1936 when it moved to the much larger
Korean community in Los Angeles. In 1910, it became known
as the Korean National Association of America. The regional
organization in San Francisco, the Korean National Association
of North America, functioned as the successor to various Korean
organizations in the United States.[7]

The Korean National Association of Hawaii at the same time
merged various branches of the old Hawaiian organization.
For Hawaii's Koreans, this amalgamation was a lull before a
major storm.[8]

In August, 1910, Japan annexed Korea. In September, the
Korean National Association of America held a protest meeting
in Honolulu and passed resolutions of opposition. One response
to the Japanese move was to train an army which could lead
in an overthrow. One of the strong Korean leaders in America,
Yong-man Pak, believed in creating the necessary military
establishment. Pak organized the Korean Youth Military Academy in Hastings, Nebraska, and enrolled twenty-seven cadets.
The academy was actually a farm which they worked by day.
Three nights each week were spent in military drill and two
were devoted to theory. The Hastings enterprise ended by
the time Pak moved to Honolulu late in 1912.[9] Following Pak's
venture at Hastings, military training centers were set up at
Kansas City, Kansas; Superior, Wyoming; and at Claremont
and Lompoc, California. Some $6,000 was budgeted by the
national association to support these enterprises.

Pak arrived in Honolulu in December, 1912, to serve as editor
of The United Korean Weekly, the publication of the Korean
National Association of Hawaii. He also supervised the training
of the Korean National Brigade at a pineapple plantation on
Oahu's Windward side. Some three hundred men who had joined
the brigade practiced and drilled daily before and after work.
By 1916 the contract with the pineapple company had ended
and a search for a new site in the Kahuku area of north Oahu
proved fruitless. Pak, in the midst of the explosive controversy
with Syngman Rhee, left Hawaii for China to attempt to create
a military base near Korea.[10]

Syngman Rhee, in 1911, following completion of his Princeton doctoral studies, had returned to Korea to work for the

Young Men's Christian Association. He soon left Korea to attend the Methodist Mission conference in Minneapolis, but his political activities had made it impossible for him to return to Korea. He chose to remain in the United States to work for Korean independence. He accepted an invitation of the Korean leaders of Hawaii, including Yong-man Pak, to come to Honolulu to be the director of the Methodist's Korean Compound. From the beginning, Rhee was surrounded with dissension and disorder. In what appears to have been a premeditated drive for power, he broke with the Methodists over educational policy and by 1914 had caused a furor. From the beginning, he refused to work with Pak and the national association.[11] By 1915 Hawaiian Koreans were divided between Rhee and Pak. When Pak left for China in 1916, he in effect gave up the struggle. In 1918, as Rhee separated from the Methodist Church to form the Korean Christian Church and the Korean Christian Institute, he secured control of the Korean National Association in Hawaii.[12]

During the Korean independence movement, three major leaders struggled for Korean freedom and against each other. This internal struggle hindered the goal of independence, or, at least, the development of any common front. The three men were Pak, Rhee, and Chang-ho Ahn.

Ahn, an early arrival in San Francisco, had organized a students' association in 1903.[13] While Pak and Rhee and their followers in Hawaii were debating the proper course to follow, military preparedness or education and diplomacy, Chang-ho Ahn remained active in California. On May 13, 1913, he organized a small group of Korean students in San Francisco as the *Heung-Sa-Dan*, the Corps for the Advancement of Individuals.[14] Its motto was "virtue, intellect, and health." Aiming at a long-range plan of elitist leadership which would take eventual control of the movement, Ahn and his corps rejected the plans of Pak and Rhee. Ahn convinced many students that his way was the correct path. In 1932, Ahn was in China where he was arrested by the Japanese for being involved with Korean bombings in Shanghai. After three years in prison, he was arrested again in Seoul, following the outbreak of fighting in China in July, 1937. The consequences of imprisonment and alleged torture led to his death in March, 1938. Ahn, during his life, particularly in the early years, was considered by Rhee a bitter foe.[15]

The year 1919 was an eventful one for the independence movement. In March, the major demonstration in Korea for independence was crushed by the Japanese. In Paris at the Peace Conference, Rhee's old friend, Woodrow Wilson, was talking about the principle of self-determination. The Korean National Association had already planned in late 1918 to send delegates to Paris. Rhee and another leader were to go to New York to work with advocates of the League of Nations. Rhee arrived in California from Honolulu and announced cooperation with his rival, Ahn. He then pursued a path of independent action, writing directly to the State Department for a passport to Paris, which was denied. The department ruled that since Koreans were subjects of Japan, only that government could issue a passport to Rhee.[16] He continued his letter writing in behalf of a free Korea. Failing to gain a satisfactory response from the State Department, Rhee left for Shanghai to meet with the Korean Provisional Government which had been formed secretly in Seoul in April, 1919. At that time, Rhee was named president. His political enemies, Pak and Ahn, were also in the cabinet—Pak as minister of foreign affairs and Ahn as director of labor. But it was not until September, 1919, that the various factions met in Shanghai and there reconfirmed Rhee as president.[17] He held that position until 1945 and the establishment of an interim government. In 1948, he became President of the Republic of Korea.

While Rhee was following his own dictates in 1919, his former leader, Philip Jaisohn, who was practicing medicine in Philadelphia, suggested that the American Korean community underwrite a magazine to publicize the Korean situation. He also thought that such an effort might unify competing Korean elements in the United States. The central headquarters of the Korean National Association organized the Korean Information Office and placed Jaisohn in charge.[18]

Jaisohn, who had become a United States citizen, had, when he returned to Korea in 1895, worked for reform and democracy. When he settled in the United States in 1898, he started devoting his life to the cause of independence. In 1925, writing to Korean students in the United States, he claimed that "Korea expects you to lead her out of the shame and misery in which she is now submerged." He called upon the students to be prepared to sacrifice themselves for Korea.[19] In May, 1919, the *Korea Review* appeared, but lasted only three years. From the East Coast, then, appeared a momentary voice for the movement, but Jaisohn's hopes for unification did not materialize.[20]

Just before Rhee departed from Hawaii in 1919 to work for independence, he participated in the further fractionalization of Hawaii's Koreans by incurring the wrath of the Korean Methodists and Pak and his followers. Pak, upon his return from China, attempted to counter Rhee's political power. In March, 1918, he formed a temporary organization which existed until Rhee separated from the Korean National Association of Hawaii. With Honolulu's Koreans divided, Pak next organized, following the *Man Sei* independence movement, the Korean National Independence League on March 3, 1919.[21] Two months later, he left for China to see how Korean military activities were progressing in Manchuria and to attend the September meeting of the Provisional Government in Shanghai. Thereafter, Pak spent most of his time in China, leaving his Hawaiian followers without leadership. He was shot to death in Peking, China, in October, 1928. With his death, the league slowly declined and its members gradually rejoined the Korean National Association.[22]

After the Shanghai meeting in 1919, Rhee attempted unsuccessfully to develop his program throughout the United States. He then returned to his power base in Hawaii. On December 20, 1921, Rhee led his followers out of the Korean National Association of America. On March 22, 1922, they organized the Korean Residents Association. The former name, the Korean National Association of Hawaii, was readopted in 1932. But the Rhee group remained separate from the mainland Koreans.[23]

Prior to the association's reorganization in 1922, Rhee had on July 21, 1921, organized *Dong-Ji Hoi,* which provided support to the Korean Provisional Government headquartered in Shanghai, and which undertook to fund Rhee in his fight against other Korean nationalistic factions in the United States and in Asia. In 1924, *Dong-Ji Hoi* members elected Rhee executive-director for life. The next year he formed the *Dong-Ji* Invest-ment Company and sold stock certificates. From the sales, the company purchased almost one thousand acres on the island of Hawaii for the purpose of making charcoal, logging and milling koa lumber, and growing vegetables. The proceeds were to support the activities of *Dong-Ji Hoi* but the 1929 depression wiped out the enterprise and the investors lost their money.[24]

Rhee had hoped that *Dong-Ji Hoi* would be equally attractive to mainland Koreans. Organizations were attempted in Butte, Chicago, Detroit, Los Angeles, and New York City. Only the one founded in Los Angeles in 1929 endured but it did not adhere too closely to Rhee's mandates.[25]

Dong-Ji Hoi's official organ, the *Korean Pacific Weekly,* indi-cated in 1944 that the association held to three mandates: 1) to adhere without deviation to the principles set forth in the March 1, 1919, Declaration of Independence; 2) to abide by the organization's rules without any discord; and 3) to aim for the economic freedom of Korea and its self-sufficiency.[26]

During its lifetime, *Dong-Ji Hoi* solicited contributions and sold bonds on the promise that these would be redeemed by an independent Korean government when it was reestablished. The association also supported the Korean Christian Institute in Honolulu until it was dissolved in 1953. For all practical purposes, the management of the two organizations was the same. From the sale of the institute's property, *Dong-Ji Hoi* in 1953 contributed $180,000 to Rhee's proposed In-Ha Technical College in Inchon. An additional $50,000 was donated to the Korean Old Men's Home in Honolulu. In 1970, *Dong-Ji Hoi* ceased operations and donated its holdings to the Korean government.[27] From the time of the forming of the Provisional Government in 1919 until World War II, Rhee relied heavily upon his Hawaiian followers for help. *Dong-Ji Hoi*, in particular, stood by him, providing both moral and financial backing.

Other groups, over the years, had supported the drive for a free Korea. The Korean National Association of America, fol-lowing Rhee's defection, fell apart in 1922. Reorganized as the Korean Association of North America, it remained moribund. Not until 1936 did California Koreans reorganize, and the national association headquarters were moved from San Francisco to Los Angeles.[28]

In Hawaii, an opposition group to Rhee came to life in the mid–1930's. The genesis of the Sino-Korean Peoples' League, according to its leader, Kilsoo Haan, was to unite the Koreans in China, Hawaii, and the mainland United States to assist China and Korea in their common fight against the Empire of Japan. The underlying goal, claimed Haan, was one of espionage. In a sense, the league was a step-child of Pak's plans. While the league did not propose to parallel the spy activities of the United States Army and Navy, its members were able to discover information, said Haan, of which the military was unaware. The league's chief project in Hawaii was spying upon the Japanese.[29] Haan, when he was on the West Coast in 1942, agitating in favor of Japanese removal from the war zone, reported that he had posed in Honolulu as a member of the Japanese Consulate staff and had gained easy access to the consulate offices where he viewed detailed blueprints of Pearl Harbor. He concluded that "it is our conviction that the best way to prepare against the Japanese is to let the American people know the Japanese plans and what the Japs and the Japanese Americans are doing in this country."[30]

Fear and hatred of the Japanese appeared to be the only unifying force among the various Korean groups through the years. Both Rhee and Haan spoke for the majority of their followers when they opposed, prior to World War II, any move for Hawaiian statehood because the Japanese would gain too much political power. But the outbreak of war on December 7, 1941, had no effect upon further merging of the two factions in Hawaii. Most Koreans supported Rhee's continuing diplomatic efforts in Washington, while Haan's league, which numbered fewer than one hundred people, insisted that aid to revolutionaries in China and undercover work provided the path to freedom for Korea.

Nine Korean associations, representing groups in Honolulu and Los Angeles, met on April 20, 1949, in Honolulu to form the United Korean Committee of America which was an all-out effort to merge the several factions. Haan's Sino-Korean Peoples' League joined with *Dong-Ji Hoi* and seven other organizations

on the condition that Haan receive a key appointment. It was
agreed that he would provide liaison between the new committee and the United States government. When he was removed from this position in February, 1942, the league then
withdrew from the new coalition. Haan moved to California
and joined with Dr. John Lechner, a Baptist minister, to become
leading spokesmen in the drive to remove the Japanese from
the West Coast.[31] Both the Provisional Government, sitting in
Chungking, China, and Rhee, in Washington, proved unwilling
to share information with the committee. When the committee
protested, Rhee countered by taking *Dong-Ji Hoi* out of the
coalition in September, 1943. The remaining groups banded
together in a common effort until the end of the war.[32]

World War II provided a curious set of circumstances for
the Koreans, particularly those in Hawaii. Active since 1910 in
the independence movement against Japan, they were in 1940
once again classified by the United States government through
its Alien Registration Act as subjects of Japan. The bombing
of Pearl Harbor made Japan and its subjects enemies of the
United States. To their dismay, Koreans now found themselves
classified as enemy aliens. In Honolulu, the first-generation
Koreans regarded the war in the Pacific as the final step to a
free Korea while their children saw the war as an attack by
Japan upon the United States. The older generation viewed all
Japanese, including those in Hawaii, with hatred but their children were much less hostile or had no concern at all.[33]

Following the December 7 attack, the status of the older
Koreans, all non-citizens, changed drastically. Hawaii Territorial
Governor Joseph B. Poindexter's executive order, issued on
December 8, greatly curtailed their usual way of life. As enemy
aliens, for example, they could not withdraw more than $200 a
month from the banks.[34] The *Korean National Herald-Pacific
Weekly* in late February, 1942, editorialized about the dilemma
confronting the Koreans:

If the Korean is an enemy of Japan, that which he is, he should
be welcomed as a friend of the allied nations. The fact that every
Korean born is an enemy born for Japan, is evidenced by the
continuous stationing of Japan's best armed forces within the Korean

peninsula at strategic points of large Korean population. And Japan has never trusted the Koreans inasmuch as they hate the Japanese.

Since December 7, the Korean here is between the devil and the deep sea for the reason that the United States considers him a subject of Japan, which the Korean resents as an injustice to his true status; and he has never renounced his national heritage in line of a Japanese subject.

In China and Russia the Korean is not considered as a Japanese and he has proved himself worthy of their sympathy and encouragement for his national aspirations. A free Korean army composed of exiled Koreans in conquerored territories is fighting side by side with the Chinese and allied forces in the Far East. Their number is yet small but their fighting valor and tactics against the enemy Japan have been recognized in admiration.

What is the status of a Korean in the United States? Is he an enemy alien? Has any Korean ever been in Japanese espionage or in subversive activities against the land where he makes his home and rears his children as true Americans?

Since 1903 the Koreans came here and have been classified as Koreans. In the national census they were enumerated as distinct nationals. In the time of national crisis, the Koreans as a minority do not desire to burden the Washington and local authorities with their complaint for an honorable and just clarification. But they do hope with almost an avidity that the ambiguity of their present status be speedily clarified so as to keep up their morale.[35]

Mainland Koreans shared the concerns of their countrymen in Hawaii. During December, 1941, they announced that they were prepared to resist the policies of Japan morally and physically—if necessary. Americans were asked to distinguish between Koreans and Japanese. Pacific Coast Koreans were soon wearing badges with the crossed flags of Korea and the United States and the motto, "Korea for Victory with America."[36]

The United Korean Committee organized a brigade, nicknamed the "Tiger Brigade," to be part of the California National Guard. Formed mostly of elderly men, the brigade was soon attached to the California Home Guard, a state organization, in part because of legal complications about a unit composed completely of aliens.[37]

Late in January, 1942, the United States Department of Justice ruled that Koreans were not required to register as

enemy aliens. On March 21, 1942, Governor Poindexter declared
that Hawaii's Koreans were no longer considered Japanese
nationals in economic matters, but they remained subject to
martial law and were considered still enemy aliens.[38]

Being mistaken as Japanese both concerned and angered the
Koreans. The United Korean Committee prepared identification
cards proclaiming, "I am Korean." But Hawaii's Office of Civil
Defense asked that racial identity be downplayed. Even so,
during the early months of the war, women began to wear
Korean dresses regularly as a means of identification. In March,
1942, Korean aliens, working on defense projects in Hawaii,
were reclassified as Japanese and issued restricted badges with
black borders. All other non-Japanese workers had white bor-
dered tags bearing their pictures. This move insulted the Koreans
who protested vehemently. They aspired to white unrestricted
badges proclaiming them as friendly aliens. The border was
not changed but the words, "I am Korean," were added to the
bottom of the badge. At the same time, Hawaiian Koreans
started wearing the crossed flags buttons as a visible sign to
the community.[39]

Following the Cairo Conference in November, 1943, between
Franklin Roosevelt, Winston Churchill, and Chiang Kai-Shek,
which promised independence "in due course," the United
States Army contacted the Korean leadership in Washington,
D.C., about forming a special unit for eventual use in Korea.
On December 10, 1943, Rhee, in a confidential note to Kingsley
K. Lyu in Honolulu, indicated that the War Department was
seeking fifty young Koreans for commando training.[40]

By the war's end, Koreans in America participated in many
ways in preparing for a free Korea. Syngman Rhee had returned
to Korea to become one of several politicians jockeying for
position while a joint United States-Soviet Commission governed
the peninsula. The United States Army, for its part, in trying
to unravel the situation and form a national government, turned
to one of Korea's long-time patriots, Philip Jaisohn, to be its
political advisor. He returned to his native land in 1947 and
served as Chief Advisor on Korean Affairs to the Commander
of the United States Army in Korea. Many Koreans wanted
him to oppose Rhee in the election for president, but he declined

to do so. He left Korea for the last time in September, 1948, for his home in Media, Pennsylvania.[41]

The dreams of Jaisohn, Rhee, and many Korean-Americans were finally realized with the founding of the Republic of Korea. The forty-year struggle seemed to have been concluded satisfactorily—at least for South Korea. The establishment of the republic in 1948 was due in no small measure to the dedication and devotion of the Korean communities in the United States.

CHAPTER XIII

Korean Search
for Economic Success

EARLY in the twentieth century, faced with political instability
in Korea and confronted with poor crops and economic
disaster, many unemployed Koreans found that the advertisements recruiting workers for Hawaii suggested an attractive
alternative. The prospect of work in the sugar fields seemed better than the immediate situation at home.[1]

The emigrants crossing from Japan to Hawaii found that the
crowded conditions of steerage class jarred their sense of the
traditional. Men and women were housed together, a new experience for a culture that segregated the sexes. Encountering
Japanese cooking on the ships, Koreans found that food seasoned
with Japanese soy was too sweet for their tastes.[2] While soy
seasoning is standard in East Asian cooking, the flavors differ
between China, Japan, and Korea. Such experiences were but
the beginning of significant changes in their lives.

Upon arrival in Honolulu, the immigrants were assigned to
plantations. Four plantations received the bulk of the Korean
men. Between 1904 and 1906, the HSPA made the following
assignments—Ewa Plantation on Oahu, 1,193; Hawaiian Sugar
Company on Kauai, 784; Hawaiian Commercial and Sugar Company of Maui, 807; and Olaa Plantation on Hawaii, 525.[3]

One of these workers, writing of his Olaa Plantation experiences, reported that the new men were soon in the fields:
"... cutting away at the cane stalks. We worked in the hot
sun for ten hours a day, and the pay was fifty-nine cents a day.
I was not used to this kind of work and I had a difficult time.
This type of work was indeed harder than the type of contract
work that I did in Russia. However, I did the best I could and
struggled along with the rest of the men."[4] The hardships that

160

they confronted, particularly those who had only recently been Korean workers, were due to their first experience of working long hours at hard common labor. Bernice Kim relates that these first immigrants told her "how some boys and even men, with fair hands blistered, faces and arms torn and scratched by the cane leaf stickers, would sit between the rows of cane and weep like children." From the outset, those unhappy Koreans, who did not find Hawaii to be a paradise, began to plan and scheme for their return to Korea or a move to the West Coast.[5]

For about five years following the arrival of the first immigrants, all Koreans were tied economically to sugar and pineapple plantations. Most were field hands; others worked as interpreters, church missionaries, or language school teachers. The plantations paid men, on the average, about sixty-five cents for a ten-hour day, while women earned fifty cents. From these earnings, the workers had to meet living expenses and repay their ship passage loan.[6]

Plantation camps segregated workers by ethnic origin. Thus, the Koreans, as the newest arrivals, found Chinese, Japanese, and Puerto Rican sections already established at most camps. The older residents and the new ones viewed each other with some curiosity. The Koreans discovered, for instance, that in using both a spoon and chopsticks while eating, they were unique, and, in their own eyes, more cultured than the Chinese and Japanese who used only chopsticks. They looked with disgust at the European and Puerto Rican habit of eating lunches with their hands, using no utensils at all. At the end of the work day, the Japanese bathed communally—a habit that violated the Korean belief in separation of sexes. The very fact that the Japanese men walked through the Korean camp wearing only towel loin cloths was particularly offensive.[7]

Plantation housing consisted of "long houses," made of rough lumber and covered with tin roofs; the houses were divided into rooms about twelve feet square where single men bunked together. Married couples were given single rooms in separate "long houses," which had no cooking facilities. Wives cooked in the open, over makeshift stoves, and meals were served in the family's one all-purpose room. Single men ate at a boardinghouse usually operated by one of the Korean women.[8] Each bachelor at Honokaa, Hawaii, in 1905 paid Mrs. Tai Yoon Kim, who had been sent by the HSPA to the Big Island plantation to run the boardinghouse, $6 a month to buy the food, cook, and serve it.

Mrs. Kim prepared meals for twenty bachelors and her husband. To stretch her limited budget took resolve and imagination. She planted watercress along a nearby stream and cultivated pepper bushes to provide the seasoning necessary for kim chee. She discovered that beef innards were free for the asking at a nearby slaughterhouse and these became part of the Kim larder. Every morning at five o'clock her boarders received a breakfast of rice, kim chee, and broth. Six days a week she packed twenty-one lunch tins with rice and dried salt fish. Dinner consisted of soup, rice, and either a soy seasoned dish of vegetables, meat, or fish, or a dish of corned beef and onions. "Burned rice tea," brewed from rice burned to the bottom of the pot, was the beverage. Every Saturday fresh beef or pork was served at dinner.

In addition to preparing the meals, Mrs. Kim, then but eighteen years of age, did the men's laundry. Each paid her one dollar a month for this service. A wood fire heated the water in her galvanized tub, which also contained brown soap and an endless pile of denim work pants and shirts. She boiled the clothes to clean them of red dirt and sweat. Each article was scrubbed on a washboard, beaten with a wooden rod, rinsed, and hung to dry. The entire wash was then starched with flour and water to be ironed with a charcoal-heated iron.[9]

Finding themselves isolated on the plantations, Koreans developed an intense group unity. A countryman was warmly welcomed at any Korean camp in the islands. This sense of identification aided the concept of village self-government. Each camp selected a *Dong Jang* or headman. To be considered for such an honorable position, one had to possess most of the following qualifications: "(1) the oldest man (presumably the wisest), (2) upright conduct, (3) honest and sincerity, (4) education."[10] The *Dong Jang* remained in his position as long as he satisfied the majority. He listened to the problems of the people, served as the final arbitrator in all disputes, meted out fines and punishments, and was the camp functionary on ceremonial occasions or when visitors arrived. To assist the *Dong Jang,* the camp men also elected a *Sah Chal,* or sergeant-at-arms. The *Sah Chal* was in reality a policeman who reported violations of the rules to the *Dong Jang.*

Camp laws and regulations were developed by all the men who also determined the system of fines. The amount and the basis of fines give an insight into some weaknesses. At one camp, the fines were assessed for: "drunkenness, $1.00; drunken brawling, $5.00; gambling in Japanese or Chinese camps, $5.00. Three offenses of any of the first two were cause enough to ask the guilty one to leave camp."[11] Fines, collected at a general meeting once a month, were used for educational support of children, care of the ill, expenses incurred at holiday times, and to send back to Korea any invalid who could not earn money to buy his passage ticket.[12]

The *Dong Jang* also arbitrated troubles arising from sexual encounters. With women few in number, problems arose. Some camps ruled that any man found guilty of a first sex offense would be fined $3.00. He could also be driven from the camp. It was possible that the woman and her husband would also be told to leave. Thus Koreans attempted to confine what could have developed into explosive situations.[13]

Most Koreans remained on the plantations until the 1920's. But from the very first, some gradually drifted into cities and towns. Unlike earlier Chinese and Japanese immigrants, and Filipinos, who came later, Koreans did not have a binding contract with the HSPA and were free to move from plantation to plantation or settle in Hilo or Honolulu.[14] In 1910, about 10 percent of the Koreans already lived in the territory's two cities. Their mobility and their search for both economic advancement and social prestige did not endear them to the HSPA. In 1909, Richard Ivers, President of the Territorial Board of Immigration, observed that they "are unreliable and the least efficient of any of our laborers."[15]

During the 1920's, many more left the plantation for Honolulu. In 1920, 1,982 Koreans worked on the sugar plantations; by 1930 the number had reduced to 484 and the decline continued slowly during the 1930's. By 1930, about 40 percent of the total Korean population resided in Honolulu. Of the several ethnic

groups that left the plantations to become independent businessmen or professionals, the Koreans and Chinese made the
transition from the fields sooner than others.[16]

One factor contributing to Korean mobility was the plantation
worker unrest during the 1920's. Leaders in the labor movement
were primarily Japanese. While many Koreans were sympathetic
to the movement's cause, they were caught in a general hatred
for all Japanese because of Japan's harsh repression of the 1919
Korean independence uprising. In the 1920 Oahu plantations
strike, led by Filipinos and Japanese, many Koreans adopted the
stance of the Korean National Association: "We do not wish
to be looked upon as strike breakers, but we shall continue to
work in the plantations and we are opposed to the Japanese in
everything." Koreans, living in Honolulu, as well as men living
on other islands, volunteered to work for the HSPA during the
strike. The HSPA accepted the offer, agreeing to pay $3 a day
in addition to the normal bonuses. This arrangement attracted
Koreans from the Neighbor Islands who came to Oahu to take
advantage of the increased wages and to help damage the
Japanese strike effort.[17] At the strike's conclusion, many settled
in Honolulu.

Koreans in Honolulu first found employment on the docks
and at the Dole pineapple cannery. The families settled in the
Liliha Street neighborhood, within walking distance of their
jobs.[18] In 1930, while only a handful remained on the sugar
plantations, most were still associated in some fashion with agriculture. A sizeable number worked on pineapple plantations.
Many had become independent farmers or worked for other
Koreans. Several had flower gardens near Honolulu and the rural
town of Wahiawa in central Oahu. About one hundred men
worked on Hawaii's Kona Coast on macadamia nut farms.

In 1930, Koreans were employed in various trades and crafts
such as carpentry, cabinet and furniture making, shoemaking,
tailoring, and laundering. They also operated rooming houses.
All enterprises required little capital investment or equipment.
The selling of men's and women's clothing proved very popular
—sixty-six men were tailors, while forty-three women worked as
dressmakers. A sizeable number of Koreans entered the professions of dentistry, medicine, and teaching.[19]

One of the more successful Korean settlements on Oahu developed at Wahiawa. Koreans in 1908 started working in nearby pineapple fields. In 1912, the United States Army commenced constructing the Schofield Barracks. The arrival of the army provided a variety of jobs in the small town. Until 1922, Japanese and Chinese small businessmen controlled the civilian trade in the barracks area. The Chinese that year sold their businesses to the Koreans and by 1924 the army's policy prohibited Japanese from working on the post. This left all civilian business to the Koreans. In 1937, they operated nine tailor shops and four shoe repair shops at Schofield and thirty-eight off-base Korean laundries. The latter competed with each other and with the barracks' laundry. It was estimated that these Koreans earned $6,000 a month from the army post. Wahiawa had several Korean store owners to attend to the wants and needs of 192 Korean families and others.[20]

But not all Koreans were content to make Honolulu, or some other part of Hawaii, their home. According to the Territorial Bureau of Immigration, between 1905 and 1916, 1,246 returned to Korea. Others hoped to return, but they had not yet acquired financial independence. Such a condition would cause loss of face at home. Thus many Koreans, like other Asians, found themselves trapped in Hawaii. At the same time, 1,084 migrated to California. The bulk of these, 857, arrived during two years, 1905 and 1906.[21] Western businesses made some efforts to recruit Korean labor in Hawaii to work in Alaska fisheries, on mainland railroads, and in mines. One railroad agent in February, 1905, went to Honolulu to recruit five thousand workers but had to be satisfied with a much smaller number. These Koreans were transported to Salt Lake City where they were employed in building and maintaining railroads in the Mountain States. Other Koreans were shipped to Seattle to work on the Great Northern Railroad. After the completion of construction, some remained as railroad maintenance workers while others became small farmers in Colorado, Kansas, Montana, Oregon, and Utah.[22]

In 1914, some section hands of the Milwaukee and Northern Pacific Railroad settled in Butte, Montana. Picture brides joined the men to establish homes at Nine Mile Canyon. The Koreans raised truck garden crops for sale in Butte. As late as 1946, thirteen families still lived there.[23]

When Alaska and Puget Sound salmon canneries recruited workers in California in 1909, fifty-three Koreans contracted for the canning season. Operators reported that Koreans, although fewer in number, and Filipinos were more desirable employees than were Japanese. However, Koreans never became a major part of the cannery work force. During the 1920's, eighteen Koreans worked one year only.[24]

Most Koreans who migrated from Hawaii to California remained, lured, as were countless thousands of people, by promises of better pay and working conditions. Koreans heard that California's climate was similar to Korea's and not like the semitropical one in the islands. Many left at a moment's notice for the West Coast, often secretly, and with their fare paid by their future employers.[25]

The exclusionists' watch-dog, the Japanese and Korean Exclusion League, reported in 1907 that some Koreans were employed chiefly as farm laborers in Southern California while a few were domestic servants.[26] The United States Immigration Commission's reports confirmed that there were few Korean agricultural workers. Those who worked in California's fields utilized the labor contractor and gang system that the Chinese and Japanese had perfected.[27]

Between 1911 and 1922, many Koreans joined the stampede into the Sacramento Valley to cultivate rice. By 1917 Chong-nim Kim was known among Koreans as the "Rice King." At the height of his operations, he farmed 2,085 acres.[28] In 1917, Chang-ho Ahn's patriotic organization, the Corps for the Advancement of Individuals, organized the North American Farming Industry Company. Issuing capital stock to the amount of $95,000, the company joined the rice boom, hoping to use its profits to construct a model village. During World War I, rice prices skyrocketed from $2.75 in 1916 to $4.95 in 1918 per one hundred pounds and remained high until 1920. That year heavy rains destroyed the crops; the resulting loss ruined most rice farmers.[29]

In central California, several Koreans had successful orchards, nurseries, vineyards, and fruit packing plants. In 1916, sixty Koreans leased 1,300 acres near Manteca in the San Joaquin

Valley and developed a sugar beet cooperative. Two brothers, Ho Kim and Hyong-sum Kim, established in 1921 a partnership in Reedley, California, which dealt in wholesale fruit and nursery products. Their enterprise, which came to include fruit packing sheds and five hundred acres of land, realized $400,000 annually. One of their major contributions was the development of new varieties of nectarines such as Le Grand and Sun Grand, which they shipped throughout the United States.[30]

The extreme racial prejudice both in rural and urban areas, experienced by Koreans, as Asians, meant that those who lived in American cities found only unskilled jobs available in restaurants and hotels, or as domestic servants. Some of these people, as had been the case in Hawaii, opened small shops to cater to their fellow immigrants.[31] Most Koreans were handicapped by lack of capital to start any large business. Los Angeles' Korean community, in the 1930's, had thirty-five fruit and vegetable stands, nine grocery stores, six trucking companies, five restaurants, three herb stores, two hat shops, one rooming house, and one employment agency. The restaurants, located in poorer neighborhoods, offered a general Oriental menu. The three herb doctors served a clientele "of Koreans, Chinese, Filipinos and Americans." The employment agency placed few Koreans—not more than five a month—but did a general business for all Asians.[32]

Prior to 1952, first-generation Koreans in the United States were virtually barred from all professions since they were not citizens. Consequently, a large number of Koreans moved to Hawaii where they were able to enter the professions.[33] Two Koreans in 1939 practiced medicine in Los Angeles but there were no engineers, dentists, or social workers. At the same time, about two hundred second-generation Koreans were attending universities and colleges. Although they made excellent academic records, they too found that the professions for which they had trained were closed to them. A trained social worker was employed as a waitress while a chemistry major found employment in a sales agency. A teacher, unable to find suitable work, managed a market.[34]

A few Koreans gained national prominence. Younghill Kang won recognition as an author in the 1930's. Born in Korea in

1903, Kang migrated to New York in 1921. After a series of menial jobs in New York and Philadelphia and some travel, he enrolled at New York University. In 1931, he published an autobiographical novel, *The Grass Roof.* In 1933, as a professor of comparative literature at New York University, he won a Guggenheim Fellowship to allow him time to write a second novel, *East Goes West.* He was the first Asian to receive this award which was renewed for a second year.[35] A more recent author is Richard Kim, a faculty member at the University of Massachusetts, Amherst. Earl Kim, a member of the Princeton University faculty, has gained attention as a composer.[36]

One American of Korean ancestry who received considerable acclaim in the world of athletics during the decade of the 1950's was Dr. Sammy Lee. Lee, who grew up in Los Angeles, attended Franklin High School, and graduated from Occidental College and the University of Southern California School of Medicine. He became a member of the United States Army Medical Corps but he gained national fame in 1948 when he won the Olympic gold medal for high platform diving. He successfully defended his title in 1952. In 1953, he became the first non-Caucasian to win the James E. Sullivan Memorial Trophy, an annual award given by the Amateur Athletic Union to the athlete who ". . . has done the most during the year to advance the cause of sportsmanship."

In 1955, Lee retired from the army and sought a home in Garden Grove, California. Realtors in that city refused to show him any houses because they claimed that Orientals drove down property values. This racial snub gained Lee additional world recognition. As he attended international athletic events, he was noted as the person who could not secure a home in his own country. He was, however, able to purchase a home in Santa Ana, California, where he started his medical practice and also directed a swimming and diving school.[37]

In 1946, Hawaiian Korean professionals practiced as accountants, architects, educators, engineers, lawyers, doctors, and druggists. A few Koreans still manufactured furniture and others were well established as retailers. Many continued their small family businesses as dry cleaners, florists, grocers, military tailors, and nurserymen. Several operated hotels and rooming houses.

Korean women, by 1950, had found jobs as actresses, entertainers, managers, nurses, and proprietors.[38]

When the Hawaiian Korean community celebrated in 1973 its seventy years of settlement in the Aloha state, it honored four of its number for individual achievements. Kwan Doo Park was one so honored. After earning his baccalaureate degree from the University of Hawaii and his master's degree in structural engineering from the Massachusetts Institute of Technology, he returned to the College of Engineering faculty at the University of Hawaii. He later gained statewide recognition for his architectural firm's pioneering use of prestressed concrete construction and engineering in the state.[39]

Another Korean in the field of scientific technology was Hawaii-born Joseph D. Park, a leading chemical engineer. Early in his career, he worked for DuPont and Frigidaire and succeeded in developing a variety of refrigerants. In 1947, he joined the University of Colorado chemistry faculty. During his professorial career, more than one hundred of his students received doctorates in chemistry. Following his retirement in 1972, Park became President of the Korean Advanced Institute of Science in Seoul. He remained there until 1974.[40]

While many American Koreans have been deeply involved in international politics, some concentrated upon the American political system. In California, Alfred H. Song, the first individual of Asian ancestry to serve in that state's senate, has had a distinguished career. Elected first in 1966, he has been twice reelected. Prior to becoming a state senator, he was a councilman in Monterey Park. In 1962, he was elected to the first of his two terms as a state assemblyman. A prominent Democrat, he has held key positions in both the state and national party organization. Born in Waipahu, Oahu, Song graduated from McKinley High School where so many political leaders of Hawaii received their secondary education. After attending the University of Hawaii, he received his baccalaureate and law degrees from the University of Southern California and was admitted to the California bar in 1950.[41]

Only a few Koreans in Hawaii have sought elective office. The most successful of these was Philip P. Minn. Born in Hana, Maui, he graduated from the University of Hawaii and served

in the army during World War II. Minn lived on Oahu's Lee-
ward shore where he had a nursery and landscape company.
His first attempt in 1954 for a place in the territorial legislature
was unsuccessful, but he was elected in 1955, remaining in the
territorial house until statehood in 1959. Elected to the Hawaii
House of Representatives in 1963 from the Ewa-Waianae district,
he served until his death in 1966. Governor John Burns appointed
Minn's wife, Momi, to serve out the term. A prominent Democrat
in her own right, she was a national committeewoman from
Hawaii. She won election to the House seat in 1966 and 1968.[42]

In 1961, Richard K.C. Lee was appointed Director of the
Hawaii State Health Department. In 1965, he assumed the
deanship of the newly created School of Public Health at the
University of Hawaii. A second Korean who has served as a
Hawaii state cabinet officer was Ke Nam Kim who was ap-
pointed state controller in 1967.[43]

Herbert Y.C. Choy was one of the four Koreans honored in
1973 by his fellow Koreans as a distinguished citizen. Born on
the island of Kauai, he graduated from the University of Hawaii
and from Harvard Law School. Admitted to the bar in 1941, he
soon found himself in the army. After service in Japan and Korea,
he returned to Honolulu to open a law partnership. One of his
partners was Hiram Fong, later a United States Senator. In
1957, Choy was named territorial attorney general. The *Honolulu
Advertiser* noted that this was the first time a Korean had held
such a position in the United States. In 1959 as the territorial
government ended, he returned to private law practice. President
Richard M. Nixon, in 1971, appointed Choy to the bench of
the Ninth Circuit Court of Appeals.[44]

A large part of the Korean flow to the United States after
1968 consisted of professionally trained people. The largest
category were physicians, surgeons, and nurses. Other fields in
which significant contributions were made were engineering and
education.[45]

Recent Korean immigrants have, however, found it difficult
to cope with the job market in the United States. Where both
husband and wife worked or sought employment, as in Los
Angeles, they frequently confronted unemployment or under-
employment. In 1973, it was judged that about 20 percent of the

Korean work force in that city was unemployed. Some three thousand were on welfare. The fact that almost all of these immigrants were well-educated exacerbated the frustration that was the result of lack of work. Trained Korean women had greater success in finding employment than did men. In late 1974, about six hundred Korean nurses and three hundred pharmacists worked in Los Angeles County. The fact that women found jobs readily created problems at home when the husband, the family head in Korea's patriarchal society, could not find work.

Only about thirty or forty Korean physicians were licensed and practicing in Los Angeles County in 1974. Some men, whether professionally trained or not, found work in service stations in or near "Little Seoul." Both men and women were employed in manufacturing wigs and women worked in beauty parlors as hairdressers. As "Little Seoul" rapidly expanded, Korean restaurants, groceries, and night clubs provided additional jobs.[46]

Koreans migrating to Honolulu after 1968 experienced similar frustrations. Well-trained people discovered that state regulations kept them out of professional fields. One college-trained pharmacist had earned in Korea the equivalent of $250 a month, considered to be a decent living wage there. In anticipation of earning more money, he brought his family to Hawaii. But that state ruled that he had to return to college before he could be licensed. Because Hawaii did not offer pharmaceutical education, he would be required to attend a university on the mainland. The only employment he found was clerking in a shoe store at $2.10 an hour—about $336 a month.[47] Another pharmacist and his family of five, considered to be upper middle class in Korea, left a five-bedroom house and a maid for a Hawaii housing project concrete cubicle, costing $81 a month. He had quit his job in a Korean hospital in search of a better living. He was confronted, like other Asian immigrants, by the language barrier, the exceedingly high cost of living in Hawaii, and the restrictive laws preventing him from entering his profession. The day after he arrived, the pharmacist responded to a newspaper advertisement and was employed waxing cars at a car wash. He reported that each time he applied for a druggist's position, the answer was simply not just "No," but a hostile attitude of "No one invited you to come here so why should you expect to get a job?" In May, 1974, he was stuffing mattresses for a bedding company at $2.30 an hour.[48]

In 1969, before the influx of new immigrants, long-time Korean Americans, as a group, were economically well off. Nationally, Korean males had a median salary of $6,435 as compared to the total population's $7,609. Hawaiian Koreans had the highest median level of groups in that state—$8,510. The state median for the general population was $8,055. In California the total male population median was $9,641 while that of the Koreans was $6,322.[49]

Employment and compensation for Koreans in the 1970's fell into two distinct patterns. Second- and third-generation Koreans who had adjusted to American life had become successful businessmen and professionals. The recent arrivals in West Coast cities, Honolulu, and New York City had yet to reach the economic level to which they aspired.

PART III

EAST INDIANS IN AMERICA

CHAPTER XIV

India, Land of Many People

INDIA, one of the major geographical subdivisions of the Asian continent, with an area of about 1,560,000 square miles, is divided politically between the present-day nations of India, Pakistan, and Bangladesh. The Indian nation comprises about the same land mass as those states of the United States east of, and including, the tier from Minnesota through Louisiana, the two Dakotas, and most of Nebraska. In the case of Pakistan, the land mass approximates the southeastern United States from Tennessee to the Gulf of Mexico and North Carolina through Florida. Bangladesh is just slightly smaller than the state of Wisconsin. The three countries' tragic dilemma is highlighted when their population is compared with that of the United States. In 1973, India's territory contained an estimated 574.2 million people while Pakistan had an estimated population of 66.75 million. Bangladesh in 1974 had an estimated crowded 71.1 million people. The total United States population in 1970 was 203.25 million.[1]

Geographic features contribute greatly to the subcontinent's diversity. Across the natural 1,600 mile-long northern frontier, reaching from Assam to Afghanistan, lie the lofty peaks of the Himalaya and the Karakoram Range. In the northwest, on the present Pakistan-Afghanistan border at 3,400 feet above sea level is the fabled Khyber Pass, a natural passageway through the Hindu Kursh, extending from the city of Peshawar to Afghanistan's capital city, Kabul. This pass opened India to invasion and trade.[2]

India's river systems have played a dominant role in the life of the two nations. In the west, the Indus traverses the Punjab, the land of five rivers, from Himalayan snows through an alluvial plain to the Arabian Sea, a course of 1,800 miles. Below the

175

junction of the five rivers, in the land of Sind, human habitation has been possible only because of irrigation systems. Sind normally receives five inches of rain annually. The upper Indus Valley of Punjab receives eight to twelve inches of rain. Its natural ground cover is that of a dry tropical forest while its dry hilly districts have a desert ecology.[3]

The Indus River Valley is separated from the Ganges River basin to the east by the extensive Thar Desert which stretches along the western border of present-day India. The highland corridor of eastern Punjab, known historically as the cockpit of India, has always provided easy access to the Ganges for the Indus hills people. Conquerors, avoiding the Thar Desert, marched through the hills into the fertile and heavily populated Ganges River Valley. This flood plain, an area of over 300,000 square miles, is watered by the Ganges and its five large tributaries. The great Hindu empires thrived along the length of "Mother Ganges," the sacred river, from the uplands around Delhi to the low lying cities of Calcutta and Dacca. The valley remains one of the world's most heavily populated regions. The upland region, the present Indian state of Uttar Pradesh, averages about twenty-five inches of rainfall annually while Bengal's range is forty to sixty inches.[4]

To the south of the Ganges River basin is the Deccan plateau which extends southward to the Krishna River. Beyond this river is South India which has, more or less, remained apart from the north, and has maintained its own ancient culture. Along the western edge of the Deccan plateau, facing the Arabian Sea, an eroded mountain wall, some 600 miles long, has isolated the people of the interior from those of the coast. The survival of these inhabitants of the Deccan plateau and those of South India depends upon the July to October seasonal monsoon. During the monsoon, rain storms from the Arabian Sea cross over the peninsula to the Himalayas. Unlike the snow-fed rivers in Northern India, the rivers of the plateau and the south are dependent upon this rain. Any lasting drought brings famine and death.[5]

The coastal land, the Western Ghats, a tropical rain forest strip lying in the path of the monsoon, receives 80 to 200 inches of rain a year. It was here that the Portuguese explorers first came—to the cities of Goa and Bombay. With the opening of the Suez Canal in the nineteenth century, Bombay surpassed Calcutta and Madras to become India's major seaport.

India has always been a land of subsistence agriculture. Its staple food, and largest cereal crop, is rice which is planted and harvested twice a year in the lower Ganges Valley, along the southeastern and western seacoasts, and in the irrigated regions of the lower Indus Valley. In the uplands, wheat is the principal crop. The upper reaches of both the Ganges and the Indus Rivers, the homeland of many early immigrants to the United States, are major wheat producers. The present Indian states of Punjab and Uttar Pradesh remain wheat centers. But there is never enough rice or wheat. In the Deccan region and in South India, cereal sorghum and millet provide the basic cereal food.

Certain specialized crops also flourish. In the south and on the plateau, groundnuts, linseed, and sesame seed are grown in abundance. Along the eastern coast and in the Ganges Valley, sugar, an indigenous plant, is produced, but it, too, is always in short supply. Cotton is also a native of India, but its boll fibers have become inferior to fibers produced elsewhere. Even so, cotton textile goods remain a major adjunct of India's agricultural economy. India produces about one-third of the world's supply of tea. It possesses about one-third of the world's cattle but these are not part of its economy since cattle are sacred. In this land, predominantly agricultural and overpopulated, disaster is always near whenever the balance of nature is disturbed to the slightest degree.

India, one of the world's oldest civilizations, dates back to paleolithic time. Excavations in South India disclose that there was a fairly advanced neolithic tribal culture. One of South India's early ethnic stocks were the Dravidians, the dark-skinned ancestors of the Tamils, now living in southeast India and Sri Lanka. The Dravidian civilization advanced into the age of metals.

India's first society, which was more complex than the Dravidian, was possibly an offshoot of the Sumerians who came into the Indus Valley some time after 3,000 B.C. and imposed themselves upon tribes already there. Excavations in Sind and

Punjab attest to the vitality of this culture. Around 1,500 B.C. it declined and then disappeared.[6]

About 2,000 B.C., Aryan tribes, with horses and chariots, moved through the mountain passes in the north and in the west. They arrived, not as a major single invasion wave, but in small groups, looking for new homes and lands for their cattle herds. Only gradually did they shift to farming. The Aryans have been described in their own writings as tall, with long heads, straight noses, prominent foreheads, and fair complexions.

The language of the Aryans relates to other languages of that day, such as those of the Hittites and the Iranians. From this language came classical Sanskrit, the language of the scholars; the modern-day regional dialects of Bengali, Gujarati, Marathi; and India's official language, Hindi. Hindi itself has at least three major dialects: Hindustani, spoken in the Delhi area; Punjabi, spoken in the Punjab; and Urdu, a Muslim derivation which is written in Arabic characters.

The culture of these Indo-Aryans has been preserved through the Vedas, the sacred books of Hinduism. In the Vedas, one reads that Indo-Aryans were warriors who worshipped war and found exhilaration in fighting. They disliked intensely their enemies, whom they described as short, black, and noseless— fit only to be slaves.[7]

The Indo-Aryans moved from the Indus lands into the Ganges River Valley, overthrew the residents, and adapted to that valley's rice economy. They developed a series of empires. The first of these, founded in the fourth century B.C., was Nanda. During the time of the Nanda Empire, Alexander the Great invaded the Punjab and marched down the Indus River. Unable to sustain his invasion, his armies retreated to the west. After Alexander's death, those Indo-Aryans who defeated his successors in the Indus Valley subsequently built the Mauryan Empire, the second major empire, which included all of the subcontinent except South India.[8]

Of great importance to India's future was the evolution of the Indo-Aryan social structure and religious thought. The Indo-Aryans at first divided themselves into three fairly mobile classes but by 500 B.C. had a well-defined caste system. The Indo-Aryans were extremely color-conscious and considered themselves racially superior. They evolved a three-class societal system which became locked into place through heredity. The classes were the Brahmins, priests; the Kshatriyas, warriors; and the Vaisyas, cultivators. The many aboriginal residents of India remained outside the system. For these, the Indo-Aryans created a fourth grouping based originally on color and ancestry, the Sudras, who could never belong to the system for they were casteless.[9]

The caste system has remained an integral aspect of Indian culture, involving one's occupation, ethnic origin, and religion. Hindu religious law set sharp differentiations between castes and provided strong penalties if an untouchable or a member of any caste broke the rules. As centuries passed, those classifications, based upon occupation, divided and subdivided into smaller and smaller units which developed their own sets of rules. Individual occupational choices became limited to the caste into which one was born.[10]

Hinduism as a systematic religion regulated day-to-day living. Several divinities oversaw the people's existence. Hinduism also advanced the concept of reincarnation whereby people were re-born as different creatures until they achieved perfection.[11]

In the sixth century B.C., two new religious streams, Jainism and Buddhism, appeared in response to Hinduism which had become highly stylized and tightly controlled by the Brahmins. Dissent over this structured interpretation expressed itself first as asceticism. The ideas, which became the precepts of Jainism, held that all things had a separate soul and that it was vital that man respect all kinds of life—animate and inanimate. One major principle was the doctrine of nonviolence which has had great impact on modern Indians such as Mahatma Gandhi and his followers.[12]

Buddhism stems from the teachings of its founder, Siddhartha. The son of a prince, Siddhartha came from the Kshatriya caste. He could not see the purpose of either a caste system or an order of Brahmin priests. Shunning Sanskrit, Siddhartha advocated his views in the vernacular language. He gave up his life of ease and wandered for many years. In time, he received a revelation and was thereafter known as Buddha, or the Enlightened One. His doctrine was enunciated as Four Noble Truths. He taught that existence means suffering, that suffering comes from desire, that when desire ceases one can escape suffering, and that the end of desire becomes possible by following the precepts of the "Eightfold Path: Right Understanding, Right Resolve, Right Speech, Right Action, Right Living, Right Effort, Right Mindfulness, and Right Meditation."[13]

Early followers of Buddha developed a religion based upon monasticism, asceticism, and contemplation. However, the spread of Buddhism through Asia came with Mahayana Buddhism, which stressed the opportunity for salvation, the need for faith, and a charitable attitude.[14] In India, this meant that salvation was possible for members of the lower castes. The Brahmins gradually accepted Buddhism as a reform interpretation and its concepts were merged into Hinduism. By the fifth century A.D., Buddhism was no longer a strong independent force in India.

During the tenth century, the Turks completed their Islamic invasion of India and remained dominant politically until surpassed by the British. This new intrusion imposed additional political, religious, and social changes upon the subcontinent. From the outset, Islam established itself as a second culture paralleling Hinduism. The teachings of Muhammad, advocated by a vigorous aggressive people, ran counter to Hinduism and there was no chance for an admixture of the two. Muslims believed in one God. The *Koran,* the revealed word through God's prophet, Muhammad, showed that there was a final judgment for man according to his works on earth, and it stressed predestination. The obligations for Muslims were direct—almsgiving, prayer five times a day, and certain religious observances. All obligations could be fulfilled directly by a Muslim who needed no interpretative religious priesthood. As the Hindu and Muslim societies developed side by side, the Muslims, in control, tolerated the Hindus and only demanded that taxes be regularly paid.[15]

In the 1500's still another Asian invasion occurred as the Moguls crossed through northern passes into India to become dominant in upper India until the close of the seventeenth century.[16] India literally became a land of many societies and small states. Just before the Mogul incursions, Vasco da Gama arrived from Portugal, seeking bases for an eastern trade. By 1600 the Dutch and English had become competitors in India. A century later France had established her major commercial interests. Throughout the eighteenth century, France and England struggled for supremacy. The French lost the final battle in 1761 and the British became the European masters of India.

For almost two hundred years, the English monarch bore the title Emperor of India. The British strove to make India one of the major cogs in its imperial system. Agriculturally and industrially, the subcontinent was developed to meet British needs.

In 1920, Mahatma Gandhi started his movement against the British. He advocated that India not become a Western satellite but that life be based upon the teachings of Hinduism, and that the village, instead of being destroyed, should develop into the basic force. For years, espousing a doctrine of nonviolence, he led the fight for freedom. One of the major problems for the British in granting independence was the centuries-old division between Hindus and Muslims. The Moslem League, founded in 1906, called for a separate nation of Pakistan—to consist of the northwestern and eastern regions of the subcontinent, where large numbers of Muslims were concentrated.

The British granted independence in 1947, creating the two nations of India and Pakistan. It has been estimated that more than eleven million Hindu and Muslim refugees moved during 1947. But independence did not bring an end to turmoil. The sovereignty of the northwest district of Kashmir remained unclear, creating a stalemate. Pakistan, divided in 1947 between East Pakistan and West Pakistan, was riven by other problems. Fifty-six percent of the people lived in East Pakistan but government control was centered in the west. After two decades of unhappiness, the Awami League declared East Pakistan independent in March, 1971. Shortly thereafter, India declared war on Pakistan and in December, 1971, recognized East Pakistan as the independent nation of Bangladesh. Bangladesh demonstrated too clearly the tragedy that befalls people of mixed cultures and religious beliefs who get caught in a power struggle between nations.[17]

By the twentieth century, the cultures of the various peoples of India remained more or less static. The caste system enervated the Hindus. The Muslims lost their dominant position during British rule, for the British had encouraged the Hindus to take over the civil service as a means of diminishing Muslim power. Besides industrialization, other Western influences impinged upon the people of India—the educational system, a public health program, and Christianity. Franciscan friars arrived with the Portuguese while Protestant missionaries came in the eighteenth century. Their efforts met with considerable success. By the time of independence in the 1940's, Christianity ranked third in the number of religious adherents.[18]

Almost all of the first immigrants to North America were Sikhs. The founder of Sikhism, the first guru, Nanak (1469–1538), sought to reconcile differences between Hinduism and Islam. He held that all men are brothers who should follow the laws of love and practice the ideal of equality. From the Muslims, he adopted the concept of one God; from Hinduism, he accepted the idea of Karma or reincarnation. But he rejected caste and the worship of idols. In 1604, Nanak's fifth successor, the guru, Arjun, collected the writings into the *Adi Granth*, the holy book of the Sikhs. The fourth guru, Ram Das, built a shrine at Amritsar which early in the nineteenth century became the site of the Golden Temple, a building that implements Nanak's ideas by combining Muslim and Hindu architectural styles. Upon its altar lies the *Adi Granth*.

The tenth, and last guru, Gobind, in 1675, organized the Sikhs into a military order, the Khalsa, the Elect, and all members of the order adopted the common surname Singh, or Lion. A ceremony of initiation, the baptism of the sword repudiated caste. Once initiated, all Sikhs were equal regardless of political or economic positions. Initiates swore abstinence from tobacco and wine and adopted the five "K's—long hair, short drawers, a large comb in the hair, a dagger and an iron bracelet." The Sikhs developed an intense sense of nationalism and organized the independent state of Punjab with Lahore as its capital. In the mid-nineteenth century, the British finally conquered Punjab and the Sikhs became part of the empire.[19] In the last half of the nineteenth century, they served in the imperial armies in Asia and Africa. Strong, tall, and vigorous, they wore tight trousers, colorful tunics, and a turban over their hair, which they were forbidden to cut. In 1971, over ten million Sikhs lived in India, mostly in the northwest. It was these tall Sikhs, with their turbans, who stood out as strangers during the first two decades of the twentieth century in British Columbia and the Pacific Coast states.

During the twentieth century, emigrants from several areas of India and Pakistan crossed the oceans to North America. The Punjab, with disputed Kashmir and the divided Sikh nation, with its Holy Shrine of Amritsar in India and its capital, Lahore, in Pakistan, has remained a major contributor of immigrants. The difficulties of daily existence and the controversy caused by partition have led many to emigrate.

Another upland area that provided substantial numbers of immigrants was the state of Uttar Pradesh, formerly the United Provinces of British India. Other areas that have contributed significant numbers of emigrants center about the major seaports. On the west coast, immigrants come from the state of Gujarat and the nearby city of Bombay. In the Ganges River Valley, the old province of Bengal was divided in 1947. East Bengal, now partly in Bangladesh, has provided through its capital city of Dacca a sizeable number of Muslim immigrants, particularly since 1965. From the Indian side of the boundary, Hindus have come from Calcutta to the United States.

Most certainly the growing complexities of the diverse problems of India and Pakistan have led those who could to seek alternative solutions for themselves and their families. After World War II and changing immigration laws in the United States, many people from the subcontinent turned to the United States as the place in which to work out their futures.

CHAPTER XV

Early East Indian Immigration to the United States and Canada

DURING the first two decades of the twentieth century, the arrival of East Indians from India's subcontinent, although small in actual numbers, caused considerable uproar along the Pacific Coast of Canada and the United States.[1] East Indian immigration, and that of other Asians, coincided with increasing American and Canadian hostility against the Japanese.

Prior to the nineteenth century, few Indians had migrated overseas from the subcontinent, for crossing the "black waters" was held to be dangerous to a Hindu's soul. Thus the large-scale emigration which started in the mid-1800's was somewhat startling. With the decline of their black slave labor, West Indian sugar plantations gained permission in 1838 to transport Indian coolie labor, but it was not until 1845 that Indians were brought in large numbers to Guyana, Jamaica, and Trinidad. Coolies arriving in Natal in 1860 marked the beginning of the South Africa Indian problem. During these same years, large numbers migrated to Mauritius to labor in the cane fields of that Indian Ocean island.[2] One hundred years later, emigrants from India were also settled throughout former British Empire territories such as Kenya, Tanzania, South Africa, and Uganda in Africa; Sri Lanka; and Fiji. A sizeable number also lived in Surinam in South America.[3]

Americans first came into contact with one aspect of Indian culture in 1893 when Swami Vivekananda, a disciple of the mystic, Shri Ramakrishna, expounded on Vedantic philosophy at the First World Parliament of Religions in Chicago and established Vedanta Society centers throughout the United States. Particularly strong were the Hindu Temple in San Francisco and the New York center.[4] Throughout the twentieth century, Indian philosophy and religion have attracted many Americans.

184

In 1901, East Indian students began coming to the United States to enroll in colleges and universities. Most had received scholarships from various Indian educational societies while others had come on their own, expecting to earn enough to finance their education. Most of the first students entered eastern institutions such as Cornell University. By 1904, some had enrolled at the University of California. Four years later, seventeen students were at Berkeley while five others were studying at California's polytechnical institute at San Luis Obispo.[5] Indian students have remained an important segment of foreign students on American campuses. Rallying together in the cause of Indian independence, those East Indians at the Berkeley campus around 1910 have become identified as that university's first political activists.

Students were only a small segment of the total immigration that comprised the first major wave of Indian arrivals. This first influx, of less than fifteen years' duration, was terminated by federal legislation in 1917. The bulk of the immigrants were unskilled agriculturalists and small entrepreneurs from the arid lands of the Punjab, the United Provinces (Uttar Pradesh), Bengal, and Gujarat. Most of those arriving at West Coast ports came from the heavily populated Punjab districts of Amritsar, Hoshiarpur, Jullundar, Ludhiana, Ferozepore, and Lahore.[6] In 1946, only the Lahore district was included as part of Pakistan; the other districts became part of India. Even though irrigation projects had reclaimed considerable land, farming remained difficult. For the inhabitants, largely Sikhs, overcrowding and economic problems provided the motivation to migrate. Few intended to settle permanently in Canada or the United States, planning, as had the Filipinos and others, only to earn enough money to return home to live a life of ease.[7] The wage level in India was between five and fifteen cents a day. From both personal knowledge and rumors, the Sikhs understood that Pacific Coast labor earned from two to five dollars a day. They did not understand that these were the wages of skilled workers and that living costs were much higher.[8] Many Sikhs had been overseas as part of the British imperial establishment, serving in the army or the constabulary. As they completed their tours of duty and returned to their homes, Punjab's problems made many of them discontented. Soon a trickle of emigrants started for Vancouver, Canada, and San Francisco.

From the outset, these East Indian emigrants, regardless of their home, culture, or religion, were called "Hindus" or "Hindoos." The United States Immigration Commission's 1911 *Dictionary of Races or Peoples* defined an East Indian as any native of the East Indies. Included were peoples ranging from the inhabitants of the Philippines to the Aryans of India. Said the commission: "It is this Aryan population of northern India that is generally called Hindu although the term also applies to a religion or to the people having a certain social organization." The commission held that any native of India was to be considered a "Hindu" for immigration purposes.[9]

During 1898 and 1899, East Indians who had been peasant farmers began to arrive in the United States. In all, they numbered fifteen immigrants. By 1900, the United States Census reported there were 2,050 East Indians resident in the United States. Most of these were non-Indians who had been born in India and some Indian students and businessmen.[10] It was not until 1904 that United States ports of entry began to register major increases. The following table shows the immigration patterns for the fiscal years 1898–99 through 1913–14:

TABLE VI
EAST INDIAN IMMIGRATION
TO THE UNITED STATES,
1898–1914[a]

Fiscal Year	Number	Fiscal Year	Number
1899	15	1907	1,072
1900	9	1908	1,710
1901	20	1909	337
1902	84	1910	1,782
1903	83	1911	517
1904	258	1912	165
1905	145	1913	188
1906	271	1914	172

[a]U.S. Dept. of Commerce and Labor, Bureau of Immigration and Naturalization, "Memoranda regarding Hindus in the United States," U.S. State Dept. Numerical File 52903/110-B.

The movement of East Indians to the United States paralleled their entry into Canada where, although citizens of the British Empire, they encountered firm resistance. As this opposition grew, more and more East Indians fled southward into the United States. The original lure of Canada for the East Indians has been traced to 1897 when several Sikhs passed through British Columbia upon their return from Queen Victoria's Diamond Jubilee in London. A few remained to settle in Vancouver.

The first sizeable influx came in 1901, following the Boxer Rebellion in Peking, China, when several Sikhs arrived in Vancouver—some on leave and others as retired soldiers.[11] But the annual number of immigrants remained small until 1905 when forty-five migrated. Most of those who came in 1905, and after, had been enticed by several Canadian enterprises, such as railroads and some small businesses owned by other East Indians. Agents, sent to India, distributed pamphlets that exaggerated the economic opportunities in British Columbia. Canadian Pacific steamship companies were interested in East Indians as a source of revenue resulting from increased ticket sales. Such were the findings of the Royal Commission of Canada of 1907.[12] According to his 1923 study, Rajani K. Das believed that the major cause of emigration was the favorable letters written by East Indians already in Canada.[13] These former soldiers saw many opportunities in this western province, which they reported to their friends and relatives in the Punjab.

The majority of those arriving in 1905 settled in Port Moody, just east of Vancouver. By 1907, the number of arrivals reached 2,124. The next year saw 2,623 East Indians enter.[14] In actuality, as the table (p. 188) shows, British Columbia received few East Indian immigrants.

Nevertheless, these people ran headlong into the bitter antagonism that British Columbia provincials had developed against all Asians. The goal of this western province was similar to the Pacific Coast states to the south—keep the land for white people only. The Chinese had been the first to come to the province, both from China and the United States. Vancouver had the second largest Chinatown in North America. After 1891, Japanese started arriving. The attempt by the provincial legislature to restrict Asian immigration in the first decade of

TABLE VII
EAST INDIAN IMMIGRATION TO CANADA,
1905–1914[a]

Fiscal Year	Number	Fiscal Year	Number
1905	45	1910	10
1906	387	1911	5
1907	2,124	1912	3
1908	2,623	1913	5
1909	6	1914	88

[a]Sushil K. Jain, "East Indians in Canada," *Research Group for European Migration Problems*, June 1971, p. 3.

the twentieth century was struck down by the dominion government in Ottawa. United States immigration policies in 1907, based upon presidential orders and the Gentlemen's Agreement, caused large numbers of Japanese to land in Vancouver. In September, 1907, reacting against this influx, a Vancouver mob rampaged through both Chinatown and the Japanese section.[15] Three days after the riot, nearly one thousand East Indians arrived in port. They joined an additional seven hundred of their countrymen who had fled into the area a few days earlier from Bellingham, Washington. Vancouver's mayor telegraphed Premier Wilfred Laurier requesting that the dominion drill hall be used to house these new arrivals. When the request was refused, some men lived in tents and others slept in the open. According to the city editor of Vancouver's *Daily Province*, at that moment "the unsophisticated Hindu, dirty, gaunt, and with the roll of pagan dry goods wrapped around his head, . . . still a British subject" was "regarded with complacency alongside the Japanese."[16] Soon, however, white residents of Vancouver came to regard East Indians as another major threat.

Those East Indians emigrating to the Pacific Coast naturally saw themselves quite differently than did the white residents. One Sikh emigrant wrote in 1909 that "of all immigrants who drift to North America, none surpasses the Hindu in picturesqueness." He described the several types of emigrants:

He comes clad in countless curious styles. Yards upon yards of cotton, calico or silk are swathed about the head of one, forming a turban, cone-shaped or round like a button-mushroom, with a wave or point directly in the middle of the forehead or to the right or left, as variable as the styles of American women's pompadours— some with a long end hanging down from the back, gracefully and somewhat coquettishly dangling over one shoulder; others with the end securely tucked into the twisted rolls that twine round and round the head. A scarlet Turkish fez tops the head of another, while a third wears an ordinary cap or hat, and the fourth goes about bare- headed.

A smart English military uniform, with the front plastered over with metal medals, a voluminous turban and a bristling beard, distin- guish the tall, lanky Sikh soldier who has served in King Edward's army in India and elsewhere. The man with the fez is usually a Mahometan and is apt to wear a long-flowing coat reaching almost to his ankles and leaving partly visible his pajamas, which fit tightly around his shins. He is sockless, and the toes of his slipper-like shoes curve fantastically over the top of his feet. The man with the Western cap wears clothes of pseudo-Occidental style, which he fondly believes to be up-to-date, measured by Western standards; but the sleeves invariably are too short and end nearer the elbow than the wrist, while the coat and nether garments are tight where they should be loose, and baggy where they should be tight. As a rule, the clothes are dilapidated in appearance and frequently second- hand, and the whole combination is grotesque except in the eyes of the newcomer himself. These specimens of the Hindoo genus homo are almost invariably workingmen or peasant-laborers.

The bare-headed Hindoo is without a coat. A longish shirt, resem- bling an artist's apron, reaches nearly to his ankles. He wears long stockings like a woman's and rope-soled half-shoes. Circling his left shoulder and waist like a marshal's sash, is a *daupata,* a strip of cotton cloth, a handsomely-embroidered piece of silk or a long, soft shawl. In many cases, instead of the long shirt, the man drapes around his legs and trunk a sheet of cotton or silk known as a *dhoti*. Again, the *dhoti* is worn in combination with the shirt, the trunk covered by the shirt, reaching just below the thigh and the *dhoti* loosely wound around the legs. This type of Hindoo is usually a religious missionary intent on spreading his cult on the Western hemisphere.

Some there are in the group straggling across the gang-plank with whose dress even the most fastidious American could find no fault. Their clothes are of the latest approved style in cut, color and mate- rial. The well-dressed East-Indians are merchants, students or men of means who are traveling merely for the sake of pleasure.[17]

The East Indians provided the Canadian government with
two problems: removal of those already living in British Columbia and cessation of additional immigration. One dominion plan
proposed transporting those in the Vancouver area to British
Honduras sugar plantations. But in 1908, most East Indians in
British Columbia were employed as wage earners; none had
any desire to become contract plantation laborers. Governmental
agencies could not find anyone who wanted to be transported
to the Central American colony.[18]

That same year, at an imperial conference held to discuss the
issue of Asian immigration to Canada, particular attention was
given to East Indians. The conference reached agreements which
effectively curtailed East Indian immigration to Canada. The
findings condemned the activities of both the Canadian companies' recruiting agents and the steamship lines. It was held
that the latter had violated Canada's immigration law's "continuous voyage" proviso excluding all immigrants who had not
travelled directly from their homeland to Canada with no stop-
overs en route. This interpretation effectively closed East Indian
immigration since no ship sailed nonstop from Indian to
Canadian ports. Additionally, with the consent of the conference,
Canada raised from $25 to $200 the amount of money that
each arriving immigrant had to have in his possession.[19] With
the implementation of these regulations in 1909, East Indian
arrivals dropped that year to a mere six and immigration from
India was effectively curtailed until after World War II.

In 1914, Gurdit Singh, a wealthy land owner in India and
in British Columbia chartered the Japanese ship, *Komaga Maru*,
and 375 Sikhs sailed directly to Vancouver, arriving in that
port on May 23. Canadian authorities, caught on the issue of
the continuous voyage, refused to allow the East Indians to
land and the ship remained at anchor in the harbor. Immigration officials prohibited the Sikhs from landing because they
did not have the mandatory $200 per person. Whenever the
Japanese captain attempted to put to sea, the passengers threatened mutiny. The matter went to court and the dominion's chief
justice held that Canada, although part of the imperial network, had the right to determine its own immigration regula-

tions. At last defeated, the Sikhs allowed the ship to sail back to India on July 25.

The policy of white Canada remained intact. The problem for the British Empire was, of course, that East Indians were as much subjects of the crown as were Canadians.[20] The crisis confronting the British was whether imperial citizenship had any real status. The imperial conference of 1917–18 dodged this question of citizenship and allowed each dominion to exercise its own immigration and naturalization control. Canada subsequently excluded any further East Indian immigration, apart from wives and children of those already domiciled in the country. In 1920, a dominion election act denied the right to vote to East Indians; the only exceptions were those who had served in World War I. The denial of this franchise lasted until 1947. As a consequence of not being able to vote, East Indians could not run for public office or practice law or medicine.[21]

CHAPTER XVI

The Drive to Restrict
East Indian Immigration

DURING the first two decades of the twentieth century, East Indians encountered those prejudicial attitudes and actions which all Asians experienced in the United States. Samuel Gompers, president of the American Federation of Labor, proclaimed in 1908 that "sixty years' contact with the Chinese, twenty-five years' experience with the Japanese and two or three years' acquaintance with Hindus should be sufficient to convince any ordinarily intelligent person that they have no standards ... by which a Caucasian may judge them."[1] Unfortunately, the West Coast's open hostility occasionally resulted in violence.

Major outbursts occurred in 1907, the first year of significant arrivals in the United States. Several hundred "Hindus," mostly Sikhs, were employed by Bellingham, Washington, lumber mills. On Thursday, September 5, some five hundred white men raided the mills, broke into bunk houses, and tried to drive the "Hindus" out of town. In the ensuing fracas, six East Indians were hospitalized, 410 gained protective custody in the Bellingham jail, and 750 fled northward about twenty-five miles to the Canadian border.[2] On September 12, British Ambassador James Bryce wrote to the Acting Secretary of State Alvey A. Adee that an investigation by the British consular service found that the majority of the Sikhs at Bellingham had fled to Canada while those at Everett, Washington, feared possible violence. Civil authorities in both cities claimed, he noted, to be quite capable of coping with any future developments. Bryce pointedly hoped that the federal government would support these officials. Adee, for his part, telegraphed Governor Albert E. Mead of

Washington to ascertain that "you are taking all proper steps on the premises...."

Mead replied that while Bellingham authorities had moved to protect the Sikhs, most had left the city. The mayor had informed him that the trouble had ended. The "Hindus are receiving and will receive full protection." The rioters had been arrested and charges levied against them. The Everett police chief indicated to Governor Mead that there was no problem in that city and that authorities remained on the alert.[3] While Bellingham's mayor promised to protect the East Indians, the exclusionists' goal was accomplished, for the immigrants fled the city. Members of the Asiatic Exclusion League agitated vociferously in Bellingham and two days later in Vancouver during the riots against the Chinese and Japanese. This larger all-out two-day attack diverted attention from the Bellingham incident.[4]

A year later, the league's September, 1908, newsletter, in reviewing the Bellingham riot and its causes, claimed that a "mob of 100 Hindus" attacked a small number of Swedish longshoremen, who fled because the East Indians were armed with knives.[5] No civil authority ever substantiated this statement.

In 1907, two other incidents occurred. On October 2, white workers in eastern Washington met East Indians migrating from Canada and forced them back across the border. A month later, in Everett, Washington, East Indian fears were realized as five hundred white men herded all "Hindoos living on the waterfront ... [into] the City Hall for protection. The next day the Hindoos packed up and left." So reported the Exclusion League which concluded that the cause of violence was the presence of Asian immigrants: "In California the insolence and presumption of Japanese, and the immodest and filthy habits of the Hindoos are continually involving them in trouble, beatings and otherwise.... In all these cases, we may say the Oriental is at fault."[6]

Three years later, on March 21, 1910, white lumbermen at Saint John, Oregon, near Portland, led in expelling "Hindu" workers. An investigation by United States Marshal Charles J. Reed revealed that the entire community was involved. The mayor and the police had not attempted to restrain the mob,

for a local election was to occur on April 4 and no elected
official wanted to antagonize voters. When the marshal and
the British consul in Portland sought support of Multnomah
County's sheriff and district attorney, they found these officials
unwilling to become involved because of their own political
problems. Reed concluded that the incident was "the usual feud
between organized labor and an alien race."[7] While the British
embassy lodged an official protest, Bryce wrote privately to
Secretary of State Philander Knox:

Of the letter I sent about this recent riot affecting British Hindu
subjects at Portland I may tell you privately the government of
India has discouraged Hindu immigration into your western states,
realizing the risks of trouble. There are however still enough of them
there to make the situation a disquieting one. I am glad to see that
the President has just been reaffirming his intentions of pressing
on Congress the need for the extending of the powers of the national
government to secure protection to subjects of other powers resident
in the United States.[8]

At the controversy's conclusion, however, Saint John, Oregon,
no longer had any "Hindu" workers.

In 1908, about one hundred East Indians were driven from
the town of Live Oak, California, a Sacramento Valley agricultural community, some ten miles north of Yuba City. They
had been camping in the area for about one week awaiting
employment on the Southern Pacific Railroad. The new arrivals
claimed they had lost about $2,500 in personal property while
local citizens charged that the robbing of hen roosts and other
petty thefts had led to their expulsion. In December, 1911,
eleven East Indians were driven from their camp by fourteen
young men of the Fair Oaks area, some eighteen miles east
of Sacramento. The "Hindus" were accused of annoying white
girls. The town in general sympathized with the action of this
vigilante committee.[9] During these years of high feeling, the
standard view, most clearly stated by the Asiatic Exclusion
League, was that everyone found the East Indian immigrants
less than satisfactory: "From every part of the Coast complaints
are made of the undesirability of the Hindoos, their lack of

cleanliness, disregard of sanitary laws, petty pilfering, especially of chickens, and insolence to women."[10]

The motivation for this increasing hostility, as expressed by the Exclusion League, was reinforced by the findings of the United States Immigration Commission's report: "The East Indians are regarded as the least desirable of all races. There is a strong local prejudice against them because of their dress, color, filthy habits, taboo of articles of food not prepared by themselves, and the primitive method of living."[11]

The Asiatic Exclusion League and San Francisco's major newspapers became quite outspoken about their fear of the "Hindu invasion." On September 29, 1910, the *San Francisco Chronicle* expressed great concern about the increased immigration: "Up to the present time, few women have come in this influx of Hindus, but it has been recently stated that the men are beginning to send for their wives." By implication the newspapers saw a replay of Chinese and Japanese immigration to California. The league and the newspaper campaign attracted some national attention as the October 1, 1910, issue of *Survey* noted that "Hindus" were the Pacific Coast's latest immigration problem.[12]

The *Survey* analyzed that opposition to "Hindu" immigration stemmed from two problems. The first was a civic and social question relative to the inability of the East Indians to assimilate because of their belief in caste, their cultural habits, the imbalance between men and women, and their lower standard of living. The second concerned itself with what to do about those already residing on the Pacific Coast.[13] The *Survey* looked at the new immigrants from the view of cultural superiority and made no effort to understand the way East Indians lived. Their basic problem was that they were different and thus did not belong.

After ten years' experience with East Indians, California's officials had not changed their views. According to the Commissioner of the State Bureau of Labor Statistics in 1920, the "Hindu is the most undesirable immigrant in the state. His lack of personal cleanliness, his low morals and his blind adherence to theories and teachings, so entirely repugnant to American principles make him unfit for association with American people." The 1920 report claimed that these remarks were only aimed at the "low caste Hindu or Sikhs."[14]

Because of far-ranging cultural differences—real and imagined, white Americans saw East Indians as strange and unwanted aliens. Imperial Valley farmers reported that the "Hindu cotton pickers" were "proud and selfish," that they did not send their earnings back to India but bought cars. The farmers claimed that they "feel so far above every one else . . . they drive right in the middle of the road."

In business transactions, said other Americans, East Indians were at best unreliable. One store owner reported that after a "well-known Hindu" cashed a check in his store, the bank reported no funds. An investigation revealed that the East Indian had had five different bank accounts, and kept transferring funds from one to another, always writing checks on the account just closed. The merchant added that there were "only three honest Hindus" in his community.

A commonly held view was that East Indians belonged to an inferior culture. An American reported that he had first encountered East Indians as sailors who all had "such greasy hair" and abided by fixed tribal customs. He discovered that these sailors belonged to two different groups and the members of one would not have anything to do with the other for their rigid religions would not allow intermingling. Since the "Hindus" could eat only freshly killed mutton, the ship carried a supply of livestock which fouled the air the passengers had to breathe. To this American, "such customs seem so crude and superstitious."[15]

Saint N. Singh in 1914 correctly concluded that all Orientals, including his own people, met such strong opposition because Americans, Canadians, and Europeans really believed that Asians belonged to less advanced races, which naturally meant inferior cultures and religions. Westerners also "knew" that all Asians lowered the white man's standard of living. Singh asserted that while each argument could be logically answered, solutions to these controversial attitudes would only come when Westerners implemented the principles they espoused and when they respected the rights of Asians.[16]

One major reason why East Indian immigrants were so badly

treated was that their numbers increased at the time of international crisis over Japanese immigration. The Gentlemen's Agreement of 1907 seemed to have solved the Japanese question at the very moment "Hindus were crowding ashore" at San Francisco. Herman Scheffauer best summed up 1910 opinion regarding "The Tide of Turbans":

Again on the far outposts of the western world rises the spectre of the Yellow Peril and confronts the affrighted pale-faces. This time the chimera is not the saturnine, almond-eyed mask, the shaven head, the snaky pig-tail of the multitudinous Chinese, nor the close-cropped bulletheads of the suave and smiling Japanese, but a face of finer features, rising, turbaned out of the Pacific and bringing a new and anxious question to the dwellers of the so-called peaceful ocean. Nor is the apparition of a race different from that of the land it threatens, but of the same ancient Aryan stock. It is not, indeed, a question of the yellow and the white, but of the Oriental and the Occidental. It is nothing more or less than a threatening inundation of Hindoos over the Pacific Ocean.[17]

Two years earlier, Agnes Buchanan had helped sound the exclusionists' tocsin when she insisted that the federal government must inform the eastern wing of the Aryans that "while the earth is large enough for us all, there is no one part of it that will comfortably accommodate both branches of the Aryan family."[18]

The Asiatic Exclusion League started its "Hindu" alert with A. E. Yoell, the League's secretary-treasurer, writing to the Secretary of Commerce and Labor on December 28, 1909, that:

The Asiatic Exclusion League respectfully protests against the wholesale landing of large numbers of Hindus who are now being admitted at this port.

The League has information that formerly these undesirable aliens came to this country through ports on the Puget Sound, but that the officers of the Immigration Bureau, both of the United States and Canadian Government, so rigidly enforced the law that they abandoned their attempts to enter in that section, and are now seeking to enter here,— and do enter to the prejudice of unemployed white citizen labor. . . .

Yoell also protested that many "Hindus" were afflicted with trachoma and yet were being admitted, in part, because of their first being cleared in Honolulu. Daniel J. Keefe, United States Commissioner General of Immigration and Naturalization, responded that each alien continued to be carefully scrutinized; there was no restriction of "Hindus" as a class of people; for that to occur, there had to be congressional action. The United States Senators from California and most Bay Area Congressmen had already notified Yoell of their support.[19] This agitation proved successful, for the next year the Bureau of Immigration tightened its regulations.

In 1911, Congressman E. A. Hayes of San Jose introduced his omnibus bill to regulate the immigration of specific Asian groups and Representative E. E. Roberts introduced similar measures during subsequent sessions.[20] Such proposals were intended to stop once and for all the immigration of any Asian.

The appointment of Anthony Caminetti as Commissioner General of Immigration by Woodrow Wilson in 1913 assured California exclusionists that federal anti-Asian immigration policy would not change. Caminetti remained in that office throughout Wilson's two terms. He had labored long in the California legislature in opposition to Asian immigration. His federal appointment ideally located him to work against such immigration and he played a key role in developing national legislation aimed against East Indians.[21]

Shortly after assuming office, Caminetti urged Secretary of Labor William B. Wilson to amend existing regulations to prevent any "Hindus and Malays" who might become a public charge in the United States from emigrating from the Philippine Islands and other American insular possessions. Caminetti claimed that while an East Indian might not be a public liability in the Philippines, he could easily become such in the United States with its higher cost of living. In December, 1913, a federal district judge ruled in a San Francisco test case that East Indians could not enter the United States just because they had been admitted earlier to the Philippines. But the burden of proof, stated the judge, lay with the immigration bureau to show that any immigrant detained at Angel Island was likely to become a public charge.[22]

Early in 1914, Caminetti began pushing to terminate East Indian immigration. His first annual report devoted considerable attention to the matter. The commissioner in Seattle reinforced Caminetti's concern:

The present administration, we think, very wisely regarded their [aliens from the Philippines] entry as a mere subterfuge. . . . A few days prior to June 30, 1913, 220 Hindus arrived from Manila. They were given a rigid examination; certificates were produced by 131 who were admitted. Eighty-nine Hindus were confined to the detention house at Seattle for several months and I am sure that the most ardent advocates for the admission of Hindu laborers would become strict exclusionists if compelled to work for a long period of time in a small building such as we have. . . . The safest plan to preclude the possibility of a Hindu invasion is for Congress to enact a suitable exclusion law.[23]

In 1914, Representative Denver Church of Fresno, California, introduced a bill to exclude "Hindu" laborers. Part of his motivation was the fact that large numbers were congregating in the Fresno area. He had the support of California exclusionists in and out of Congress. The Californians again gained the support of the South in their continuing fight against Asian immigration as Senator "Cotton Ed" Smith of South Carolina introduced a companion measure in the upper house. Church also had a staunch ally in his fellow Californian, Commissioner General Caminetti, who continued to issue statements calling for the end of "Hindu" immigration.[24]

Church's bill was referred to the House Committee on Immigration and Naturalization where he had support of the committee chairman, John Burnett of Alabama and committee members Albert Johnson of Hoquium, Washington, and John Raker of San Francisco—the latter two long-standing anti-Asianists. The key witness for the exclusionists was Caminetti who was more an advocate for California than a representative of the Bureau of Immigration and Naturalization. In urging exclusion, he did not hesitate to play upon Southern fears: ". . . in order to stop a menace that is now upon the people of the Pacific coast, and upon the people of the United States, as conditions existing in the West are like those generally existing throughout the South. . . . and that when you open the door and throw down the bars to 300,000 people of India, it will not be only California, nor the Pacific coast that will get a share of these but the South will likewise have its proportion." Representative Raker then led Caminetti through a series of questions relative to the number of "Hindus" in California after the Commissioner General indicated a total of 6,656 legal "Hindu" residents. He then hedged by indicating that there had been no exact count since 1910 (which according to the Bureau of Census was 2,544), but he judged that "there are between 20,000 and 30,000 . . . in California and the Pacific Coast States alone; certainly a great many more than the record shows."[25] Representative Church in his testimony affirmed that California alone had thirty thousand "Hindus." Raker now had evidence from two different sources that "Hindus" numbered thirty thousand on the Pacific Coast and therefore constituted a menace. But others on the committee were unable to arrive at the same total after doing their own arithmetic. The immigration bureau by this time had already effectively restricted the East Indians and there was no need for any legislation other than to placate Pacific Coast exclusionists. Church's bill was tabled.[26]

American nativists were successful in 1917 when Congress passed over President Wilson's veto, his second on such a measure, an immigration restriction act. The new law, under consideration since the 1911 recommendations of the immigration commission, included for the first time a literacy test while section 3 of the act created what was known as the "barred zone."[27] All Asians living within that area which included India, Southeast Asia, the Indonesian islands, New Guinea, and parts of Arabia, Afghanistan, and Siberia were excluded.

During the congressional debates on the "barred zone," an East Indian member of the University of Iowa faculty, Sudhindra Bose, wrote British Ambassador Cecil Spring-Rice, asking what steps the embassy had taken to protest this discriminatory act. Spring-Rice replied: "No protest was lodged against the clause excluding Hindus from the United States since it is considered that the Embassy could not properly interfere in a matter of domestic legislation." Bose, in checking with the Chinese and

Japanese embassies, found that both had protested all restrictive and discriminatory legislation.[28] East Indians had no official voice of their own in Washington, D. C., at that time because they were under British rule. British officers were more concerned about the growing anti-British sentiment that East Indians had created in the United States. One possible way to control the growth of radical ideas was for the ambassador not to protest about exclusion of East Indian immigrants.

Caminetti's 1918–19 report, which indicated that the "barred zone" concept had been successful, urged that Africa and other parts of Asia be included. He noted that while the "barred zone" was aimed primarily at East Indian migration, the law had effectively closed the doors to an estimated population of five hundred million people.[29]

But this federal legislation did not still West Coast voices. Senator James Phelan of California in 1919 presented a resolution prepared by the Native Sons of the Golden West which again claimed that the numbers of Chinese, Japanese, and "Hindus" were rapidly increasing in California and that these unassimilable people created race problems that might well lead to armed conflict. Said the resolution, "the only way to solve a race problem is to stop it before it begins."[30] California continued its attack against Asian immigration in its 1920 report, *California and the Oriental*. This effort, aimed at the Chinese, Japanese, and "Hindus," consistently found the "Hindus" unfit to live in California. The thrust of such attacks was aimed at finding ways to drive out these East Indians who had established themselves as workers or businessmen. They were not able to establish legally permanent residences in the United States until 1946.

CHAPTER XVII

East Indian Immigration to the United States, 1909–1974

ALTHOUGH Canada had closed its doors in 1909, East Indian entry into the United States continued for another five years. The United States Immigration Commission noted that while the number of East Indians in the continental United States had not been specified by race, the 1900 census had reported that 2,050 residents had been born in India. The commission concluded that most of these were East Indians.[1] That number, however, when compared to immigration reports, appears excessive. H.A. Millis, who had supervised the commission's West Coast study, said that most East Indians in the United States prior to 1907 were students or businessmen residing along the Atlantic seaboard. Between 1907 and 1914, almost six thousand East Indians arrived either directly from India, via Canada, or from the Philippines. As the numbers began to increase in 1907, West Coast immigration officials began to reject more and more East Indians on the grounds that they were liable to become public charges.[2]

In 1910, these controls ran counter to the needs of Western railroads for migrant labor. This demand led to some relaxation of immigration regulations. Those East Indians who cleared immigration at Angel Island in San Francisco Bay in 1910 were taken in tow by railroad agents who sent them to various construction camps where they earned $1.80 a day.[3]

Yet, by late April, 1910, Commissioner General Keefe directed Hart H. North, Commissioner of Immigration at San Francisco, to observe these guidelines: 1) no law prohibited the admission of "Hindus" and the bureau of immigration "will not inject race as the basis of rejection"; 2) many "Hindus" had arrived in poor physical condition and therefore an "exacting physical examination is in order"; 3) "no public charge will be admitted"; and 4) there had to be a source of immediate employment. "If there is none, the Hindu might be rejected."[4] Keefe was reacting, in part, to pressure from A.E. Yoell, Secretary-Treasurer of the Asiatic Exclusion League. Yoell had claimed in December, 1909, that East Indians brought diseases. Keefe pressed this same point in his directive.[5]

During the late summer and early fall of 1910, various federal officials, expressing similar concern about the growing number of emigrants from India, suggested that control was essential. On August 11, 1910, William R. Wheeler, a member of the immigration commission, wrote to Charles P. Neil, United States Commissioner of Labor, that the "influx of Hindus at this port [San Francisco] [was] assuming alarming prospectus [*sic*] .... It seems to me that the administration is justified in adopting any policy which will keep these undesirables out." Wheeler, when he had been Assistant Secretary of Commerce and Labor, had ruled that East Indians could not migrate from Canada to the United States—an adaptation of Canada's "continuous voyage" concept.[6]

On the same day, William Michael, United States Consul General in Calcutta, wrote Secretary of State Philander Knox to confirm an earlier cablegram: "Five hundred Punjabis sailed this week Calcutta for San Francisco. Undesirable. Refuse admission." Michael claimed additionally that he had examined each person's purpose for emigration. He denied travel visas to almost all who were not taking their families. He reported concern about the immigrants' moral character, views on "sedition in India," labor qualifications, and educational and financial conditions. He found that the next group he examined evaded his questions. He soon discovered that recruiting agents in the Punjab had coached them in their answers and that they were purchasing tickets to Hong Kong and other way points (such as the Philippines).[7]

By September, 1910, the Bureau of Immigration and Naturalization kept a watchful eye on the situation. Keefe warned the Commissioners of Immigration at El Paso, Honolulu, Montreal, San Francisco, and Seattle that agents and subagents of some steamship lines were recruiting "Indian coolies to migrate to the United States."[8]

On September 27, the San Francisco immigration office reported that twenty-five "Hindus" had first landed in Honolulu to avoid the physical examination administered at Angel Island. The *San Francisco Examiner* immediately charged that the East Indians had learned that health examinations were much more lenient in Honolulu and so they cleared immigration there for easy access into California. Keefe replied that the bureau was working on the matter.[9] A carbon copy of this reply was sent to A.E. Yoell.

The *San Francisco Chronicle* claimed that hookworm had been discovered in the recent East Indian arrivals and that rigid physical examinations would reduce by half the number of "Hindus" admitted.

Angel Island authorities had already implemented the Commissioner General's directive and the number of rejections had sharply increased. In the first quarter of 1910, 519 East Indians were admitted and 39 rejected. In the third quarter, 299 were admitted and 388 turned back. By the fourth quarter, immigration through San Francisco had virtually stopped when only four were cleared and 303 returned to India.[10]

Keefe's 1910 directive was continued for the remainder of the Taft administration. In 1911, 517 East Indians were admitted; 861 were barred. During the Wilson administration, tight control continued and an exclusion program was enacted. Between 1911 and 1920, about 1,460 East Indians were admitted while 1,782 were prohibited from entering the United States. Another fourteen hundred returned voluntarily to India while the United States deported 235.[11]

The United States Immigration Commission estimated that by 1910 there were some five thousand East Indians in the United States while a 1930 Bureau of Census recapitulation of the population of "minor races" reported that in 1910 there were only 2,544 "Hindus" in the United States. The vast majority, 2,478, lived in Western states—California had 1,948, Oregon had 305, and Washington had 161.[12]

While East Indians were migrating to the West Coast along with Koreans and Filipinos, only a handful settled in the Hawaiian Islands. Between 1905 and 1910, 629 men and one woman arrived in Honolulu; 434 continued to California while

125 and the woman returned to the Orient.[13] The sugar plantations, at the time these first East Indians arrived, had satisfied
their needs with Filipino labor and there was no need for these
South Asian immigrants. In 1908, the Asiatic Exclusion League
reported that there was a plan to "induce the Hindoos to go. to
the Hawaiian Islands to work on the plantations."[14] But there
was never any large influx of East Indians to these Pacific Islands.

Prior to 1910, a considerable number of East Indians crossed
the international border from British Columbia and migrated
southward into Washington and Oregon. Many continued to
California and joined those arriving directly from India. In
California, they settled primarily in the Marysville-Yuba City
area of the Sacramento Valley, in the San Joaquin Valley around
Stockton, and in the Imperial Valley.[15]

The 1920 census reports reflected the government's restrictive
policies. The Pacific Coast experienced a slight decline while
New York gained about two hundred East Indians since 1910.
The total in the United States was 2,495, a decrease of forty-nine
in ten years. The majority, 1,961, remained in the West. In 1920,
almost all East Indians lived in rural areas. The largest urban
cluster was in New York City—123. San Francisco had forty-six
residents and Los Angeles had only twenty-three.[16]

While visas for the purpose of establishing residences were
no longer issued to "barred zone" inhabitants, East Indians continued to enter the United States. During the 1920's, more than
one thousand students arrived. While all were expected to return to their homeland, some arranged to remain. During the
same decade, probably as many as three thousand entered the
United States illegally. In 1923, the United States Consul at
Karachi, India, reported that many high school boys and laborers
from the Punjab wanted to go to Mexico or the United States
in order to: "achieve the advantages of the better livelihood and
social equality as reported to them from numerous relatives who
have penetrated the United States apparently through the overland boundaries of Canada and Mexico. . . . The most recent
communications from Sikhs and Moslems in the Punjab appear to
contemplate immigration to Mexico and this condition is reported to forewarn the land frontier immigration officials."[17]
Many Sikhs and Hindus crossed the Mexican border while

Muslims from Punjab and Bengal jumped ship in Atlantic ports. While some illegal aliens were arrested and deported, others managed to blend into the small East Indian communities in California and in large Eastern cities.[18]

By 1930, according to the Bureau of Census, only 3,130 East Indians lived in the United States; this number declined to 2,405 in 1940. About two-thirds still lived on the Pacific Coast, mostly in California.[19]

During World War II, after Chinese nationals were granted the right of immigration and naturalization, a movement for the same rights for East Indians started. In March, 1944, Representative Emanuel Celler of New York, a long-time friend of East Indian immigration, and Representative Claire Booth Luce of Connecticut introduced parallel measures in the House of Representatives providing for an annual quota of one hundred immigrants and granting naturalization.[20]

A few months earlier, in December, 1943, Senator Langer of South Dakota introduced a bill to grant citizenship to all East Indians who had come to the United States before 1924 and had resided there permanently. The Celler and Luce measures received the most support since these accomplished the goals of the East Indians living in the United States, but all three measures died in committee.[21]

During the 1945 congressional session, Representative Everett Dirksen of Illinois joined Celler and Luce in reintroducing immigration and naturalization bills while Senators Joseph Ball of Minnesota and Arthur Capper of Kansas sponsored similar legislation in the Senate. President Franklin Roosevelt favored these measures and wrote to the House committee giving support, but Congressman Robert Ramspeck of Georgia was able to have the proposals tabled. While Roosevelt's death left the matter in limbo, Harry S. Truman quickly let it be known that his administration favored a quota and naturalization. Ramspeck's objections were neutralized by the new President and the Celler bill, quickly clearing committee, was approved by the House in October, 1945. After some delay, the Senate passed the measure and President Truman signed it into law on July 2, 1946, the same day he signed a similar act regarding Filipinos.[22]

East Indians were able to emigrate to the United States and

this federal legislation set in motion the second wave of migra- tion. Following the separation of the subcontinent into the two nations of India and Pakistan, both new nations were allocated a quota of one hundred immigrants each. Between 1948 and 1965, 6,474 East Indians entered the United States. Of these, 5,774 were non-quota immigrants, mostly husbands, wives, children, and other dependents of American citizens. Those already here brought their families while single men returned to their villages to seek brides.[23]

Those new quota immigrants who arrived after World War II, but prior to 1965, were mostly professionals and their families. Whereas the first wave of immigrants had been rural Punjabis, the newer arrivals came mostly from the larger cities such as Bombay and Calcutta. Those who settled in San Fran- cisco, for example, were largely from Bombay and spoke Gujarati.[24] Throughout the 1940's, the number of East Indians remained static. Most were still concentrated in California and the New York area. The 1950 census reported the total nonwhite foreign East Indian population was 2,398.[25]

This influx of new immigrants, although still small, spread, so far as it can be determined, throughout the United States. The problem for the researcher is that, since 1950, census re- ports have not separately identified East Indian residents in the United States. In 1960, there were 8,746 nonwhites of foreign- born East Indian stock while in 1970 the number had increased to 13,149.[26] The actual number of East Indians from India and Pakistan residing in the United States can only be approximated. Jacoby's study has suggested that in 1950, after discounting the diplomatic corps and merchants, there were actually between 1,200 and 1,500 permanent residents.[27]

The 1950, 1960, and 1970 census figures showed a growth pat- tern similar to that of other Asian countries. As Tables VIII and IX in the Appendix show, the number of foreign-born Indians and Pakistani increased most in the northeastern and north central part of the United States. New York, where the United Nations headquarters was located, had become the lead- ing state in the number of East Indian residents. All geographical areas, except the West, experienced a substantial growth in the number of foreign-born East Indians over the twenty-year period,

1950–70. By 1970, East Indians appeared to be more evenly distributed throughout the country than any other Asian group.[28]

TABLE VIII
INDIAN AND PAKISTANI IMMIGRANTS ADMITTED
INTO THE UNITED STATES, 1965–1974[a]

Year	Indians	Pakistani	Year	Indians	Pakistani
1965	582	187	1970	10,114	1,528
1966	2,458	347	1971	14,310	2,125
1967	4,642	646	1972	16,926	N.A.[b]
1968	4,682	673	1973	13,124	N.A.
1969	5,963	851	1974	12,779	2,570

[a]U.S. Immigration and Naturalization Service, *Annual Reports, 1971*, p. 54; *1974*, pp. 3 & 59.
[b]N.A.—Not available.

Since enactment of the 1965 immigration law, the third wave of new arrivals from India and Pakistan has continued to increase dramatically. The pattern established in the years after World War II has continued as professional men, their wives, and children seek a new environment. As has been the case with recent Filipino and Korean immigrants, these East Indians were young—three out of five were under thirty years of age and one out of seven was less than ten years old.[29] The new wave of immigrants, as Table VIII shows, has come predominantly from India. Between 1965 and 1974, Indian immigration has increased 2,095.7 percent as 85,580 Indians emigrated to American shores. At the same time, the number of Pakistani emigrants increased 1,274.3 percent with more than nine thousand migrating.[30]

This third wave has contributed significantly to the stream of Asian immigrants arriving in the United States. A more mature American citizenry has been able to accept these Asian people. This had not been possible in the earlier decades of the twentieth century. What their impact upon American culture will be, only the future will determine.

CHAPTER XVIII

The Indian Independence Movement in the United States

IN 1926, the *San Francisco Chronicle* concluded that every East Indian was, to varying degrees, a nationalist in the struggle for independence from British rule. The newspaper saw this nationalism ranging from moderate viewpoints, which found solutions coming from within the law, to extremist ones, espoused by radicals and revolutionaries.[1]

British officials, perhaps, were not able to draw such a fine line regarding the political views of their opponents. For about forty years, East Indian activists utilized the United States as one of their bases of operations in the drive for independence. Political protest first began in the United States in 1908 under the leadership of Taraknath Das, a political activist who had fled the Bengal to avoid imprisonment. While a student at the University of Washington, he and some friends started publishing the *Free Hindustan,* first in Vancouver, British Columbia, and then in Seattle. He continued publishing the monthly magazine after he moved to New York City. The enterprise lasted for about three years.[2]

Between 1910 and 1920, the major nationalist activities were centered in California, particularly in San Francisco. The moving spirit was Har Dayal, a "high caste Hindu" native of Delhi. Following completion of his master's degree at the University of the Punjab in 1905, he received a state scholarship to attend Oxford. After a short time, he repudiated the scholarship and became politically active both in England and in India. By 1911 he was lecturing in California at Stanford University but his growing political enterprises proved an embarrassment for David Starr Jordan, the university president. This led to Har Dayal's resignation in the summer of 1912. He then traveled

209

about the Pacific Coast, talking about the need of revolution.[3]
In May, 1913, under his leadership, the Hindu Association of
the Pacific Coast was organized to tie together the Hindu in-
tellectuals and the many Sikhs in the three coast states. That
fall, Har Dayal, aided by Das, Ram Chandra and others, formed
a new activist party, Ghadr. Ghadr is an Arabic word meaning
revolution. Chandra became editor of the party's newspaper.[4]

As a consequence of hints from the British embassy, United
States immigration officials came to see Har Dayal as a dangerous
anarchist. He was arrested in March, 1914, after the Bureau of
Immigration had prepared charges against him. The warrant,
served in San Francisco, claimed that he was an undesirable
alien. As such, he was subject to deportation to India. After
being interrogated by the bureau, he fled to Switzerland. He then
moved to Berlin where during World War I he was attached to
the Indian section of the German General Staff.[5]

The Pacific Coast activities of Das and Har Dayal stirred the
British government to seek removal of both from the United
States. The British effort to prevent the awarding of United
States citizenship to Das, which coincided with Caminetti's
campaign against East Indians, was to no avail as Das was
granted citizenship by a federal court in San Francisco on June
9, 1914. As for Har Dayal, British Ambassador Cecil Spring-Rice,
learning of the pending United States deportation action, asked
to be apprised before Har Dayal was sent to any British possession.[6]

Following the flight of Har Dayal from the United States,
Ram Chandra assumed leadership of the Ghadr party. Organiza-
tional efforts continued among the East Indians on the Pacific
Coast and with the outbreak of World War I, about four hundred
East Indians left San Francisco on the S.S. *Korea,* bound for
Calcutta. Chandra had smoothed over differences between
Hindus and Muslims and convinced some Muslims to join the
expedition which was under the direction of Jawala Singh, a
Sikh. The expedition failed and Singh received a life sentence in
a Singapore prison.[7]

The Germans, meanwhile, sent an East Indian, Heramba Lal
Gupta, to the United States to lead in developing revolutionary
plots against the British government in India. All that the

Ghadr party attempted, however, failed, largely due to poor
planning, the work of British intelligence, and no real support
for the movement in India.[8] Additionally, the Hindus, Muslims,
and Sikhs kept mistrusting each other, but the Ghadr party
continued. In February, 1916, Chandra K. Chakravarty was sent
by the German government to replace Gupta as an undercover
agent. Sir William Wiseman, chief of British intelligence in the
United States, and his agents, aware of Chakravarty's German
affiliation, arranged for the New York City police to learn about
a bomb plot. This led to a raid of Chakravarty's office. His subsequent arrest for violation of United States neutrality laws and
his confession brought the desired results for the British agents.
The United States government, which had already broken
diplomatic relations with Germany, now saw the Ghadr party
as a seditious organization and moved against it.[9] When the
United States entered the war, Indian revolutionaries were
regarded as traitors.

On April 7, 1917, Ram Chandra and sixteen other East Indians
in San Francisco were taken into custody; by July, 105 indictments
were issued, charging all with conspiracy to violate the neutrality
laws. Only thirty-five persons were brought to trial; seventeen
were East Indians. The trial lasted five months and ended in
a disaster as a consequence of the deeply held suspicions of
the different religious factions. A Sikh, and one of the defendants, Ram Singh, smuggled a gun into the courtroom, approached
Ram Chandra, and killed him. Singh in turn was killed by a federal marshal. At the trial's conclusion, all but one of the defendants were found guilty. The fourteen East Indians received sentences ranging from four to twenty-two months.[10]
While there were many protests about the treatment of the
defendants and the deportation of other East Indians, the tragic
end of the trial and continuing internecine strife blunted any
impact by the Ghadr party. Following the war's end in 1918, the
United States lost interest in keeping the party under surveillance
and it revived somewhat. For another ten years, the San Francisco party headquarters issued an assortment of publications.[11]

Elsewhere in the United States during World War I, other
East Indians active in the independence movement were
harassed with threats of deportation by the immigration service.

Sailendra Nath Ghose, one of the activists, was arrested and charged in March, 1918, with writing a malicious letter to the President of the United States. Accused of being an agent of a foreign government without registering with the Secretary of State, his bail was set at $10,000 and he was in jail for six months because he could not raise the money. When his case appeared on the court docket, Judge Learned Hand reduced bail to $1,000. Ghose, in 1919, noted that six other East Indians also faced deportation because of their political activities. They were, however, being charged, said Ghose, with moral turpitude, making false statements when entering the United States, and the likelihood of becoming public charges. He maintained that these claims stemmed solely from the insistence of British officials in the United States that the activists be deported. He noted that Bhagwan Singh, one of the six, had had his bail increased from $3,000 to $10,000 and that the Department of Labor had concluded deportation hearings while refusing Singh the right to present evidence in his own behalf. Singh had been serving a federal prison term at McNeil Island and his deportation hearing was held and decided three weeks before his sentence expired. Removed from prison, he was deported to India to face additional punishment there, described as "probably quite horrible."

Ghose felt a similar fate was in store for Santokh Singh and Taraknath Das, both of whom were in Leavenworth federal prison.[12] Das, found guilty of charges brought by federal authorities, was sentenced to twenty months in prison. He served sixteen of these. While he was in prison, the British asked the United States to start deportation proceedings. The case came to court only to be dismissed by the federal judge, for Das, as a United States citizen, could not be deported.

Several years later, in 1924, Das claimed that his American citizenship saved him from the fate of others not so fortunate. Senator Hiram Johnson, chairman of the Senate Immigration Committee, asked Das what the effect would have been if he had been deprived of his citizenship and deported to India. He replied: "Well, it ... will all depend on the mercy of Great Britain, and there are instances in the past where several persons were hanged. ... the British Government has full right to put any person in prison for an indefinite period and send them to forts and confine them for indefinite periods, without giving any trial whatsoever, for the safety of the Empire."[13] Small wonder that East Indian activists in the United States, knowing this, fought against deportation.

Following the 1917 indictments against the West Coast Ghadr party, British officials turned to the restraint of Lal Laijat Rai, an active member of the Indian National Congress in India who had first visited the United States in 1906 and had returned in 1914 to enlist American public opinion for the Indian cause. Rai was considered by most observers to be a moderate in the Indian nationalist movement. Devoting the next five years to the cause, he founded the India Home Rule League of America, gave lectures, published the periodical *Young India*, to which he frequently contributed, and wrote a book. He worked with those American politicians who appeared to be anti-British or who had constituencies that might be.[14]

In December, 1917, the British embassy asked the State Department to suppress Rai's recent writings. The department informed the embassy in February, 1918, that this would happen. Rai was questioned several times by various United States security agencies during 1917–18. When the British government in India learned of the possibility of his deportation, considerable concern was expressed. In the United States, Rai created only a small stir; in India the effect of his propaganda would be greatly increased. The Viceroy of India indicated that this had already been the conclusion regarding the San Francisco Ghadr extremists. British pressure was able to prevent Rai's deportation until 1919.[15] With Rai's removal, the Home Rule League collapsed, but his efforts showed the way for future groups who also relied upon "educated Indians and American liberals."[16]

In January, 1919, Robert Morss Lovett, editor of *Dial*, called attention to the plight of the East Indians and in March, 1919, he helped found the Friends of Freedom for India. Taraknath Das and Sailendra Ghose were the two most active members but the organization also attracted several Americans. The Friends of Freedom lost its momentum when Das enrolled in the doctoral program at Georgetown University. This American organization and others concerned about India's freedom disappeared by 1922.[17]

After the promulgation of the Atlantic Charter in 1940, the number of East Indian activists for independence again increased in the United States. During World War II, the India League of America, under the direction of Sirdar Jagit Singh and the India Welfare League, led by Mubarak Ali Khan, strove for independence for India and naturalization rights for East Indians in the United States. The India League of America under the guidance of a capable executive committee, which showed the force of Singh, drew upon the ranks of Eastern United States liberalism in the struggle for independence. Khan's India Welfare League was really an adjunct of the All–India Muslim League in India.

Indian groups remained very active between 1944 and 1946 in the fight for naturalization. The India League and its monthly periodical *India Today* presented the views of the Indian National Congress. An arm of the league, The National Committee for India's Freedom had been organized in 1944 to keep Americans apprised of the independence movement. At the same time, the India Association for American Citizenship provided publicity about the educational and scientific achievements of East Indians in the United States. Periodicals such as *India News* and *The Orient and the U.S.A.* presented other viewpoints about the fight for freedom.[18]

Even as the struggle for citizenship rights was fought out in Congress, East Indian groups in the United States continued to reflect the deep religious and political splits in India. The India League of America was essentially oriented against the Muslims while the Muslim's India Welfare League endorsed the stand calling for separation of Pakistan from India.[19]

East Indian agitation for independence gave concern to many people in the United States because of their own cultural ties on the one hand with Great Britain. Yet, on the other hand, many people saw the need for equal justice and freedom for all people. Except for the repression and injustice of the World War I period, the United States government kept a hands-off attitude over the matter of Indian independence. With the settlement in 1946 and 1947 of the issues of American citizenship for East Indians and freedom for India, Indian nationalists at home and in the United States soon found a new controversy—the growing conflict between India and Pakistan—which divided East Indian communities in the United States.

CHAPTER XIX

Citizenship for East Indians

EAST Indians quickly became interested in determining their civil and political rights in the face of harassment. The controversy over their citizenship rights provides a classic example of inequity when rights are based upon a classification system that stems from the narrowness and rigidity of prejudicial thinking. Prejudice and discrimination usually flourish when one group tries to categorize other groups in broad terms and to assign certain characteristics to members of these groups. Time and time again, East Indians who were seeking citizenship were acknowledged as worthy by their opponents, who usually stated that the class action was not aimed at them but at other undefined strangers of their group. Unfortunately, these individuals were part of that larger group. The unfairness with which East Indians were treated rankled deep in the hearts of those in this country and of their compatriots in India.[1]

In 1907, as East Indians started to apply for naturalization, United States Attorney General Charles J. Bonaparte issued an opinion, which had a stultifying effect, that natives of India were not eligible for citizenship for they were not "free-white born." Four Muslims, in effect challenging Bonaparte's view, sought and gained citizenship—two in 1908 and two in 1909.[2] From these first applications, the semantical debate arose over the meaning of such words as Aryan, Caucasian, and "free white." Between 1912 and 1914, five East Indians were admitted to citizenship while sixty more gained this privilege between 1916 and 1923.

In 1909, the United States protested the granting of citizenship to Bhicaji Franji Balsara, a native of Bombay. Having lost in district court, the federal government appealed to the United States Court of Appeals in 1910.[3] This court ruled unanimously for Balsara. The opinion held:

Congress intended by the words "free white persons" to confer the privilege of naturalization upon members of the white or Caucasian race only. This we think the right conclusion and one supported by the great weight of authority. . . . We think that the words refer to race and include all persons of the white race as distinguished from black, red, yellow or brown races which differ in so many respects from it. . . . Difficult questions may arise and Congress may have to settle them by more specific legislation, but in our opinion the Parsees belong to the white race and the District Court properly admitted Balsara.[4]

In 1913, following two years of litigation, a federal court judge agreed with the arguments of Ahkoy Kumar Mozumdar, a former resident of Calcutta, that he was indeed a free white person according to the United States Revised Statutes, Section 2169. Judge Frank Rudkin, who had earlier refused Mozumdar the right of citizenship, now reversed himself. Relying upon the Balsara decision, he held that "it was the intention of Congress to confer the privilege of naturalization upon members of the Caucasian race only." Rudkin's interpretation was that any "high-caste Hindu of pure blood" who contended that he was a member of the Aryan race was entitled to naturalization as a white person.[5]

Taraknath Das, who had been an Indian political activist in India and in the United States, encountered difficulties when he applied for naturalization papers in 1912. When he reapplied in 1914 in San Francisco, the United States naturalization examiner there lodged a protest regarding Das's qualifications. United States Commissioner of Naturalization Raymond F. Crist, stated in 1926 that the United States attorney in 1914 had all the facts regarding Das's revolutionary activities, and had decided that Das understood and would uphold the principles of the United States Constitution.[6] Judge Maurice Dooling in 1914 ruled that "the applicant is a high caste Hindu of the Aryan race. It has been held that the words 'free white person' as used in the Section 2169 Revised Statutes falls within the meaning of the words as therein construed, and will be admitted."[7]

The issue of race, nevertheless, remained unsettled and in some doubt. A federal court in Pennsylvania disagreed that

"Hindus," while thought of as Caucasians, fit the definition
"white person." But two years later, a district court in California
held that "Hindus" could be naturalized.[8]

The issue of citizenship for both Japanese and East Indians
arrived in the United States Supreme Court in the early 1920's.
On November 13, 1922, Justice George Sutherland delivered
the court's opinion denying citizenship to Takao Ozawa.[9] In
rendering his opinion, Sutherland cited the cases involving
Mozumdar and Mohan Singh. He wrote:

With the conclusion reached in these several decisions we see no
reason to differ. Moreover, that conclusion has become so well established by judicial and executive concurrence and legislative
acquiescences that we should not at this late day feel at liberty to
disturb it, in the absence of reasons far more cogent than any that
have been suggested.

The determination that the words, "white person" are synonymous
with the words, "a person of the Caucasian race" simplified the
problem, although it does not entirely dispose of it. Controversies
have arisen and will no doubt arise again in respect of the proper
classification of individuals in border line cases.[10]

The Supreme Court was already considering one of these
"border line cases," namely, Bhagat Singh Thind's claim of
citizenship. Thind, of Amritsar, Punjab, emigrated to the United
States in 1913. During World War I, he was drafted into the
army, served six months, and received an honorable discharge.
He subsequently applied for citizenship in an Oregon district
court. The judge, not overly concerned as to whether or not a
"high class Hindu coming from the Punjab was ethnologically
a white person," rested his decision to award citizenship upon
the earlier Mohan Singh and Balsara cases. The United States
then attempted to cancel Thind's citizenship because of the
1917 immigration act. The Oregon district court dismissed this
action and continued Thind's citizenship.[11] The court of appeals
upheld the district court and the issue was then sent to the
United States Supreme Court. On February 19, 1923, with
Justice Sutherland delivering the opinion, the Supreme Court
held that East Indians were not eligible for United States

citizenship. The issue, in Sutherland's mind, revolved around the word Caucasian.

"Caucasian" is a convention word of much flexibility . . . and while it and the words "white persons" are treated as synonymous for the purposes of [the Ozawa] case, they are not of identical meaning. . . .

In the endeavor to ascertain the meaning of the statute we must not fail to keep in mind that it does not employ the word "Caucasian" but the words "white persons," and these are words of common speech and not of scientific origin. The word "Caucasian" not only was not employed in the law but was probably wholly unfamiliar to the original framers of the statute in 1790.

Sutherland, after discussing the definitions of Aryan and Caucasian, concluded that the words of familiar speech, as used by members of the First Congress, were intended to include only people whom they knew as white. Thus anyone else, such as a high-caste Hindu or any other East Indian, was not a "white person" and therefore ineligible.[12]

The fact that the Ozawa and the Thind cases, both dealing with citizenship for Asians, depended upon the meaning of Caucasian, has led to considerable speculation about Sutherland's decisions. Ray E. Chase and S. G. Pandit in 1926 concluded that the test in the Ozawa case was race, not color, while in the Thind case the determination was color, not race. The Justice's mental dexterity perplexed the two authors.

While there was "little protest" and much "sorrow" over the decision in India, the *Modern Review* of Calcutta did note that Sutherland, whose ruling prevented high-caste Hindus from becoming United States citizens, was himself a naturalized citizen, born in Buckinghamshire, England. The review thought "it may be that he has not been able to forget his inherited prejudices against the natives of India."[13]

Following the Thind decision, the United States Immigration and Naturalization Service sought to cancel the citizenship of all East Indians. By the end of September, 1926, forty-three had had their citizenship cancelled and the cases of another twelve were pending. The citizenship of both Mozumdar and Singh, whose earlier cases were reference points in the Ozawa decision, was annulled.[14]

Highly educated East Indians, such as Taraknath Das and Sailendra Nath Ghose, determined to counter what Das called the creation of "stateless persons." Chief Justice William Howard Taft, in a letter to Das, conceded that those East Indians who had been granted citizenship were victims of injustice. With such encouragement, Das, who was one of the twelve whose citizenship was in jeopardy, asked Senator David Reed of Pennsylvania to introduce a joint resolution to ratify the citizenship of sixty-nine East Indians and to protect the right of citizenship of American women who had married East Indians.

Meanwhile, Ghose had convinced Senator Royal Copeland and Representative Celler, both of New York, that all Indians should be considered as white persons and hence eligible for citizenship.[15] Both Reed's resolution and Copeland's bill were tabled. The two men tried again in 1927 and 1928 but to no avail.[16] The strong exclusionist alliance against Asian immigration was too powerful.

In California, after the Thind decision, the federal government started action in June, 1923, to repudiate the citizenship of Sakharam G. Pandit. A member of the California bar, who had practiced law in both state and federal courts and who had been appointed a notary public, Pandit countered the federal effort with the claim of res judicata—that the original federal court in 1914 after hearing the government's protest to his naturalization had granted citizenship and no subsequent challenge had been made. Thus, said Pandit, he was entitled to the 1914 opinion which had been made by a court of competent jurisdiction. The district court and the circuit court of appeals in the 1920's agreed with Pandit while the Supreme Court refused to hear the case.[17]

This case stopped other retroactive reversals of citizenship, but not without some struggles. In Michigan, Mohamand Ali, a World War I veteran, won decisions in both the district court (1925) and the appeals court (1927). Shankar Laxman Gokhale of Schenectady, New York, an engineer employed by General Electric since 1912, had his citizenship cancelled by both district and circuit courts. Gokhale appealed to the United States Supreme Court who granted a writ of certiorari. The writ concurred that he had been entitled to citizenship and the other courts did not have the power to revoke it.[18]

Equally disastrous to East Indians in California was that state's anti-alien land law which restricted land ownership to "aliens eligible to citizenship."[19] After the Thind decision, the *Sacramento Bee* editorialized:

The decision of the United States Supreme Court, that Hindus are not eligible to American citizenship, is most welcome in California.

The decree in a test case brings Hindu holders of land in this State, and likewise all descendants of Hindus, within the mandatory provisions of the California anti-alien land law.

There must be no more leasing or sale of land to such immigrants from India.[20]

California's Board of Control calculated in 1920 that "Hindus" owned eleven city lots and 2,099 acres of farm land. In addition, they leased or had under crop contract another 86,340 acres. Altogether, they controlled about 11 percent of the total acreage occupied by Chinese, Japanese, and "Hindus." The board raised the question at that time as to the eligibility of "Hindus" to citizenship and their right to own land.[21]

In September, 1923, the British chargé d'affaires, H. G. Chilton, wrote to the State Department expressing concern about the property rights of the "British Indians" in the United States, particularly in California. The British embassy hoped that those East Indians who had to dispose of their property would be granted an interval of time in order to avoid total loss arising from the California land law escheat proceedings, and to warn other East Indians about the problem caused by the Thind case.

While the British embassy carefully noted that it had no "desire to impugn the right of the United States Goverment to determine what persons are eligible for United States citizenship," it was concerned about the impact of possible escheat proceedings upon East Indians. Three months later, the embassy, after asking for clarification on the cancellation of Tulsa R. Mandal's citizenship, noted that property confiscation had begun. Secretary of State Charles Evans Hughes, in his reply of April 2,

1924, indicated there was no purpose in a delay to protect the rights of East Indians because they had no rights in the first place. The only response that the British government made to Hughes in June, 1924, was that it hoped the Indians could sell at a fair market price since "the fact that these various Estates will be thrown upon the market more or less simultaneously will tend to reduce prices. . . ." The embassy reported that it had collated a list of ninety-five Indians who owned about 1,868 acres worth an estimated $1,328,000. Missing from the list, as the embassy itself noted, were any Imperial Valley landholders.[22]

On August 16, 1924, Hughes sent a copy of the British embassy's June 2 letter to California Governor Friend Richardson to ascertain the governor's opinion on the reasonableness of the British request for additional time during which the property could be sold. Richardson asked California's Attorney General, U. S. Webb, to draft the state's reply. Webb's statement, consistent with his long anti-Asian stand, held that there could be no postponing of the effective date, for it had been the intent of the law that all ineligible aliens dispose of illegal lands as quickly as possible. He added that several district attorneys had started escheat proceedings against East Indians and that all East Indians who owned land would be involved. The attorney general could see no reason to draw any distinction between those who had acquired land illegally prior to the passage of the 1913 land act and those who had done so afterward. He concluded that, even though there were major differences of opinion between California and the British embassy on the issue, the interests of California and the East Indians could be resolved.[23] California officials, it was clear, intended to remove the East Indians from their lands.

The Department of State, between 1924 and 1928, received numerous requests about the rights of "Hindus" to own land. These inquiries asked for a copy of the treaty and for an interpretation as to any right East Indians as British subjects had to hold land. In each instance the State Department dodged the issue by not answering the question but merely providing conventions and legal citations for lawyers to check. During these years, the department indicated that it was reluctant to make any statement since there was no judicial decision in the matter of land tenure. Thus for five years following the Thind citizenship issue, the question of land ownership remained unresolved. Only in California were there some foreclosures.[24] According to a 1946 article by a Sikh writer, the denial of citizenship made every East Indian suffer. Those who had been most severely imposed upon were those California agriculturalists who, while acknowledged as great farmers, could not own land or lease in their own name. According to D. P. Panda and Mme. Kamadelvi, California white landowners leased or rented land to the Hindustani and then in some instances "betrayed the trust by making off with the crop on the land."[25]

During the 1920's in India, some attempts to protest the Thind case and Pacific Coast discrimination were made, but these were constrained by British imperial rule. Proposed local Indian legislation sought to deny citizenship and restrict missionary activities and business ventures to all Americans. While these were vetoed by the central government, the 1926 legislature passed the Indian Naturalization Act which prohibited citizenship to nationals of any country which denied the same right to Indians.[26]

The most publicized incident regarding East Indian dissatisfaction over American attitudes occurred in 1929 when Rabindranath Tagore, India's Nobel Prize in Literature recipient, made a trip to North America. Tagore had accepted an invitation to lecture at a Canadian national conference on education at Victoria, British Columbia. While there, he received invitations to visit several American universities. He lost his passport in Vancouver and applied for another from the American consul in that city who asked the standard questions which Tagore felt to be an affront. He received a new passport, but the treatment and the racial attitudes he encountered in Los Angeles led him to cancel his tour and return to India. In 1916, Tagore had expressed the view that "America is the only nation engaged in solving the problems of race intimacy. Its mission is to raise civilization by permitting all races entry and widening the ideal of humanity." His 1929 experience led him to say in anger: "Jesus could not get into America because, first of all, He would not have the necessary money, and secondly, He would be an Asiatic."[27]

During the 1930's, the issues of naturalization rights and enforcement of the alien land laws were allowed to float without any real effort at resolution. The major problem for the East Indians residing in the United States, legally or illegally, was that since they were not citizens, they were ineligible for any federal relief programs during the depression.[28] After considerable effort, Mubarak Ali Khan, leader of the India Welfare League, and two of his associates convinced Representative Samuel Dickstein of New York to introduce a bill granting citizenship to all East Indians who had been residing in the United States prior to 1924.[29]

One of the motivations for this bill was to counter the Immigration Service's recent efforts to deport illegal entrants. Some three hundred had been deported between 1935 and 1940. Two East Indian writers, in calling for "Justice for Hindus," protested that even if there were some technical flaw about their entry, it was unjust, after a period of fifteen years, to deport them. Most of these people had built businesses and established homes and families. The writers argued that these men were not engaged in undesirable activity but had only violated some immigration regulations.[30]

While the East Indian leaders and their expert witnesses attested to the Indians' Aryan origin at the 1939 Congressional hearing, exclusionists leveled strong opposition. The American Federation of Labor mounted the heaviest attack through its spokesman, Paul Scharrenberg of the California federation. In 1939 he used the standard argument about allowing one iota of change: "First, it will be the people who are here in our country now, the Chinese, Japanese, and Hindus, who want to be naturalized. Then they will find some other means of breaking some other little hole in the immigration law here and there or elsewhere, and on behalf of the American Federation of Labor I plead with you very earnestly and sincerely not to permit the smallest loophole in our present immigration restriction law so far as orientals are concerned."[31]

Another financial supporter of the California Joint Immigration Committee, the Native Sons of the Golden West, let California's Congressional delegation know its position through its monthly publication, the *Grizzly Bear*, when it declared that

HR 7110 "must be defeated. Its adoption will be followed by repeal of the Exclusion law and a demand that naturalization be extended to others."[32]

East Indians in 1940 determined to keep pressing for the right of citizenship. In San Francisco, Khairata Ram Samras filed a petition in federal court challenging the Thind decision. In a letter to the editor of *Nation*, Samras noted that "discrimination against Hindus in respect to naturalization is not only capricious and untenable but, in violation of constitutional provisions." He anticipated rejection by the lower court and was prepared to appeal to the Supreme Court in behalf of an estimated four thousand East Indians, one-fourth of whom were married to American citizens. Samras's own citizenship problem was quickly resolved when he was drafted into the United States Army which led to his securing citizenship.[33]

World War II and the Atlantic Charter put new pressures upon the United States to examine more closely its relations with India. The major problem, of course, was that India remained part of the British Empire under the direction of Winston Churchill and Roosevelt did not wish to antagonize the Prime Minister.

The East Indians gained citizenship and political rights in 1946 but continued to experience racial prejudice and discrimination in some parts of the United States. Since 1965 the number who have become citizens has markedly increased. Between 1966 and 1972, some 2,972 East Indians received United States citizenship. Many more planned to become naturalized.[34] Moreover, they shared a desire on the one hand to exercise their political rights, while on the other maintaining their own cultural identity.

CHAPTER XX

Economic Struggles by East Indians

THE first East Indians in British Columbia found ready
employment as unskilled laborers in saw and shingle mills,
the fishing industry, the railroads, and various provincial public
utilities. Some became truck gardeners while others cleared
stumps from recently cut-over areas which gave the province
more usable land for farming, industry, and housing.[1] While
East Indians remained few in number, they were well received.
In 1911, a writer in the *Victoria Daily Times* indicated that
"they are industriously employed in the many forms of manual
labor for which they appear to have both special adaptation
and desire."[2] East Indians remained unskilled because they
were not given the chance to secure more training or more
advanced jobs.

At first, wage levels, when compared to economic conditions
in the Punjab, seemed to be more than satisfactory. But the
cost of living in British Columbia was so much greater that
their earnings barely enabled them to survive. Finding themselves in financial trouble, and needing jobs, they accepted
employment at lower wages than did others. This willingness
in time proved a threat not only to British Columbia but to
their own standard of living.[3]

By 1913, almost half of the East Indians in British Columbia
worked in agriculture; others were employed by factories, lumber
mills, and railroads.[4] Many Sikhs, who comprised the bulk of
the first migration wave, continued to prosper.

When the British Columbia Legislative Assembly examined
its Asian immigrant problem in 1927, the estimate was that
about 1,100 "Hindus" were concentrated in Vancouver and its
suburbs of North Vancouver and Port Moody. More Hindustani,
particularly Sikhs, lived in Vancouver than in any other Canadian

or United States city at that time. The provincial capital, Victoria, also had a sizeable settlement. The legislative report showed that, in 1924, 609 "Hindus" worked in sawmills and 150 worked in other industries.[5] Their number remained at a low level until after World War II when revised Canadian immigration laws allowed the immigration of highly skilled workers and professionals who found a greater number of economic opportunities open to them.[6]

Those East Indians who came to the Pacific Coast states from about 1905 to 1914 also found employment as unskilled laborers. In the Midwest and East, there were some merchants and factory workers as well as scholars, journalists, and writers.[7]

The Pacific Northwest lumber industry was one of the first to hire East Indians. By 1906, they worked primarily as "yard men" in Puget Sound mills from Bellingham to Tacoma. They were paid higher wages than were their countrymen in British Columbia who soon moved southward in quest of greater earnings. In Oregon, East Indians also found jobs in lumber towns such as Astoria, Bridal Veil, and Linton. Though they were paid higher wages than the Japanese (but less than white Americans), opinions varied about their worth. Employment in the mills was of short duration. By 1925, only ninety-four East Indian sawmill workers were employed in the state of Washington.[8]

Rajani K. Das, in his 1923 study, felt the Hindustani had in fact proven to be good lumber workers. At that time, Northwest mills and forest camps were the third largest Pacific Coast employers of East Indians, one indication of company satisfaction. Others in the Northwest worked on Northern Pacific and Southern Pacific railroad construction and maintenance crews.[9] But white worker hostility, which the East Indians had faced in Bellingham, Everett, and elsewhere, in addition to the Northwest's rainy cold climate, led many men to move farther south into California. The *Red Bluff News* reported in 1907 that "every train that comes from the North and passes this city has from one to twenty and often more of this new pest."[10]

They entered California from the North by riding the Southern Pacific Railroad or from the East by sailing into the port of San Francisco to become part of the migratory agricultural work

force. Other "Hindus," or "Ragheads," as Californians called
the Sikhs, worked briefly in industrial enterprises. In Portland,
Oregon, around 1910, some twenty worked in a rope factory,
"one of the few instances," according to the immigration commission, "where they found inside employment." In California,
some found employment at the New Idria quicksilver mines in
southeastern San Benito County, while others worked in pot-
teries and quarries.[11]

East Indians first arrived in the Sacramento Valley in 1906.
The following summer some two hundred were recruited to
help construct the Northern Electric Company railroad in the
Marysville-Yuba City area. The Western Pacific Railroad at the
same time was extending its line from Marysville up the Feather
River canyon. There is evidence that the increased immigration
in 1910 was linked to the needs of these California railroads.
The Asiatic Exclusion League erroneously claimed that the
railroad "had 300 of them at work [in 1907] at track work, but
has since discharged them owing to their inability to perform
arduous labor."[12] The company actually increased the number
to 1,700, some of whom helped drill the three-mile Spring
Garden Tunnel near the head of the canyon, giving the railroad
access to the high country.[13]

Railroad construction gave only short-range employment while
California agriculture has provided many jobs for many years.
After completing the electric railroad, several East Indians drifted
into farm work, first in the Newcastle fruit orchards southeast
of Marysville. During the remainder of 1908 and 1909, others
found jobs as unskilled farm laborers on Chico sugar beet farms,
San Joaquin Delta ranches around Stockton, the Vaca Valley
fruit orchards west of Sacramento, and Fresno's vineyards. A
few moved into Tulare County and beyond to Southern California. Those working in sugar beets were scrutinized by the
immigration commission which observed:

[The East Indian] is, of course, generally complained of on account
of his uncleanliness, but this complaint is irrelevant in a consideration of his efficiency as a beet worker. So far as present experience
goes, the East Indian is a slow but honest, steady, and exceedingly
tractable worker. He is averse to enter into contracts, because he

does not understand the contract system, but it is said that his aversion has been overcome after his confidence has been gained by his employers.[14]

East Indians found ready employment as California's farmers sought to break the monopoly held by Japanese farm laborers. In 1908, the wages of East Indians ranged from twenty-five to fifty cents a day less than that earned by Chinese or Japanese workers. One Stockton area rancher paid white labor $30 a month and board (calculated by the United States Immigration Commission as equivalent to $1.65 a day), $1.70 a day to Japanese, while East Indians received $1.10.

The reaction of white farm owners to East Indians was mixed and judgments regarding them as laborers were too often blurred by racial prejudice. Although the commission's facts suggested otherwise, H. A. Millis commented unfavorably:

Though they have commended themselves to some ranchers, they have generally been regarded as distinctly inferior to laborers of other races and not cheap labor at the wages which they have been paid. In few cases have they displaced any other race; usually they have done the work not desired by other races, or have been employed when other laborers were not available at the customary or even a higher wage.[15]

East Indians seemed to have gained acceptance as workers and were considered not to pose an economic threat to any other group. In 1914, Dr. Sudhindra Bose testified before the House Committee on Immigration relative to "Hindu labor" that these West Coast laborers did not undercut white workers. He claimed:

Now, the Hindu laborers demand the wages of unskilled labor. They do not demand the high wages demanded by the skilled laborer, just for the simple reason that they have not efficient and skilled labor. They are, nevertheless, demanding and striving to get as high wages as any other laborers, and they are never underbidding or underselling white labor by demanding lower wages. The average wage of unskilled labor runs from $1.25 to $1.75 a day.... From this it will be evident that the Hindu laborer is no pauper and that they do not undersell white labor.[16]

But their ability as laborers was never really the issue with white exclusionists.

The East Indians organized themselves into work gangs ranging from three to fifty members, but were much less structured than the crews of other Asian immigrants. These groups existed because most Sikhs did not understand English and could not find jobs for themselves. The gang boss, who spoke English, served as the interpreter and gave work orders. He did not receive a commission from his crew's wages but was paid a higher hourly wage for serving as interpreter. The larger work gangs frequently used their leader as a job scout. The gang joined him after he found work. Most scouts, according to the immigration commission, did quite well: "Their success in finding employment has been due in most districts to a scarcity of other laborers. They are very persistent in looking for work, and many employers ascribe their employment to their frequent application for work. In some places where they seemed to be desperate in their needs they have attempted to force employers to hire them and have entered the fields to begin work so that they had to be driven off."[17]

The Bridge Land and Navigation Company in the San Joaquin Delta employed "Hindus" to clean its ditches. According to an official, the Japanese would not accept such jobs and the Chinese had become too old. He added: "But the Hindus are very efficient at this work. They are paid $3.50 a day [in 1930]; the boss of the gang gets $4.00 but he works under the worst conditions in water up to his waist...."[18]

By the early 1920's, most East Indians worked in California. Three permanent labor groups had evolved in that state's major agricultural valleys: Sacramento, San Joaquin, and Imperial. Although the groups were small in number, they provided some stability and exerted considerable peer influence upon the much larger group of itinerant workers who followed the crops and faced annual periods of seasonal unemployment.[19]

Many East Indians moved from the ranks of labor to that of farm operator. Between 1910 and 1920, these men leased or purchased farm land in one of the three valleys. Edward A. Brown, Chief Sanitary Engineer for the California State Commission of Immigration and Housing, confirmed in 1919 that "Hindus" had located in major agricultural districts. While many were employed as "squat labor," he asserted that their "number is growing less, for the change from the employed to employer or lessee is rapidly placing the Hindu in the position of 'little land lord.' The Hindu will not farm poor land. He wants the best and will pay for it. Consequently the American owner who can get a big rental for his land desires the Hindu. He will pay."[20]

East Indians usually started by leasing acreage on a cash or share basis for one to three years. The size of their holdings varied with the type of crops. Only 2 percent of California's farmlands was owned or leased by Asians at the end of 1919— a total acreage of 623,752; the East Indians farmed 88,450 acres of this.[21]

The first East Indian farmers started in the fruit orchards of Folsom, Loomis, and Newcastle in the foothills of the Sierra Nevadas. Others located themselves by 1913 in the Sacramento Valley communities of Marysville, Colusa, Willows, Chico, Gridley, and the rice center of Biggs, where they became successful businessmen and rice producers. They and the Japanese developed the arid hardpan ground into profitable rice fields. By 1919 they leased 35,175 acres and owned 1,218 acres of rice land.[22] Several East Indians, as had been the case with the Koreans, were known locally as "Hindu rice kings." After 1920, with the enforcement of the anti-alien laws and the severe drop in the price of rice, the East Indians joined the Japanese and Koreans in abandoning their Colusa and Glenn County rice lands.[23]

East Indians first appeared in the San Joaquin Delta in 1907 where they found employment on Woodward Island near Stockton in asparagus and sugar beets. Some leased land near Holt where they planted potatoes, onions, celery, and beans, but when these efforts failed, the men moved south to the Imperial Valley or north to the rice fields. Most East Indians in the delta remained farm laborers who settled mostly in Stockton and in other farm communities such as Holt, Lodi, and Sando. By 1919 East Indians owned or leased only about 4,500 acres in the delta.[24]

Many workers and some owners congregated in the central part of the San Joaquin Valley, with the largest number in and around Fresno. Smaller groups lived at Clovis, Exeter, Hanford, Lone Star, Madera, and Porterville, with a few in Bakersfield to the south. Rajani K. Das's study indicated that by the 1920's the Fresno area had the highest concentration of Hindustani in the Pacific Coast states.[25]

The turbaned immigrants proved to be a major factor in developing the Imperial Valley agricultural economy. Arriving first in 1910 to assist in the first large cotton crop harvest, East Indians made a favorable impression because of their willingness to work hard and for long hours. For several years their numbers increased. Some soon leased land to grow cotton and other crops such as alfalfa, barley, corn, and melons. By 1920 they had leased 32,380 acres in the valley. About two hundred East Indians lived near the major centers of Brawley, Calexico, El Centro, and Holtville. That year, however, many East Indians suffered losses when the cotton crop failed and prices declined drastically. Many had to declare themselves bankrupt.[26] But, by the time of World War II, others still farmed these specialty crops.[27]

In 1935, according to Theodore Fieldbrave, an East Indian American citizen, about 4,500 East Indians resided in the United States (the 1930 census count was 3,130). There were three thousand Pacific Coast farmers, one thousand skilled workers, merchants, and traders in the Eastern United States, about five hundred students scattered throughout the nation and twenty-five to thirty "Hindu Swamis and Yogis." Those immigrants who first entered Atlantic Coast seaports, said Fieldbrave, were mostly Bengalese Muslim sailors who found factory jobs in the large industrial centers of New York, Pittsburgh, Detroit, Milwaukee, Chicago, St. Louis, and New Orleans.[28]

About two hundred worked in the Detroit auto industry. In New York City, 290 East Indians worked in various occupations while another 150 worked across the Hudson River in the New Jersey counties of Essex and Passaic. Some of these were employed in the Paterson silk mills and dye factories.[29]

A few of the first East Indian immigrants became successful merchants in the larger American cities. Sidar Jagjit Singh, president of the India League of America in the 1940's, was one such merchant who sold Indian wares to New Yorkers.

Singh was typical of many who opened small shops to sell the varied goods and crafts produced in India. Singh, for his part, operated a store that specialized in Indian silks and cottons.[30] In several major cities, East Indian immigrants have been successful restaurant owners, bringing to Western palates taste pleasures which have evolved over centuries. The recipes of India are a combination of the foods of many national and ethnic groups who have crowded into the subcontinent.

In Hawaii, two brothers, Jhamandas and Gobindram Watumull, combined their talents and skills over several decades to develop a major merchandising firm. The Watumulls were born in Hyderabad, Sind Province. Jhamandas Watumull left India for the Philippines when he was sixteen to live with an elder brother and to work in the textile mills. By 1909 he and a partner opened a small import store in Manila. In 1913, the firm, following American troops to Hawaii, opened the first East India Store on Fort Street. His brother, Gobindram, came to the territory in 1917 from India to manage operations while Jhamandas returned to Manila. Gobindram, educated as an irrigation engineer, had worked for a time on Indus River irrigation projects. His marriage to Ellen Jensen of Oregon cost her her citizenship for many years because of the Thind case. The East India Store in downtown Honolulu prospered and the enterprise expanded until in 1957 it included ten stores, a Waikiki apartment house, and mercantile developments in Waikiki and Kailua.[31]

Jhamandas Watumull moved to Honolulu in 1956 to join his sons and brother. After his brother's death, Jhamandas continued to expand the Hawaiian operations. In 1973, after fifty-nine years of continued success, twenty-nine Watumull stores sold a wide range of goods.[32]

In 1942, Gobindram Watumull founded the Watumull Foundation to provide scholarships to enable Indian students to receive their education in the United States and then work in India. The foundation also proposed to support an academic chair in Indian culture at the University of Hawaii and to provide travel funds for scholars and professionals in India to come to the United States. The foundation also established a chair in American History in India and travel funds for American scholars and professionals to visit India.[33] In 1976, the foundation still sustained academic interests related to India.

One East Indian who gained a national reputation in science and journalism was Gobind Behari Lal. Born in Delhi, he graduated from the University of Punjab and received a graduate degree from the University of California. He became science editor for the Hearst publications; his home newspaper was the *New York American.* Lal wrote many scientific articles and books. In 1937, a series of news stories relative to the tercentenary celebration of Harvard University won for him and four others the Pulitzer Prize for Reporting.[34]

Indian writers, reviewing the accomplishments of East Indians in the United States, described the successful immigrants as merchants, traders, philosophers, journalists, writers, chemists, and scientists who lived in large Eastern and Midwestern cities.[35] In 1940, only 4 percent of all East Indians were in this category. About 30 percent worked in industry and various trades. The rest still were connected with agriculture, largely as laborers.[36]

During World War II, California's East Indians still lived in the same areas as before the war. Stockton remained the headquarters of all East Indians, regardless of creed or caste. In the Sacramento Valley, they remained in the fruit and rice districts. About two thousand laborers who worked in and around Sacramento made that city their home.[37] In the Imperial Valley, many occupied key positions in agriculture—as laborers, contractors, managers, or owners.[38]

About 210 East Indians developed Arizona's desert lands between Tucson and Phoenix, particularly in the Salt River Valley. Most of these farmers leased or owned 2,500 to 3,000 acres, registered in their children's or wives' names to circumvent legally Arizona's alien land law. Three East Indians together controlled five thousand acres in the Salt River Valley where they grew wheat, barley, and various vegetables. At Casa Grande, Divan Singh owned, in his wife's name, about 1,600 acres where he employed from two to three hundred people. Many others were truck farmers utilizing small parcels of land about 160 acres in size. Most grew lettuce. When Senator William Langer visited the Arizona settlements in 1944, he was impressed with the productivity of the East Indian farmers. He reported that D. J. Khan, after securing three thousand acres of worthless land at twenty-five cents an acre, had utilized the Salt River Valley's irrigation system to make the land produce specialty crops.[39]

S. Chandrasekhar, writing in 1944, summed up the motivation and the results of the first wave of immigration: "The basic reason for their migration to this country, economic betterment, seems to have been satisfied. They did not become millionaires but there was none of the chronic rural indebtedness and poverty of the average peasant in India."[40]

During the 1920's and 1930's, East Indian merchants and professionals preferred to be inconspicuous because of the efforts of the United States to deport activists and illegal entrants. Senator Langer, who championed their fight for citizenship, admitted being surprised at the intellectual attainment of many East Indians. In New York City, he discovered a large colony of doctors, dentists, scientists, and scholars. During testimony before the Senate Committee on Immigration in 1944, witnesses identified some fourteen East Indian scholars and scientists in key positions in American industry and in universities.[41]

East Indians, because of their small number in the United States and their recent acquisition of citizenship, have not been active in American politics. One Sikh immigrant who achieved political success was Dalip Singh Saund. Born in Amritsar, India, in 1899, he received his B.A. at the University of Punjab. He came to the United States in 1920 to earn his master's and doctor's degrees in mathematics at the University of California. He then moved to the Imperial Valley where, from 1930 through 1953, he was a lettuce farmer near Westmoreland, California. He also manufactured and sold a chemical fertilizer.

Saund became a United States citizen in 1949 and one year later was elected judge of the Westmoreland Judicial District. At that time, legal training was not a prerequisite to qualify as a judge in small local courts. Although elected, he was denied his judgeship, for he was successfully challenged on the point that he had not yet been a citizen for one year, a qualification for the office. He was, however, reelected the following year

when he was eligible. He remained in that elective office until
1957 when he assumed his seat in the United States House
of Representatives. In 1954, he was elected chairman of the
Imperial Valley Democratic Central Committee.

In 1956, as Saund sought election to Congress as the representative from Imperial and Riverside Counties in California,
a petition was filed in the California courts to bar him from
the November ballot on the grounds that he had not been a
United States citizen for seven years. The California Fourth
District Court of Appeals ruled that by January 3, 1957, when
Saund would take office, if he were successful in his bid, he
would have been a citizen the requisite amount of time.[42]

Saund was victorious and became a member of the Eighty-
Fifth Congress. During his first term, he received a signal honor
for a freshman Congressman by being appointed to the House
Committee on Foreign Relations. He was reelected in 1960.
During his campaign for a third term, in 1962, a massive stroke
incapacitated him. He nevertheless continued his campaign from
his hospital bed, but he lost. He remained an invalid, dying in
1973 at the age of seventy-three.[43]

During the 1950's and 1960's, fewer East Indian unskilled
laborers migrated but more professionals and their families
left India and Pakistan for the United States. While the brain
drain had started prior to 1965, the changed immigration law
accelerated the movement. In 1967, over 50 percent of all
Indian and over 25 percent of all Pakistani emigrants came
from the professional classes. In 1969, the percentage for Pakistan remained about the same, while the percentage for India
declined to just under 50 percent.[44]

While the economic levels and prior educational training of
East Indian immigrants shifted significantly upward following
World War II, the motives of the emigrants remained the
same—the desire to improve one's status and to escape the
grinding poverty as well as some of the problems in India
and Pakistan. Families came to the United States to seek a
better environment and greater opportunities for their children.
Their reasons proved to be no different from those of other
Asian and European immigrants.

CHAPTER XXI

East Indian Homes in the United States

THOSE East Indians who comprised the first wave of immigration were confronted with the pressures of having to adjust to living in the United States and Canada while maintaining personal ties with their homeland. A large number who could not cope with social prejudice and economic discrimination returned home. Others were deported for illegal entry or for leading their countrymen into various movements for Indian independence. Those who did remain in the United States, voluntarily or not, adapted as best they could to their new economic environment while retaining most of their own social customs. Those living in California experienced more adjustment difficulties than did those living in isolated family units in the East.

While the first immigrants encountered strong hatred and much misunderstanding, a large part of the difficulties in adaptation was attributed to the East Indians themselves. Most arrived as illiterates and remained in that condition, learning little of the English language. Their inability to communicate and their desire to continue their own customs tied them to small isolated groups and separated them from the dominant culture.[1]

Most observers, even those with biased opinions, found the Sikh immigrants, who comprised most of the first influx, to be rather distinguished in appearance. According to one account, a typical Sikh "was tall, broad-shouldered, black bearded. His *pagri* [turban] was an immaculate, pale blue. He might have been an Oriental prince from the looks of him. But he was only a Sikh from the Punjab wandering along a Sacramento street gazing curiously at the shop windows."[2]

Dominion Immigration Inspector Alexander S. Munro, who met the Sikhs as they disembarked in Vancouver in the early

1900's, was favorably impressed. He too described them as "tall—broad shouldered and deep winded; muscular and robust—men who can patiently put up with a hard struggling life." He opined that East Indians had quick perceptions and high levels of intelligence equal to that of any recent British Columbia immigrant.[3]

However, for at least two decades, East Indians on the Pacific Coast suffered because of misunderstanding and intolerance. An example of such prejudicial thinking, reflecting a pro-Christian bias, is seen in a comparison of the motives of East Indian and Korean immigrants in the *Missionary Review of the World*:

In the little college town of Claremont, California, there are about forty Hindus and as many Koreans, but the contrast between them, even as they walk the streets, is startling. They have come to America for widely different purposes. The Hindus come merely for the sake of two dollars a day ranch wages; the Koreans come for education, secular and religious. The Hindus, intensely suspicious of Americans, fear proselytizing, cling to their distinctive clothes and to all the insignia of their strange cult—the turban of white or pink or yellow or black, the long black hair done up with comb and iron disc. They want to learn only enough English to make a living and do business. They harbor terrible grudges and are frequently in the local courts for stoning each other. They are shrouded in superstition, dead to American thought, dead to everything save the glitter and clink of two-dollars-a-day.[4]

The Sikhs, bewildered by these prejudices, withdrew to become self-sufficient in their own ways. At a time when most American men had shaved off beards and mustaches, the long hair and beards of the tall Sikhs attracted both attention and unfavorable comment. The Sikhs' turbans also distinguished them and led other Californians to use the pejorative term, "Raghead."

Religious taboos about certain foods also set East Indians apart. Hindus and Sikhs ate no beef and they could not eat food prepared by people of different religions while Muslims could not eat pork. All had reservations about eating with people who did not share their particular religious views.[5] A California camp of East Indians, during 1910, might encompass members of several religions and/or castes, forced to live together because of housing difficulties. But each subgroup formed separate eating arrangements with the food prepared by one of its members: "As a rule they will not purchase meat which has been prepared by other hands, and are thus limited ... to poultry and lambs butchered by themselves. In fact, they eat little meat. They subsist chiefly upon unleavened bread cooked as pancakes, upon vegetables, such fruit as they happen to be harvesting, and milk when they can get it."[6]

At the height of American agitation against East Indians, the generic term *Hindu* led many writers to emphasize the caste system as a major problem preventing assimilation. In actual practice, the caste system had little importance in the United States or in other overseas East Indian settlements. In the United States, where most early immigrants were farm laborers, the traditional job classifications of India did not pertain. The shortage of East Indian women also broke down the rigid lines. Another significant factor was that the majority of the immigrants to the Pacific Coast were Sikhs whose religion had repudiated the concept of caste. Those feelings about caste which existed among the first immigrants related mostly to social position and prestige, but the inherited caste rights of privilege and the rigid separation into classes were not observed.[7]

Their self-imposed isolation, readily supported by the white majority, resulted in substandard housing for the East Indian. Farm laborers, for example, received "free lodging in 'shacks,' barns, or other outbuildings, or, more frequently, live in the open. They usually have no furniture and sleep in blankets. They generally cook upon a grate placed over a hole in the ground and frequently eat standing, without plate, knife or fork."[8] In California's agricultural cities of Sacramento and Stockton, East Indians lived crowded together in cheap rooming houses as did other newly arrived immigrants.[9]

The lopsided East Indian male-female ratio was another major adjustment problem. At first this was of little concern since most men intended to return home. While white exclusionists claimed that women had not migrated because of the "peculiar reluctance of the Hindoos to expose their women to the shameless gaze of the western unbeliever," the East Indians found it "a singular fact ... that in America almost the

entire Hindu population is male, as the United States Government has never allowed, except in a few cases, the families of
the laboring men to enter." A similar policy had been followed
by the Canadian government until the early 1930's.[10]

As the possibility of returning to India became less possible
for East Indians, they sought wives from non-Indian groups.
Prior to World War II, most wed Mexican-Americans. The
largest number of such marriages occurred in the Imperial
Valley and even there it involved only about sixty couples.
Some Muslims in the eastern United States married blacks while
many East Indians who attended American universities married
women of European ancestry.[11] According to the *San Francisco
Chronicle*, by 1926 some 150 women had married "high caste
Hindus." Most lost their citizenship because of the Thind
decision.[12] East Indians, unlike other Asian immigrants, were
able to marry freely in California for the miscegenation laws,
aimed at blacks, Malays, and Mongolians, did not apply to
"Hindus or Mexicans."[13]

As already indicated, different religious beliefs helped set
East Indians apart from the dominant American society. The
early immigrants were adherents of three basic religions—Hinduism, Sikhism, and Mohammedanism. The religion that had the
most followers, prior to World War II, was Sikhism. Somewhere
between 50 and 60 percent of the East Indians residing in the
United States in 1960 were Sikhs. There was also a sizeable
number of Muslims.[14]

Prior to 1946, Hinduism was confined largely to Indian students and American followers. In 1914, the Hindu Society of
America existed primarily to attend to the welfare of students
in this country. An international organization, it had in 1914 two
hundred members at all major American universities.[15]

Hinduism first gained attention within the United States in
1893 when Swami Vivekananda attended the Parliament of
Religions in Chicago where he outlined that aspect of Hindu
philosophy known as Vedantism. From this beginning developed
the Ramakrishna Order which sent twenty-one swamis to the
United States. By 1933 the order still had ten swamis laboring
in the states. But there was no doubt that the greatest swami
was Vivekananda. He was remembered as "The silver-tongued

swami [who] served ... Hindustan in the capacity of a John
the Baptist, ... He seems to have won an instant way into the
hearts of American men and women, and his personality is very
much alive in the hearts of thousands of Americans of the highest
intellect and culture."[16]

The Ramakrishna swamis were missionaries working to extend
Hinduism in America. Many ashrams (religious centers) were
built throughout the United States where people could listen
to the swamis but American Protestant leaders at first dismissed
this effort. In 1913, George Hinman, Pacific District Secretary
of the American Missionary Association, claimed the Hindu
Temple in San Francisco had "no message for the friendless
people of India. It is an American religious fad."[17] In 1920,
San Francisco still had the only Hindu temple in the United
States although Boston and New York each had a center. A
religious service in 1920, conducted by a swami at the temple
on Christmas morning, drew about sixty people, only two of
whom appeared to be from India.[18]

During the 1930's, the Vedanta Society of America, headquartered in Calcutta, was responsible for the work of Ramakrishna. It had centers of varying size throughout the United
States to which leaders, high-caste Hindus, were sent from Calcutta to labor in the ashrams without remuneration.[19]

Another group of swamis, less spiritually motivated than
those of the Vedanta Society, saw an opportunity for economic
gain in the United States. One East Indian Christian, writing
in the 1930's, claimed: "Most of them have taken up this profession for what they can get out of it. They have discovered
that Americans, especially women, are curious creatures and
will 'fall for' anything or anybody who looks odd or mysterious."[20]
A Sikh immigrant in 1909 had already identified such men:

The Hindoo fortune teller in America is a bird of passage, flitting here,
there and everywhere, evading those States where it is a criminal
offence for him to follow his profession. He travels all the time, from
town to town, county to county, State to State and coast to coast.
He plies his trade wherever he can, and usually makes a success
of it, for there is a mystical charm attached to him in the eyes of
credulous people seeking to peer into the future. It is sufficient

that he comes from the "East." It must follow that he is a "wise man."[21]

Hinduism, in one form or another, has had an impact upon the lives of many Americans. In the early 1970's, for example, Guru Majarai Ji, only thirteen years old and the proclaimed leader of the Divine Light Mission, arrived in Los Angeles. The son of a holy man who had died in 1966, Ji had been designated as the new guru. (Later, when he found life in the United States to be more pleasant than in India, his mother, who had remained in India, announced that he was no longer leader.) But at the height of his influence in the United States, there were ten Divine Light Mission ashrams that followed Ji's instruction. In New York City, the mission occupied the two top floors of an old townhouse in lower Manhattan. A typical gathering consisted of fifty people who watched Ji on videotapes and then engaged in a session of *satsang*—a time of talking about what each person still needed to learn.[22] Other Americans, searching for spiritual expression, adopted the practice of Yoga. In the past decade, many young Americans have joined Hare Krishna in their search for a religious outlet.

Between 1946 and 1965, most of those attending Hindu religious centers were non-Indian, but a change slowly occurred. As Indians from Bombay and Calcutta began arriving after 1946, San Francisco's "Old Temple" soon filled to capacity and a new temple was built on Vallejo Street to accommodate these new Hindu immigrants. Los Angeles had had a temple for several years and new temples were built in Berkeley and Sacramento.[23]

East Indian Muslims in California were concentrated in the Imperial Valley and the Sacramento Valley. Sacramento was the organizational center with the Moslem Association of America headquartered there. Northern California Muslims had two other organizations as well. In the Imperial Valley, the Moslem Association provided funeral and burial services while the Pakistan House provided recreational activities. The Imperial Valley non-Sikhs organized themselves into the Hindustani Welfare and Reform Association.[24]

From 1910 to 1970, the Sikhs remained concentrated in the Imperial, Sacramento, and San Joaquin Valleys. By 1960 the

Sikh center in Stockton had declined, remaining important only because its Sikh Temple filled religious needs and served as a hostel for elderly Sikh men.[25] Stockton had become the major center as early as 1907, and by 1909 the Pacific Coast Khalsa Diwan Society had organized a temple. In 1919, it built a new temple to serve the religious needs of the Sikhs. The society, while developed by the Sikhs, maintained from the very beginning that its doors were open to all Indians, regardless of religion or caste. The society over the years aided students from India and contributed to India's educational programs and political causes.[26]

In 1948, Sikhs formed a temple organization in the Imperial Valley and remodeled the Buddhist Center in El Centro as their religious headquarters.[27] By 1970 Sikh temples were also located in Los Angeles and Yuba City. The Yuba City temple was the spiritual home for a growing East Indian community estimated to range between three and six thousand people. When some 150 Sikhs from the San Francisco Bay Area gathered in 1969 to celebrate the 500th anniversary of the founding of their religion, it was estimated that there were more than ten thousand followers in California.[28]

Sikhism has had an impact upon Americans. In 1974, some 150,000 Americans, after examining several Asian religions such as Buddhism, Hinduism, and Sikhism, selected the latter because it appeared to be more robust and less introspective than the others. Many joined the faith and accepted the name Singh. For some, particularly those in the armed forces, the matter of letting one's hair grow and the wearing of a turban caused dissension between the new believers and those in authority.[29]

One of the stronger Sikh organizations in California, the Indian Society of Yuba and Sutter Counties, was founded in 1945 as Stockton's importance faded. A study of some nine hundred East Indians, who lived along the Feather River north and south of Yuba City, revealed that about 450 East Indians used the name Singh as a last name and over seven hundred used Singh as part of their total name.[30]

As the Sacramento Valley East Indian settlements enlarged, there was a growing demand for renewed cultural identity. In 1958, the Sikhs in Yuba and Sutter Counties split the India

Society to form a second organization—the India American Cultural Society, whose task was to plan social programs oriented around four events. The first of these was Baisakhi Day, in honor of the founding of the Sikh religion. Previously, the celebration occurred only at the Stockton Temple but by 1964 Baisakhi Day had become an important event in Yuba City as well. The second celebration, either in December or January, depending upon the lunar calendar, was Gobind Day, honoring the birthday of Gobind Singh, the last Sikh guru. The other two events were political in nature. The first, Martyrdom Day, May 10, commemorated all who had given their lives for Indian independence. Almost all martyrs were Sikhs. The other, Republic Day, was held each January 26 to commemorate the adoption of India's 1947 constitution.[31]

As a consequence of the restrictive immigration policies in force before 1965, some East Indians feared that their culture was losing its significance.[32] The fact that there were so few East Indians and that they had remained culturally isolated gave credence to this view. In 1951, Yusuf Dadabhay, a sociologist, concluded in his study that when East Indians were excluded from free access to the white community, they had been unable to develop fully. Consequently they had moved into the Mexican-American culture which accepted them. Dadabhay made it clear that he was not attempting "to prove that Hindustanis lose their ethnicity entirely in the Mexican subculture, but the fact of intermarriage is regarded as evidence of mutual acceptance."[33]

Dadabhay showed what had happened to fifty of the early immigrants in Santa Clara County, Stockton, and Sacramento who remained apart from other East Indians and from the larger society around them. For some reason, he ignored the larger settlements in the Imperial Valley and Yuba City. These fifty people had not chosen to live in East Indian neighborhoods but settled amidst Mexican communities around the fringes of towns. As a matter of fact, East Indians were frequently identified as Mexicans—a factor which led, said Dadabhay, to easy relations between the two people. Throughout the state, where farm labor was utilized, they worked side by side.

A major assimilative force between East Indians and Mexicans were marriages which gave to the former both social and community contacts. The Mexican wife, with her relatives, provided an entry for her husband into the larger Mexican community. Of the fifty East Indians interviewed, twenty-six had wives in the United States, twenty-two of whom were Mexicans. Their children were raised predominantly in the Mexican culture. Dadabhay's study notwithstanding, the question of the vitality of an East Indian culture in the 1950's remained unanswered.[34]

As newer immigrants asserted themselves in the 1960's, the sagging cultures and their traditions revived and prospered. The arrival of East Indian wives and families provided a great impetus. Most of the women continued to wear saris, their traditional dress, while only about 10 percent of the men wore traditional garb as they felt more keenly the need to conform in the business community.[35] While most of the newer immigrants were more adaptable and moved somewhat more easily into American life, the older generation remained apart. That group, living in rural areas, had adjusted to economic demands, but their social acculturation remained slight.[36]

CHAPTER XXII

Challenge and Opportunity

EAST Indians, Filipinos, and Koreans have been arriving on American shores for the past seventy years. But, during the first sixty years, as immigration records show, the number of people coming from each land was small. Although their cultures and traditions were different, their purposes for migrating were generally the same. These pioneers accepted the challenge of adapting to a new life in America. Their impact and influences have been felt both in the United States and in their homelands. Starting anew in twentieth century America was not easy for these Asians, for they faced discrimination and hostility as had other immigrants. Interestingly, many of these first Asians, and those who followed later, may well have found such hostility a relative matter when compared to economic and political conditions in their own nations. But most expected better of the United States than they received.

Almost all of the first Asian immigrants, as was the case with other immigrant groups, have remained unknown, struggling to provide for themselves and their families. Perhaps their greatest contribution has been to their children who have gained immeasurably more in economic and political freedoms.

Most significantly, the immigrants have had a major impact upon relatives and friends who remained behind in the Asian homeland. The financial contributions, seemingly meager in American terms, made a great difference in the economic status of their families. Letters from immigrants and travelers, the American press and movies, a belief in American ideals, and internal conditions in their countries motivated other East Indians, Filipinos, and Koreans to follow when they could. These new arrivals, part of the marked increase of the last ten years, will continue the process of adaptation started earlier in this century.

246

In 1976, the United States looked back at what had been accomplished in the past two hundred years. An international seminar, held at the East-West Center in Honolulu, examined the meaning of the American Revolution to Asians and Americans. A consensus developed which suggested the ideas of the revolution were in fact universal ones—freedom, liberty, equality, and justice—for which mankind has striven through all ages. Following the Declaration of Independence, many Americans had the opportunity to translate these ideas into action. The human imperfection, however, said the seminar's participants, was that reality never corresponded with the ideal.

Since the American Revolution, opportunity for economic betterment and the goal of individual freedom have remained two major lodestones. People crossed the ocean, first from Europe, to accept the risk of building new careers and new homes. Then came Asians with their diverse cultures and nations to take up the challenge.

As the history of American immigration demonstrates, people reluctantly left home and did so generally because of political persecution or depressed economic conditions. This movement of millions and millions of people has been a uniquely American phenomenon in the history of man. It was, and obviously still is, perceived as a drastic alternative to enduring at home. In 1976, those from the Philippines, Korea, Bangladesh, India, and Pakistan followed in the footsteps of earlier immigrants as they sought new opportunities in the United States.

They and their countrymen know, as do many Americans, that those American Revolution concepts, such as equality and justice, are not uniformly applicable to all people in the United States. The record of the United States' immigration policy and its intolerance and discrimination against Asians, as documented in this book and elsewhere, does not gibe with what is professed to be the American purpose.

Those Filipinos, Koreans, and East Indians, in the face of such intolerance, have met the challenge of living in the United States and have contributed to a multifaceted society. Their very endurance has forced a reassessment of the nineteenth century Anglo-Saxon view that the United States was a melting pot blending a homogeneous people. Instead, all people have continued to maintain modified, frequently out-of-date, versions of the cultures they brought with them or inherited. These Asian immigrants have helped to demonstrate that America remains a multi-ethnic nation and that their presence has contributed to a better sense of purpose.

TABLE I

FILIPINO IMMIGRANTS AND RESIDENTS

Year	Arrivals[1]	U.S. Census Reports[2]	California[3]	Hawaii[4]	New York[5]	Illinois[6]	Washington[7]
1910	—	2,767	5	2,361	1	3	17
1920	869	26,634	2,674	21,031	496	164	958
1930	5,651	108,260	30,470	63,052	1,982	2,011	3,480
1940	55	98,535	31,408	52,659	2,978	1,930	2,222
1950	595	122,707	40,424	61,071	3,719	N.A.	4,274
1960	2,954	176,310	65,459	69,070	5,403	3,587	7,110
1970	31,203	343,060	138,859	93,915	14,279	12,654	11,462

[1]U.S. Immigration and Naturalization Service, *Annual Report, 1931*, p. 261; ibid., *1943*, table 5; ibid., *1953*, table 13A; ibid., *1970*, p. 5; ibid., *1973*, p. 56. Prior to 1960, Filipino arrivals to Hawaii were not included in the national figures.

[2]U.S. Bureau of Census, *Characteristics of Population, 1970*, I, 262.

[3]U.S. Bureau of Census, *Characteristics of Population, California, 1960*, pt. 6–86; ibid., *1970*, I, pt. 6–58.

[4]U.S. Bureau of Census, *Characteristics of Population, Hawaii, 1970*, I, pt. 13–28.

[5]U.S. Bureau of Census, *Characteristics of Population, New York, 1960*, I, pt. 34–51; ibid., *1970*, I, pt. 34–73.

[6]U.S. Bureau of Census, *Characteristics of Population, Illinois, 1960*, I, pt. 15–58; ibid., *1970*, I, pt. 15–89.

[7]U.S. Bureau of Census, *Characteristics of Population, Washington, 1960*, I, pt. 49–26; ibid., *1970*, I, pt. 49–41.

TABLE II
FILIPINO POPULATION IN U.S. BY GEOGRAPHICAL AREA

Geographical Area	1910[1]	1920[2]	1930[3]	1940[4]	1950[5]	1960[6]	1970[7]
Northeast	1	1,844	3,240	4,587	6,186	10,650	31,424
North Central	14	382	3,804	3,569	4,079	8,600	27,824
South	109	446	1,750	3,851	4,408	10,720	31,979
West	35	3,930	36,407	35,086	46,963*	146,340	251,833
	(22%)**	(60%)	(81%)	(73%)	(77%)	(83%)	(73%)
California	5	2,674	30,470	31,408	40,424	65,459	138,859
	(3%)	(41%)	(67%)	(65%)	(66%)	(31%)	(40%)
Hawaii	2,361	21,031	63,052	52,659	61,071	69,070	93,915
	(94%)	(74%)	(52%)	(52%)	(50%)	(34%)	(24%)

[1] U.S. Bureau of Census, *Population, 1930,* II, 58–59.
[2] Ibid.
[3] Ibid.
[4] Ibid., *1940,* II, 52.
[5] U.S. Bureau of Census, *Nonwhite Population by Race, 1950,* 3B–20.
[6] U.S. Bureau of Census, *Characteristics of Population, 1970,* I, 281.
[7] Ibid., I, 293; U.S. Bureau of Census, *Hawaii, 1970,* I, pt. 13–28.

*From 1910 to 1950, Hawaii's population is not included as part of the West's total. After statehood in 1959, its number of Filipinos is included as part of the West's count.

**From 1910 to 1950, the West's and California's percentages are based upon the total mainland population; Hawaii's percentages are based upon both the mainland and Hawaii. The 1960–1970 percentages reflect the number of Filipinos in all states.

TABLE III
FILIPINO POPULATION IN U.S. BY CITIES

Cities	1910[1]	1920[2]	1930[3]	1940[4]	1950[5]	1960[6]	1970[7]
Chicago	3	154	1,796	1,740	1,249	2,725	9,497
Honolulu	87	2,113	4,776[8]	6,887[9]	17,376[10]	21,807	29,481
Los Angeles	—	253	3,245	4,498	7,117	7,681	19,392
New York	—	159	572	627	4,027°	4,281	11,207
Philadelphia	—	236	549	660	N.A.	1,812	2,675
San Diego	—	48	394	799	N.A.	3,615	9,074
San Francisco	3	948	4,576	3,483	11,803°°	7,456	10,415
Seattle	—	458	1,614	1,392	2,744	3,755	5,830
Stockton	—	—	—	—	6,511	2,364	3,899

[1] U.S. Bureau of Census, *Population, 1930*, II, 80.
[2] Ibid.
[3] Ibid.
[4] U.S. Bureau of Census, *Nonwhite Population by Race, 1940*, p. 6.
[5] U.S. Bureau of Census, *Nonwhite Population by Race, 1950*, 3B–65 and 3B–83.
[6] U.S. Bureau of Census, *Characteristics of Population, 1960, California*, I, pt. 6–136; 141; 143; *Hawaii*, I, pt. 13–31; *Illinois*, I, pt. 15–107; *New York*, I, pt. 34–107; *Pennsylvania*, I, pt. 40–133; *Washington*, I, pt. 49–56.
[7] U.S. Bureau of Census, *Characteristics of Population, 1970*, I, 331–33.
[8] U.S. Bureau of Census, *General Population Characteristics, Territories, 1930*, p. 48.
[9] U.S. Bureau of Census, *General Population Characteristics, Hawaii, 1940*, p. 5.
[10] U.S. Bureau of Census, *General Population Characteristics, Hawaii, 1950*, pt. 52–22.
° Represents New York–Northeastern New Jersey Metropolitan Area.
°° Represents San Francisco–Oakland Metropolitan Area.

TABLE IV
KOREAN IMMIGRANTS AND RESIDENTS

Year	U.S. Census Reports	California	Hawaii	Illinois	Montana	New York	Pennsylvania	Washington
1910[1]	461	304	4,533	—	13	4	—	8
1920	1,677	772	4,950	32	18	30	9	98
1930	1,860	1,097	6,461	76	115	105	9	25
1940[2]	1,711	1,088	6,851	54	90	114	23	12
1950[3]	(1,146)*	(621)	7,030	(25)	N.A.	(121)	(16)	(28)
1960[4]	(14,231)**	(3,690)	(4,079)	(2,224)	(33)	(330)	(319)	(364)
1970[5]	70,598***	16,684	9,625	3,803	132	6,109	2,639	1,693

[1]U.S. Bureau of Census, *Population, 1930*, II, 58–59; *Territories, 1930*, p. 49.

[2]U.S. Bureau of Census, *Population, 1940*, II, 52; ibid., *Nonwhite Population by Race, 1940*, p. 2.

[3]U.S. Bureau of Census, *Nonwhite Population by Race, 1950*, 3B-82; *Hawaii, 1950*, p. vi.

[4]U.S. Bureau of Census, *Characteristics of Population, 1960*, I, 366; *Characteristics of Population, 1960, California*, I, pt. 6–489; *Hawaii*, I, pt. 13–201; *Illinois*, I, pt. 15–474; *Montana*, I, pt. 28–184; *New York*, I, pt. 34–431; *Pennsylvania*, I, pt. 40, 549; *Washington*, I, pt. 49–200; Robert C. Schmitt, *Demographic Statistics of Hawaii, 1778–1965* (Honolulu: Univ. of Hawaii Press, 1968), p. 120.

[5]U.S. Bureau of Census, *Detailed Characteristics of Population, 1970*, I, 594; *Detailed Characteristics of Population, 1970, California*, I, pt. 6-1147; *Hawaii*, I, pt. 13–196; *Illinois*, I, pt. 15–841; *Montana*, I, pt. 28–271; *New York*, I, pt. 34–709; *Pennsylvania*, I, pt. 40–744; *Washington*, I, pt. 49–351.

*Figures in parentheses denote nonwhite foreign-born Koreans in the U.S. in 1950.

**Figures in parentheses denote nonwhite foreign-born Korean stock in the U.S. in 1960.

***Prior to 1960 Koreans in Hawaii were not included as part of the national total.

TABLE V

KOREAN POPULATION IN U.S. BY GEOGRAPHICAL AREA

Geographical Area	1910[1]	1920[2]	1930[3]	1940[4]	1950[5]	1960[6]	1970[7]
Northeast	4	47	135	164	180	1,987	13,985
North Central	26	111	203	186	151	1,561	13,419
South	1	18	49	99	75	2,230	12,024
West	430*	1,045	1,472	2,321	740	8,753	31,170
	(95%)	(93%)	(79%)	(83%)	(64%)	(62%)	(44%)
California	304	772	1,097	1,088	621	3,690	16,684
	(66%)	(69%)	(58%)	(47%)	(54%)	(26%)	(24%)
Hawaii	4,533	4,950	6,461	6,851	7,030	4,079	9,625
	(92%)**	(81%)	(78%)	(71%)	(86%)	(29%)	(14%)

[1] U.S. Bureau of Census, *Population, 1930*, II, 58–59; Schmitt, p. 120.

[2] U.S. Bureau of Census, *Population, 1930*, II, 58–59; *General Population Characteristics, Territories, 1930*, p. 49.

[3] U.S. Bureau of Census, *Population, 1930*, II, 58–59; *General Population Characteristics, Territories, 1930*, p. 49.

[4] U.S. Bureau of Census, *Nonwhite Population by Race, 1940*, p. 2; ibid., *General Population Characteristics, Hawaii, 1950*, 52–vi.

[5] U.S. Bureau of Census, *Nonwhite Population by Race, 1950*, 3B–82; ibid., *General Population Characteristics, Hawaii, 1950*, 52–vi. The 1950 figures represent Koreans who were nonwhite foreign-born.

[6] U.S. Bureau of Census, *Characteristics of Population 1960*, I, 623–26. The 1960 figures represent nonwhite foreign-born Korean stock.

[7] U.S. Bureau of Census, *Detailed Characteristics of Population, 1970*, I, 1071–79.

* Hawaii's Korean population is not included as part of the West's total until 1960.

** Hawaii's percentage of the total population in the United States since 1910 is based upon the residents of both Hawaii and on the mainland.

TABLE VI

KOREAN POPULATION IN U.S. BY CITIES

Cities	1910[1]	1920[2]	1930[3]	1940[4]	1950[5]	1960[6]	1970[7]
Chicago	—	27	64	39	48	297*	1,666*
Honolulu	460	1,319	2,604	—	4,802	3,592	3,375
Los Angeles	14	84	345	482	330	2,034**	5,363
New York	4	18	86	N.A.	116	536	3,394
San Francisco	39	77	143	81	90***	724***	996
Seattle	1	37	15	6	23	172	472

[1] U.S. Bureau of Census, *Population, 1930*, II, 80; *Territories, 1930*, p. 48.

[2] U.S. Bureau of Census, *Population, 1930*, II, 80; *General Population Characteristics, Territories, 1930*, p. 48.

[3] U.S. Bureau of Census, *Population, 1930*, II, 80; *General Population Characteristics, Territories, 1930*, p. 48.

[4] U.S. Bureau of Census, *Population, 1940*, II, 114.

[5] U.S. Bureau of Census, *Nonwhite Population by Race, 1950*, 3B-83; Andrew W. Lind, *Hawaii's People*, 3rd ed. (Honolulu: Univ. of Hawaii, 1967), p. 50.

[6] U.S. Bureau of Census, *Detailed Characteristics of Population, 1960, California*, I, pt. 6-492, 496; *Hawaii*, I, pt. 13-220; *Illinois*, I, pt. 15-476; *New York*, I, pt. 34-434; *Washington*, I, pt. 49-201.

[7] U.S. Bureau of Census, *Detailed Characteristics of Population, 1970, California*, I, pt. 6-1174-77; *Hawaii*, I, pt. 13-201; *Illinois*, I, pt. 15-476; *New York*, I, pt. 34-434; *Washington*, I, pt. 49-357.

*Based on nonwhite foreign-born stock.

**Includes Long Beach-Los Angeles Metropolitan Area.

***Includes San Francisco-Oakland Metropolitan Area.

TABLE VII
EAST INDIAN IMMIGRANTS AND RESIDENTS

Year	Arrivals[1]	U.S. Census Reports	California	Illinois	New York	Michigan	Washington
1900[2]	9	2,050	—	—	—	—	
1910	1,782	2,544	1,948	1	14	—	161
1920	—	2,544	1,723	33	204	38	85
1930	110	3,130	1,873	87	320	181	53
1940[3]	3	2,405	1,476	41	243	113	23
1950[4]	153	2,398*	815	107	515	123	33
1960[5]	391	8,746**	1,586	493	1,382	443	213
1970[6]	10,114	13,149	1,585	1,214	2,738	534	173

[1]U.S. Immigration and Naturalization Service, *Annual Report, 1900,* p. 9; *1910;* ibid., *1931,* 222; ibid., *1957,* p. 37; ibid., *1961,* p. 43; ibid., *1971,* p. 40; *Monthly Labor Review,* LVII (1943), 1204.

[2]U.S. Immigration Commission, *Japanese and Other Immigrant Races,* I, 325; U.S. Bureau of Census, *Population, 1930,* II, 58–59.

[3]U.S. Bureau of Census, *Nonwhite Population by Race, 1940,* p. 2.

[4]U.S. Bureau of Census, *Nonwhite Population by Race, 1950,* 3B–82.

[5]U.S. Bureau of Census, *Detailed Characteristics of Population, 1960,* I, 366; *Detailed Characteristics of Population, 1960, California,* I, pt. 6–489; *Illinois,* I, pt. 15–479; *Michigan,* I, pt. 24–663; *New York,* I, pt. 34–718; *Washington,* I, pt. 49–357.

[6]U.S. Bureau of Census, *Detailed Characteristics of Population, 1970,* I, 598; *Detailed Characteristics of Population, 1970, California,* I, pt. 6–1169; *Illinois,* I, pt. 15–847; *Michigan,* I, pt. 24–663; *New York,* I, pt. 34–718; *Washington,* I, pt. 49–357.

*The census count for 1950 reflects a sample of nonwhite foreign-born. The counts for 1960 and 1970 reflects nonwhite of foreign-born stock.

**For 1960 and 1970 the figures represent the combined foreign-born stock from India and Pakistan.

TABLE VIII

EAST INDIAN POPULATION IN U.S. BY GEOGRAPHICAL AREA

Geographical Area	1910[1]	1920[2]	1930[3]	1940[4]	1950[5]	1960[6]	1970[7]
Northeast	30	306	540	374	751	2,440	5,117
North Central	7	136	368	223	429	2,776	2,231
South	29	92	149	169	245	1,230	3,654
West	2,478	1,961	2,109	1,639	973	2,300	2,152
	(97%)	(75%)	(67%)	(66%)	(36%)	(27%)	(21%)
California	1,948	1,723	1,873	1,476	815	1,586	1,585
	(77%)	(69%)	(59%)	(60%)	(34%)	(17%)	(16%)

[1]U.S. Bureau of Census, *Population, 1930*, II, 58–59.
[2]Ibid.
[3]Ibid.
[4]U.S. Bureau of Census, *Nonwhite Population by Race, 1940*, p. 2.
[5]U.S. Bureau of Census, *Nonwhite Population by Race, 1950*, 3B–82. Figures are for nonwhite for-eign-born only.
[6]U.S. Bureau of Census, *Detailed Population Characteristics, 1960*, I, 623–26. Figures for 1960 and 1970 represent nonwhite foreign stock from India and Pakistan.
[7]U.S. Bureau of Census, *Detailed Population Characteristics, 1970*, I, 1087–88.

TABLE IX
EAST INDIAN POPULATION IN U.S. BY CITIES

Cities	1910[1]	1920[2]	1930[3]	1940[4]	1950[5]	1960[6]	1970[7]
Chicago	1	32	79	38	73	68	713
Los Angeles	5	23	71	60	107	397*	250
San Francisco	68	46	44	29	118**	325**	265
Seattle	69	10	5	9	20	163	50
New York	14	123	240	213	532***	1,097	1,647
Philadelphia	1	8	19	24	34	176	226
Stockton	—	6	7	—	24	—	31

[1] U.S. Bureau of Census, *Population, 1930*, II, 80.

[2] Ibid.

[3] Ibid.

[4] U.S. Bureau of Census, *Population, 1940*, II, 114.

[5] U.S. Bureau of Census, *Nonwhite Population by Race, 1950*, 3B–83. Figures are for foreign-born only.

[6] U.S. Bureau of Census, *Detailed Population Characteristics, 1960, California*, I, pt. 6–492, 496; *Illinois*, I, pt. 15–476; *New York*, I, pt. 34–434; *Pennsylvania*, I, pt. 40–555; *Washington*, I, pt. 49–201. Figures are for nonwhite foreign stock.

[7] U.S. Bureau of Census, *Detailed Population Characteristics, 1970, California*, I, pt. 6–1174, 1177, 1179; *Illinois*, I, pt. 15–847; *New York*, I, pt. 34–720; *Pennsylvania*, I, 40–753; *Washington*, I, pt. 44–357.

*Long Beach is included as part of the Los Angeles Metropolitan Area in 1960.

**Oakland is included as part of the San Francisco Metropolitan Area in 1950 and 1960.

***Northeastern New Jersey is included as part of the New York Metropolitan Area in 1950.

Notes and References

Chapter I

1. *U.S. Statutes at Large*, LXXIX, 911–22; *New York Times*, Oct. 6, 1965, p. 1. The enactment of this statute ended quota restrictions for the Asia-Pacific Triangle. The 1965 act placed all unused national quotas into a common pool which qualified aliens from oversubscribed countries could utilize during the interim period, July 1, 1965–June 30, 1968. After 1968, 170,000 immigrants from the Eastern hemisphere could be admitted with no more than 20,000 coming from any one country. However, certain groups could be, and were, exempted from this ceiling. Political refugees were but one example of exemption. See *U.S. News & World Report*, June 14, 1971, p. 12, and U.S. Dept. of Justice, Immigration and Naturalization Service, *Annual Reports, 1964–75; Time*, July 5, 1976, p. 18.

2. Stephen Jurika, Jr., "The Political Geography of the Philippines," Ph.D. dissertation, Stanford Univ., 1962, p. 17.

3. Ibid., pp. 17–18; E. H. Dobby, *Southeast Asia*, 7th ed. (London: Univ. of London Press, 1960), p. 319.

4. Dobby, p. 320; *World Almanac & Book of Facts, 1975* (New York: Newspaper Enterprise Assoc., 1974), p. 401.

5. Dobby, p. 320; Iwao Tsuchiya, "Fluctuations of Rainfall in Southeast Asia," in Masatoshi M. Yoshino, ed., *Water Balance of Monsoon Asia* (Honolulu: Univ. of Hawaii Press, 1971), pp. 217–39.

6. Dobby, pp. 326–37; Jurika, pp. 42, 46–48, 57–61.

7. Jurika, pp. 143–46; Henry T. Lewis, *Ilocano Rice Farmers* (Honolulu: Univ. of Hawaii Press, 1971), pp. 25–26.

8. Jurika, pp. 81–91, 93.

9. Edward G. Bourne, *Spain in America, 1450–1580* (New York: Harper & Bros., 1904), pp. 126–27.

10. Jurika, p. 130; Roman R. Cariaga, *The Filipinos in Hawaii* (Honolulu: Filipino Public Relations Bureau, 1937), pp. 15–16.

11. Jurika, pp. 132–34; Cariaga, pp. 14–15.

12. Julius W. Pratt, *America's Colonial Experiment* (New York: Prentice-Hall, 1951), pp. 193–94.

13. *Sunday Star-Bulletin & Advertiser* (Honolulu), Feb. 23, 1975, p. A-24.

14. Pratt, pp. 195–201.

15. Hartzell Spence, *Marcos of the Philippines* (New York: World Publishing Co., 1969), pp. 22–23; Pratt, p. 64.

16. Pratt, pp. 201–202.

17. Ralston Hayden, "The United States and the Philippines," *Annals of the American Academy of Political and Social Science*, CXXII (Nov. 1925), 38–39.

18. Ibid., pp. 39–40; Pratt, pp. 206–10; 297–304.

19. Pratt, pp. 304–10.

20. *U.S. Statutes at Large*, LX, 128–59, 413, 1363.

21. Sung Yong Kim, *United States-Philippine Relations, 1946–1956* (Washington, D.C.: Public Affairs Press, 1968); Alvin H. Scaff, *The Philippine Answer to Communism* (Stanford: Stanford Univ. Press, 1955).

22. Jurika, p. 95.

23. Ibid., pp. 97–106; Dobby, p. 340.

24. Jurika, p. 108. In 1902, a schism occurred in the Philippine Roman Catholic Church; the branch that broke away became known as the Aglipayan, or Philippine Independent Church. In time the Aglipayan Church subdivided, one wing affiliating with Protestant denominations.

25. Lewis, *Ilocano Rice Farmers*, pp. 82–84.

26. Roman Cariaga, "Some Filipino Traits Transplanted," *Social Process*, II (1936), 20–23.

Chapter II

1. Dorita Clifford, "Motivation for Ilocano Migration," *Proceedings of Conference on International Migration from the Philippines* (Honolulu: East-West Center Population Institute, 1975), p. 25; *Time*, July 6, 1976, p. 19.

2. Carlos P. Romulo, *I Have Walked with Heroes* (New York: Holt, Rinehart and Winston, 1961), pp. 130–54; Emory S. Bogardus, "American Attitudes toward Filipinos," *Sociology and Social Research*, XIV (1929), 59–63.

3. Walter J. Ballard, "Filipino Students in the United States," *Journal of Education*, LXVII (1908), 272.

4. William A Sutherland, *Not by Might* (Las Cruces, New Mexico: Southwest Publishing Co., 1953), pp. 8–36; "Statement of Camilo Osias," U. S. House, Committee on Immigration and Naturalization, *Hearings to Return to Philippine Islands Unemployed*

Filipinos, 72 Cong., 2 sess. (1935), p. 35. Camilo Osias, Resident Commissioner for the Philippine Islands in 1935, had come to the United States in 1905 as a *Pensionado.*

5. "Statment of Dr. Diosado M. Yap," U.S. House Committee on Immigration and Naturalization, *Hearings Providing for Naturalization of Filipinos, Nov. 22, 1944,* 78 Cong., 2 sess. (1944), p. 52.

6. Benicio T. Catapusan, "Problems of Filipino Students in America," *Sociology and Social Research,* XXVI (1941–42), 146–51; Jose C. Alba, "Filipinos in California," *Pacific Historian,* II (1967), 41; Bruno Lasker, *Filipino Immigration to Continental United States and to Hawaii* (Chicago: Univ. of Chicago Press, 1931), pp. 369–74.

7. Mary Dorita Clifford, "Filipino Immigration to Hawaii," M. A. thesis, Univ. of Hawaii, 1954, pp. 12–14.

8. Ibid., p. 19; Cariaga, *Filipinos in Hawaii,* p. 5.

9. Clifford, "Filipino Immigration," pp. 21–22; Hawaii, Territorial House of Representatives, Committee on Agriculture and Immigration, *Report on Resolution Requiring Inquiry into the Question of Filipino Immigration,* 1911 Sess., p. 8.

10. Richard Ivers, "Statement on Immigration Prepared by Mr. Ivers, President, Board of Immigration for Federal Immigration Commission," Honolulu, 1909, typescript, Hawaiian Collection, Univ. of Hawaii Library.

11. Hawaii, House Territorial Report, 1911 Sess., p. 8; Mary Dorita Clifford, "The Hawaiian Sugar Planters' Association and Filipino Exclusion," in *The Filipino Exclusion Movement, 1927–1935* (Quezon City, Philippines: Institute of Asian Studies, Occasional Papers No. 1, 1967), p. 15; Clifford, "Filipino Immigration," pp. 35–36.

12. Sanford A. Platt, *Immigration and Emigration in the Hawaiian Sugar Industry* (Honolulu, n. p., 1950), p. 12.

13. Clifford, "Hawaiian Sugar Planters and Filipino Exclusion," p. 17; Clifford, "Filipino Immigration," pp. 38–42; Edna C. Wentworth, *Filipino Plantation Workers in Hawaii* (San Francisco: American Council, Institute of Pacific Relations, 1941), p. 30. By 1915, recruits were also secured from Bohol, Iloilo, Leyte, and Negros Oriental.

14. Cariaga, *Filipinos in Hawaii,* pp. 18–19.

15. Ibid., p. 19; Lewis, *Ilocano Rice Farmers,* p. 4; Wentworth, p. 30.

16. U.S. Bureau of Labor Statistics, *Monthly Labor Review,* XXIII (1926), 634.

17. Ibid., p. 685; "Quezon Papers on Filipinos in Hawaii, 1914–1943," Hawaiian Collection, Univ. of Hawaii Library, pp. 31–45.

18. Clifford, "Filipino Immigration," pp. 54–55.

19. See Appendix A, Table II.

20. Clifford, "Hawaiian Sugar Planters and Filipino Exclusion," pp. 21–22; see Appendix A, Table II.

21. Cariaga, Filipinos in Hawaii, pp. 19–20; Virgilio Menor Felipe, "Hawaii: A Pilipino Dream—An Oral Biography" in "Searching for the Promised Land: Filipinos and Samoans in Hawaii," Nancy Foon Young, ed., Univ. of Hawaii, College of Education General Assistance Center, [1973] mimeographed, pp. 22–23; Dolores Quinto, "Life Story of a Filipino Immigrant," Social Process, IV (1938), 71–72.

22. Felipe, p. 23.

23. Lewis, pp. 26, 147.

24. Quinto, p. 71.

25. "Testimony of Manuel Roxas," U. S. House, Committee on Immigration and Naturalization, Hearings on Exclusion of Immigration from the Philippine Islands, 71 Cong. 2 sess. (1930), p. 112.

26. Honorante Mariano, "The Filipino Immigrants in the United States," M.A. thesis, Univ. of Oregon, 1933, pp. 7–15.

27. Quinto, pp. 74–75.

28. Felipe in "Hawaii: a Pilipino Dream" recounts a crossing made after 1915 under regulated recruiting.

29. See Appendix A, Tables I, II and III.

30. U. S. Statutes at Large, XLVIII, 462–63; Clifford, "Hawaiian Sugar Planters and Filipino Exclusion," pp. 25–26.

31. Riley H. Allen, "The Filipino in Hawaii," The Philippines in Hawaii (Honolulu, n. p., 1948), p. 23.

32. Slator M. Miller, "Report to Mr. H. A. Walker, President, Hawaiian Sugar Planters' Association on 1945–1946 Filipino Emigration Project" (Honolulu [1946]), pp. 1–24; H. Brett Melendy, "Filipinos in the United States," Pacific Historical Review, XLIII (1974), 523, 545.

33. San Francisco Call, Sept. 22, 1903, p. 7; Emory S. Bogardus, "American Attitudes towards Filipinos," Sociology and Social Research, XIV (1929), 63–64.

34. Clifford, "Filipino Immigration," pp. 37, 47.

35. See Appendix A, Table III. Detroit in 1930 had a Filipino population of 605. On the West Coast, Oakland had 572. See Albert W. Palmer, "Who are the Orientals in America?" Missionary Review of the World, LVII (1934), 265.

36. California, Department of Industrial Relations, *Facts about Filipino Immigration in California* (Sacramento, 1930), p. 11 (hereafter cited as California, *Facts*).

37. Ibid., pp. 12–13, 37–38; Lasker, p. 351; Mariano, pp. 20–21.

38. Carey McWilliams, *Brothers under the Skin*, rev. ed. (Boston: Little Brown and Co., 1964), pp. 25–26.

39. *Filipino Nation*, Nov. 1932, p. 14.

40. See Appendix A, Tables I, II and III.

41. *San Francisco Chronicle*, April 21, 1934; p. 1; April 26, 1934, p. 4.

42. U. S. Immigration and Naturalization Service, *Annual Report, 1957*, p. 37; *Annual Report, 1961*, p. 43; *Annual Report, 1970*, p. 64.

43. See Appendix A, Tables I and II.

44. *San Francisco Chronicle*, Aug. 5, 1956, p. 15; Aug. 25, 1957, p. 2; California, Department of Employment, Farm Placement Service, *California Annual Farm Labor Report—1961* (Sacramento, 1962), p. 29. For the next few years, the U. S. Dept. of Agriculture continued to tinker with the idea, but in March, 1965, Secretary of Agriculture W. Willard Wirtz announced that no new foreign farm contract workers would be admitted. See *San Francisco Chronicle*, March 8, 1965, p. 31. The last year that workers were sent was 1963 when a total of 124 was reported. See U. S. Immigration and Naturalization Service, *Annual Report, 1972*, p. 69.

45. See Appendix A, Tables I, and II and III; U. S. Immigration and Naturalization Service, *Annual Report, 1973*, pp. 48–52.

46. Peter Smith, "A Demographic Overview of Outmigration from the Philippines," *Proceedings of Conference on International Migration from the Philippines* (Honolulu: East-West Population Institute, 1975), p. 12; Charles B. Keely, "Philippine Migration: Internal Movements and Emigration to the United States," *International Migration Review*, VII (1973), 180–86.

47. Hawaii, Commission on Manpower and Full Employment, *Report of the State Immigration Service Center* (Honolulu, 1972), pp. 44–47.

48. Ibid., p. 54.

Chapter III

1. Commonwealth Club of California, "Filipino Immigration," *Transactions*, XXIV (1929), 312–20.

2. McWilliams, *Brothers Under the Skin*, p. 238.

3. Manuel Buaken, *I Have Lived with the American People* (Caldwell, Idaho: Caxton Printers, 1948), p. 169; E. S. Bogardus,

264   ASIANS IN AMERICA

Anti-Filipino Riots (San Diego: Ingram Institute, May 15, 1930), pp. 7–8.

4. *San Francisco Chronicle*, Jan. 22, 1936, pp. 7–8.

5. *U. S. Statutes at Large*, XXXII, 691–92.

6. Ibid., XXXIV, 606. When the Revised Statutes were enacted, the wording of Sec. 2165 read that "an alien may be admitted to become a citizen of the United States in the following manner and not otherwise. . . ." Interestingly, the words, "free white person," of the 1790 act were not included. The Revised Statutes in Sec. 2169 added the words "aliens of African nativity and persons of African descent" to conform to the wording of the 1870 act. Attention was called in 1875 to the omission of Sec. 2165, but only Sec. 2169 was amended to include "free white persons." The many subsequent court cases turned on the interpretation of the key section, 2165. See Consulate General of Japan, *Documentary History of Law Cases Affecting Japanese in the United States, 1916–1924* (San Fransicso, 1925), I, 22.

7. *In re Alverto*, D. C. 198 Fed. 688. Other cases were *In re Rallos*, D. C. 241, Fed. 686; *In re Lampitoe*, D. C. 232, Fed. 382; *United States v. Balsara*, 180 Fed. 694.

8. *In re Bautista*, 245 Fed. 765.

9. *U. S. Statutes at Large*, XL, 542.

10. *In re Geronimo Para*, 269 Fed., 643; *Toyota v. United States*, 268 U. S. 402.

11. *U. S. Statutes at Large*, XXXIX, 874; XLIII, 168; Garel A. Grunder and William E. Livezey, *The Philippines and the United States* (Norman, Okla., Univ. of Oklahoma Press, 1951), 205–33.

12. Maximo C. Manzon, *The Strange Case of the Filipinos in the United States* (New York: American Committee for Protection of Foreign Born, 1938), pp. 5–6; McWilliams, p. 243.

13. *Roque Espiritu De La Yala v. U. S.*, 77 Fed. 988; *In re Rena*, 50 Fed. 606.

14. *Filipino Nation*, March 1930, pp. 21–47.

15. *San Francisco Chronicle*, April 10, 1942, p. 16; Adeva to Quezon, Jan. 7, 1943, Washington, D. C., Manuel L. Quezon Papers, National Library of the Philippines, Ermiita, Manila.

16. *San Francisco Chronicle*, Jan. 15, 1934, p. 10.

17. John Burma, *Spanish-Speaking Groups in the United States* (Durham, N.C.: Duke Univ. Press, 1954), p. 142; Benicio T. Catapusan, "Filipino Immigrants and Public Relief in the United States," *Sociology and Social Research*, XXIII (1938–39), 546–54.

18. *Manila Daily Bulletin*, March 20, 1939, as quoted in Adeudato

J. Agbayani, "The Resident Commissioner of the Philippines to the United States," Ph.D. dissertation, Univ. of Santo Tomas, Manila, 1946, p. 160.

19. U. S. *Congressional Record,* 75 Cong. 3 sess. (1938), p. 4260; 76 Cong. 1 sess. (1939), pp. 3144, 9207; 77 Cong. 1 sess. (1941), p. 122; 78 Cong. 1 sess. (1943), pp. 1373, 4841, 9300.

20. U. S. House, Committee on Immigration and Naturalization, *Hearings on Authorizing of Naturalization of Filipinos,* 78 Cong., 2 sess. (1944), pp. 1–40; *Congressional Record,* 78 Cong., 2 sess. (1944), pp. 368, 1901, 4685; 79 Cong., 1 sess. (1945), p. 58.

21. *U. S. Statutes at Large,* LX, 416, 1353; LXVI, 248; LXXIX, 911–22.

22. Bienvenido N. Santos, "Filipinos in War," *Far Eastern Survey,* XI (1942), 249–50; *New Republic,* May 18, 1942, p. 665; Basilio Valdes, "Memorandum for His Excellency the President," Oct. 25, 1942, Washington, D.C., Quezon Papers.

23. Jaime Hernandez, "Findings and Observations on the Social and Economic Conditions of the Filipinos on the Pacific Seaboard," Aug. 7, 1942, Quezon Papers; Joaquin M. Elizalde to Quezon, Washington, D. C., Jan. 22, 1943; Adeva to Quezon, Jan. 1, 1943, Quezon Papers.

24. Adeva to Quezon, Jan. 7, 1943; Elizalde to Quezon, Jan. 22, 1943, Quezon Papers.

25. Letter to Editor, *Asia and America,* XLIII (1943), 560; Memorandum, J. C. Dionisio, "Conditions among Filipinos in America," Feb. 15, 1944, Quezon Papers; Elizalde to Quezon, Jan. 22, 1943, April 7, 1943, Quezon Papers. On April 23, 1943, Elizalde informed Quezon that Arizona's attorney general had reversed the 1939 ruling and Filipinos could hold title to farm lands. See Elizalde to Quezon, March 23, 1943, Quezon Papers.

26. Manuel Buaken, "Life in the Armed Forces," *New Republic,* Aug. 10, 1943, p. 279.

27. Adeva to Quezon, Jan. 7, 1943, Quezon Papers.

28. *San Francisco Chronicle,* April 10, 1946, p. 3.

29. Iris Buaken, "You Can't Marry a Filipino," *Commonweal,* March 9, 1945, pp. 534–36.

30. *California Statutes,* 34 Sess. (1901), 335.

31. Nellie Foster, "Legal Status of Filipino Intermarriage in California," *Sociology and Social Research,* XVI (1932), 447–52.

32. *Rolden v. Los Angeles County,* 129 Calif. 267; *San Francisco Chronicle,* March 30, 1933, p. 1.

33. *California Statutes,* 50 Sess. (1933), 561.

34. In 1939, Arizona prohibited marriage between white women and "Hindus" and Malays. Nevada and Utah prohibited marriage with Malays but common law marriage was valid. Wyoming prohibited marriage with Malays and whites. The Western states of New Mexico and Washington and the territories of Alaska and Hawaii had no prohibition. Oregon's law was a bit vague because of the ambiguous meaning of the word *Mongolian*. See Iris Buaken, pp. 536–37.

35. *Perez v. Sharp*, 32 Calif., 2nd Series, 711.

36. Randall Risdon, "A Study of Interracial Marriages Based on Data for Los Angeles County," *Sociology and Social Research*, XXXIX (1954), 92–95.

37. *Stockton Record*, Jan. 1, 1926, p. 13; Jan. 1, 1927, p. 2.

38. Buaken, *I Have Lived with the American People*, pp. 94–97; Burma, *Spanish-Speaking Groups*, pp. 152–53.

39. California, *Facts*, pp. 73–74; E. S. Bogardus, *Anti-Filipino Race Riots*, pp. 3–16.

40. Quoted in Buaken, *I Have Lived with the American People*, p. 169.

41. Ibid., pp. 169–70.

42. California, *Facts*, p. 75; Buaken, *I Have Lived with the American People*, pp. 97–105; *San Jose Mercury*, Jan. 11–23, 1930.

43. Lasker, pp. 13–19; *Filipino Nation*, Jan. 1931, p. 21; March 1931, p. 36.

44. *San Francisco Chronicle*, Aug. 10, 1933, p. 3; Sept 11, 1934, p. 15; Sept. 12, 1934, p. 23; Sept. 14, 1934, p. 10.

45. Commonwealth Club of California, *Transactions*, XXIV (1929), 320; Lasker, p. v; California, *Senate Journal*, 48 Sess. (1929), p. 2690.

46. *San Francisco Chronicle*, Jan. 30, 1931, p. 41.

47. *U. S. Statutes at Large*, XLIX, 478–79; H. Brett Melendy, "California's Discrimination Against Filipinos, 1927–1935," in *The Filipino Exclusion Movement, 1927–1935* (Quezon City, Philippines, Institute of Asian Studies, Occasional Paper No. 1, 1967), p. 10.

48. McWilliams, *Brothers Under the Skin*, p. 243.

Chapter IV

1. Memorandum, J. C. Dionisio to Quezon, March 7, 1944, Quezon Papers.

2. D. F. Gonzalo, "Social Adjustments of Filipinos in America," *Sociology and Social Research*, XIV (1929), 166–72.

3. Ibid., pp. 172–73.

4. Letter, Dora Eckenrode to Editor, *Filipino Students' Magazine*, I (1905), 36.

5. Lauriel E. Eubank, "The Effects of the First Six Months of World War II on the Attitudes of Koreans and Filipinos toward the Japanese in Hawaii," M. A. thesis, Univ. of Hawaii, 1943, pp. 106–07.

6. Melendy, "Filipinos in the United States," pp. 538–39; Bogardus, "American Attitudes towards the Filipinos," pp. 59–65; Danilo E. Ponce, "The Filipinos in Hawaii," in Nancy Foon Young, ed., "Searching for the Promised Land—Filipinos and Samoans in Hawaii," pp. 14–15.

7. U. S. House, Committee on Immigration and Naturalization, *Hearings Providing for Naturalization of Filipinos, Nov. 22, 1944*, 78 Cong., 2 sess. (1944), p. 49.

8. Ibid., pp. 50–52.

9. Stanley D. Porteus and Marjorie E. Babcock, *Temperament and Race* (Boston: Gorham Press, 1926), pp. 58–59.

10. Ibid., pp. 60, 64–67; Ponce, pp. 15–16.

11. *San Francisco Chronicle*, Dec. 5, 1931, p. 13.

12. *Seamen's Journal*, XLII (1928), 100.

13. C. M. Goethe, "Filipino Immigration Viewed as a Peril," *Current History*, XXXIV (June, 1931), 354.

14. Social Science Institute, Fisk Univ., "Orientals and their Cultural Adjustment," (Social Science Source Documents, #4, 1946), pp. 112, 119.

15. Carlos Bulosan, *Sound of Falling Light: Letters in Exile*, Dolores S. Feria, ed. (Quezon City, n. p., 1960), pp. 191–92.

16. Social Science Institute, p. 132; Emory Bogardus, "Filipino Immigrant Attitudes," *Sociology and Social Research*, XIV (May–June, 1929), pp. 472–74; Burma, pp. 144, 152; U. S. House, Committee on Immigration and Naturalization, *Hearings to Provide for Return to Philippine Islands*, 72 Cong., 2 sess. (1933), pp. 8–9; Romulos, p. 132; Melendy, "Filipinos in the United States," p. 539.

17. Bogardus, "Filipino Immigrant Attitudes," p. 474.

18. Dorteno B. Inez, "The Question of Race Pops Again," *Commonwealth Chronicle*, 1936, p. 8.

19. *Monterey Peninsula Herald*, Aug. 25, 1930, clipping in James E. Wood Collection, Bancroft Library, Univ. of California, Berkeley.

20. John H. Burma, "The Background of the Current Situation of Filipino-Americans," *Social Forces*, XXX (1951), 42–43; R. T. Feria, "War and the Status of Filipino Immigrants," *Sociology and Social Research*, XXXI (1946), 49; Melendy, p. 539; Burma, *Spanish-Speaking Groups*, p. 144; U. S. House, Committee on Immigration

268

and Naturalization, *Hearings on Return to Philippine Islands of Un-employed Filipinos*, 72 Cong., 2 sess. (1933), pp. 8–9.

21. Albert W. Palmer, *Orientals in American Life* (New York: Friendship Press, 1934), pp. 94–102.

22. *Filipino Nation*, VII (1931), 38; VI (1929), 23; VIII (1931), pp. 22, 32.

23. Ponce, "Filipinos in Hawaii," p. 15; McWilliams, *Brothers Under the Skin*, p. 239.

24. Felipe, pp. 34–35; Cariaga, *Filipinos in Hawaii*, pp. 67–68.

25. Lillian Galedo and Theresa Q. Mar, "Filipinos in a Farm Labor Camp," in "Asians in America" (Davis, Calif.: Univ. of California Asian American Research Project Working Publication No. 3, 1970, mimeographed), p. 58.

26. *Philippine Free Press* (Manila), 1929, as quoted in Lasker, pp. 133–34.

27. U. S. Commission on Law Observance and Enforcement, *Report on Crime and the Foreign Born*, Report No. 10, June 24, 1931, p. 362.

28. Norman S. Hayner, "Social Factors in Oriental Crime," *American Journal of Sociology*, XLIII (1938), 908–19; Buaken, *I Have Lived with the American People*, pp. 146–54.

29. Burma, "Background of Current Situation," *Social Forces*, XXX (1951), 45–46.

30. U. S. House, Committee on Immigration and Naturalization, *Hearings*, 71 Cong., 2 sess. (1930), p. 35.

31. U. S. House, Committee on Immigration and Naturalization, *Preliminary Hearing Subject to Revising Immigration from Countries of the Western Hemisphere*, 71 Cong., 2 sess. (1930), p. 226.

32. Interview by James Woods with Charles F. Crook, Deputy Labor Commissioner, San Joaquin County, Feb. 1930, James E. Wood Collection, Bancroft Library.

33. Buaken, *I Have Lived with the American People*, p. 173.

34. Benicio T. Catapusan, "Leisure-Time Problems of Filipino Immigrants," *Sociology and Social Research*, XXIV (1939–40), 544–49; Trinidad A. Rojo, "Social Maladjustment among Filipinos in the United States," *Sociology and Social Research*, XXI, (1937), 454–55.

35. Paul G. Cressey, *The Taxi-Dance Hall* (Chicago: Univ. of Chicago Press, 1932).

36. McWilliams, *Brothers under the Skin*, pp. 238–39.

37. Catapusan, p. 547.

38. Virginia Lord and Alice W. Lee, "The Taxi Dance Hall in Honolulu," *Social Process*, II (1936), 46–50.

39. *Filipino Nation,* VI (March 1930), p. 20.

40. Catapusan, pp. 548–49; Benjamin Menor, "Filipino Plantation Adjustments," *Social Process,* XIII (1949), 49.

41. *San Francisco Chronicle,* May 17, 1936, p. 3.

42. Ibid., Jan. 22, 1936, p. 13.

Chapter V

1. Burma, *Spanish-Speaking Groups,* p. 140; McWilliams, *Brothers under the Skin,* pp. 236–37.

2. Burma, *Spanish-Speaking Groups,* p. 140; Melendy, "Filipinos in the United States," pp. 526–27.

3. "Memorandum of Hilario C. Moncado," U. S. House, Committee on Immigration and Naturalization, *Hearings on Exclusion of Immigration from Philippine Islands,* 71 Cong., 2 sess. (1930), p. 138; Trinidad A. Rojo, "Filipino-American Contacts," Mss., Bancroft Library, Univ. of California, Berkeley; *Filipino Nation,* VII (1931), 36.

4. Emory S. Bogardus, "The Filipino Immigrant Problem," *Sociology and Social Research,* XIII (1929), 472–79; Catapusan, "Problems of Filipino Students in America," *Sociology and Social Research,* XXVI (1941–42), 150–51.

5. Melendy, "Filipinos in the United States," pp. 527–28; Lasker, *Filipino Immigration,* p. 21; Burma, *Spanish-Speaking Groups,* p. 140; "Immigration Problems on the Pacific Coast," *Current History,* XXXIII (1930–31), 726–27.

6. California, *Facts,* p. 12.

7. Buaken, *I Have Lived with the American People,* pp. 58–59.

8. Paul Scharrenberg, "The Filipino Problem," *Public Affairs* (Honolulu, 1929), pp. 45–54; Bogardus, "Filipino Immigrant Problem," p. 474; Hubert Phillips, "The Oriental on the Pacific Coast," *Nation,* CXXXII (1931), 13.

9. California, *Facts,* pp. 72–73.

10. Buaken, *I Have Lived with the American People,* pp. 188–89.

11. *Statistical History of the United States from Colonial Times to the Present* (Stamford, Conn.: Fairfield Publishers, 1965), p. 95; California, *Facts,* pp. 12–13.

12. Benicio Catapusan, "The Filipino Labor Cycle in the United States," *Sociology and Social Research,* XIX (1934), 61–63.

13. California, *Facts,* pp. 57, 66; Lloyd H. Fisher, *The Harvest Labor Market in California* (Cambridge, Mass.: Harvard Univ. Press, 1953), p. 7.

14. Paul S. Taylor, *Mexican Labor in the Imperial Valley* (Berke-

ley: Univ. of Calif. Publications in Economics, 1928), pp. 3–7, 34.

15. Palmer, *Orientals in America*, pp. 84–85; see Appendix A, Table III.

16. Buaken, *I Have Lived with the American People*, pp. 194–95.

17. Fisher, *Harvest Labor Market*, pp. 6–7.

18. Melendy, pp. 536–37; McWilliams, p. 237; Burma, *Spanish-Speaking Groups*, p. 141; Buaken, *I Have Lived with the American People*, p. 87.

19. U. S. House, Select Committee to Investigate the Interstate Migration of Destitute Citizens, *Hearings*, 76 Cong., 3 sess. (1940), pp. 2529–38; Fisher, p. 40; California, *Facts*, p. 70.

20. Palmer, *Orientals in America*, pp. 80–81.

21. Buaken, *I Have Lived with the American People*, p. 197.

22. Federal Writers' Project, "Unionization of Filipinos in California Agriculture," Oakland, Calif., typescript [n.d.]), p. 2; Phillips, p. 13.

23. Interview by James Wood with Paul Lewis, San Joaquin County Horticulture Commission, Feb. 15, 1930, James E. Wood Collection.

24. Interview, Wood with Crook, Feb., 1930, James E. Wood Collection.

25. Buaken, *I Have Lived with the American People*, pp. 37–38; Interview by James Wood with Mrs. Marcuello, Stockton, Calif., Feb. 7, 1930, James E. Wood Collection; address by H. C. Carrasco, State Labor Commissioner, Aug. 2, 1940, James E. Wood Collection; Philippine Islands, Dept. of Commerce and Communications, Bureau of Labor, *Activities of the Bureau of Labor*, 1930, p. 6.

26. Palmer, *Orientals in America*, p. 80.

27. Carey McWilliams, "Exit the Filipino," *Nation*, CXLI (1935), 265.

28. Harry Schwartz, *Seasonal Farm Labor in the United States* (New York: Columbia Univ. Press, 1954), p. 83; Carey McWilliams, *Factories in the Field* (Boston: Little, Brown, 1939), p. 118.

29. Schwartz, pp. 92–93; Fisher, *Harvest Labor Market*, p. 29; Melendy, *Filipinos in the United States*, p. 529.

30. Bogardus, "American Attitudes towards Filipinos," pp. 65–66.

31. Burma, *Spanish-Speaking Groups*, p. 143; Buaken, *I Have Lived with the American People*, p. 196.

32. McWilliams, *Factories in the Field*, p. 212; *Filipino Informer*, II (Feb. 11, 1928), 4, (April 21, 1928), 1; Taylor, *Mexican Labor . . .* , p. 54; *San Francisco Chronicle*, June 26, 1930, p. 15; Phillips, "The Oriental on the Pacific Coast," p. 13.

33. Burma, *Spanish-Speaking Groups*, p. 142; Manzon, *Strange Case of Filipinos*, pp. 9–10.

34. *San Francisco Chronicle*, Sept. 25, 1934; *Brawley News*, Nov. 20, Dec. 19, 1935, as quoted in Fisher, p. 39.

35. The Trade Union Unity League was affiliated with the Cannery and Agricultural Workers Industrial Union, a Communist-backed union, which attempted to carry on the I.W.W. tradition. See Helen B. Lamb, "Industrial Relations in the Western Lettuce Industry," Ph.D. dissertation, Radcliffe College, 1942, p. 196.

36. Lamb, p. 189; McWilliams, *Factories in the Field*, pp. 213–14. McWilliams records that eight of those arrested were convicted of violating the Criminal Syndicalism Act of 1919 which had been aimed at preventing the I.W.W. from developing in California. Seven of the defendants were sent to San Quentin prison. For background on the 1919 act, see H. Brett Melendy and Benjamin F. Gilbert, *The Governors of California* (Georgetown, Calif.: Talisman Press, 1965), pp. 325–29.

37. Federal Writers' Project, "Unionization . . . ," p. 11.

38. Lamb, "Western Lettuce Industry . . . ," pp. 247–62.

39. *Philippine Mail* (Salinas, Calif.) as quoted in Lamb, pp. 271–72; McWilliams, "Exit the Filipino," p. 265.

40. McWilliams, *Factories in the Field*, pp. 254–59; Lamb, 374–80.

41. Yamato Ichihashi, *Japanese in the United States* (Stanford: Stanford Univ. Press, 1932), p. 154; U. S. Immigration Commission, *Report*, XXIII, 407.

42. Mariano, "Filipino Immigrants . . . ," p. 33.

43. Rojo, "Filipino-American Contacts."

44. California, Bureau of Labor Statistics, *The Alaska Salmon Canneries* in *Appendix to Legislative Journals*, 40 Sess. (1913), III, 51–53.

45. Manuel L. Quezon to Frank McIntyre, Jan. 14, 1914; memorandum, L. M. Garrison, Sec. of War, to Attorney General, Jan. 22, 1914, Quezon Papers.

46. Buaken, *I Have Lived with the American People*, pp. 198–203; 206–11; Lasker, *Filipino Immigration*, pp. 356–57.

47. Mariano, pp. 34–35.

48. U. S. House, Committee on Immigration and Naturalization, *Hearings on Exclusion of Immigration from Philippine Islands*, 71 Cong., 2 sess. (1930), pp. 234–35.

49. *U. S. Statutes at Large*, XLIX, 1992–93; Manzon, *Strange Case . . .* , pp. 11–12.

50. Buaken, *I Have Lived with the American People*, pp. 213–14; *Western Worker* (San Francisco), June 1, 1932, p. 4.

51. Santos, pp. 249–50; *Newsweek,* Nov. 9, 1970, pp. 32–33.

Chapter VI

1. Felipe, "Hawaii: a Pilipino Dream," p. 26; Quinto, "Life Story of a Filipino Immigrant," p. 76.

2. Philippines, *Report of the Director of Labor to His Excellency the Governor-General of the Philippine Islands,* [Hermenegildo Cruz] (Manila) in *Bureau of Labor Bulletin,* VII (March, 1926), 5. Hereafter cited as Cruz.

3. Quinto, p. 77; Wentworth, *Filipino Plantation Workers . . .,* p. 56.

4. Cruz, p. 5; Wentworth, pp. 49–51, 56.

5. Cruz, p. 6.

6. Felipe, pp. 28–29.

7. Wentworth, pp. 53–54.

8. Felipe, p. 27.

9. Cruz, p. 8.

10. Felipe, p. 30.

11. John E. Reinecke, "The Big Lie of 1920," typescript, Hawaiian Collection, Univ. of Hawaii Library, p. 2; *Filipino Nation,* V (1929), 17.

12. Roman Cariaga, "The Filipinos in Hawaii: A Survey of the Economic and Social Conditions," M. A. thesis, Univ. of Hawaii, 1936, pp. 90–92; Wentworth, p. 54.

13. Sylvester K. Stevens, *American Expansion in Hawaii, 1842–1898* (Harrisburg, Pa.: Archives Publishing Co. of Penn., Inc., 1945), p. 144.

14. The strike was led by the Japanese High Wage Association.

15. Lawrence H. Fuchs, *Hawaii Pono: a Social History* (New York: Harcourt, Brace & World, Inc., 1961), pp. 212–13; "August 2, 1919 Labor Contract," Quezon Papers, Univ. of Hawaii, pp. 31–45; M. A. Fonseca to Quezon and Osmeña, May 29, 1922, Quezon Papers, pp. 95–96; "Wage and Bonus Schedule Effective on and after Nov. 1, 1921," Quezon Papers, pp. 130–31.

16. Fuchs, p. 214.

17. Pablo Manlapit, "Pablo Manlapit," Mss., Hawaiian Collection, Univ. of Hawaii Library; Herbert A. Probasco, "Japanese and Filipino Labor Unions and the 1920 Plantation Strike in Hawaii," Mss., Hawaiian Collection, Univ. of Hawaii Library.

18. Fuchs, pp. 215–25; Probasco, "Japanese and Filipino Labor Unions," pp. 19–36; Reinecke, "The Big Lie of 1920," pp. 3–4; Victor Weingarten, *Raising Cane: a Brief History of Labor in Hawaii,*

(Honolulu: International Longshoremen's and Warehousemen's Union, 1946), pp. 26–29.

19. Fonseca to Quezon and Osmeña, pp. 95–96; Pablo Manlapit to Quezon, Oct. 25, 1922, Quezon Papers, Univ. of Hawaii, pp. 100–102.

20. W. F. Babbitt to Quezon, Jan. 11, 1923, Quezon Papers, Univ. of Hawaii, pp. 118–24.

21. Fuchs, pp. 114, 233.

22. Ibid., p. 235.

23. Fred K. Makino to Manuel Quezon, Nov. 16, 1925, Quezon Papers, Univ. of Hawaii, pp. 251–54.

24. *Filipino Informer*, II (March 3, 1928), 1.

25. Manlapit, "Pablo Manlapit."

26. J. K. Butler to Quezon, Dec. 2, 1933, Quezon Papers, Univ. of Hawaii, pp. 302–303.

27. Fuchs, p. 236.

28. *San Francisco Chronicle*, June 22, 1933, p. 12; James Shoemaker, "Labor Conditions in Hawaii," *Monthly Labor Review*, LI (1940), 1321; Weingarten, pp. 34–35.

29. Weingarten, *Raising Cane*, p. 37.

30. James Shoemaker, "The Economy of Hawaii in 1947," U. S. Bureau of Labor Statistics, *Bulletin 1948*, #926, p. 184.

31. Fuchs, p. 249.

32. Shoemaker, "Labor Conditions in Hawaii," pp. 32–33, 44.

33. Cruz, p. 4.

34. See Appendix, Table III.

Chapter VII

1. *Pacific Citizen* (Salt Lake City), Jan. 6, 1945, p. 4.

2. Fuchs, *Hawaii Pono*, pp. 356–59.

3. Institute of Labor Economics, Univ. of Washington, "Job Opportunities for Racial Minorities in the Seattle Area, 1948," pp. 8, 19–20. The San Francisco-Oakland Metropolitan Area in 1950 had 4,674 Filipino males and 393 females in the work force. The males were distributed between: service workers—41.8%; farm labor—17.5%; operatives—11.1%; craftsmen—7.5%; managers—2.3%; professionals—1.2%. Thirty-three percent of the female workers were domestic servants and the rest were scattered among several occupations. See *Monthly Labor Review*, VIII (1958), 1132. For a view of the Filipinos in Minnesota in the late 1940's, see the report of Governor Luther W. Youngdahl's Interracial Commission of Minnesota, *The Oriental in Minnesota* (St. Paul, 1949).

4. Calif. Dept of Industrial Relations, *Californians of Japanese, Chinese and Filipino Ancestry* (San Francisco, 1965), p. 12.

5. Andrew W. Lind, *Hawaii's People*, 3rd ed. (Honolulu: Univ. of Hawaii Press, 1967), pp. 75, 77.

6. Ibid., pp. 76, 78.

7. *Newsweek*, Nov. 9, 1970, pp. 32–33; Alfredo N. Munroz, *The Filipinos in America* (Los Angeles: Mountainview Publishers, 1971), pp. 107–13.

8. U. S. Bureau of Census, *Japanese, Chinese and Filipinos in the United States, 1970*, pp. 149–53. Filipino males in California were listed in the following categories: clerks, 8,000; professionals, 4,305; services, 3,500. In Hawaii 3,595 were in the service trades while there were 2,741 clerks and 866 professionals.

9. Lind, p. 100; Calif. Dept. of Industrial Relations, *Californians . . . Filipino Ancestry*, p. 14; *Honolulu Star-Bulletin*, Sept. 10, 1973, p. B-1.

10. Joint Strategy and Action Committee, Inc., *Grapevine*, IV (Oct. 1972), 1.

11. See Appendix A, Table III.

12. *San Francisco Chronicle*, Feb. 23, 1973, p. 6.

13. *San Francisco Examiner & Chronicle*, Feb. 23, 1969, p. A–20.

14. Ibid.; "California Living," May 13, 1973, pp. 16–17; *San Francisco Chronicle*, Nov. 28, 1968, p. 5.

15. *San Francisco Examiner & Chronicle*, "California Living," May 13, 1973, p. 16.

16. Galedo and Mar, "Filipinos in a Farm Labor Camp," pp. 53–56.

17. Ibid., pp. 56–57.

18. Ibid., p. 57.

19. Ibid., p. 58.

20. Schwartz, *Seasonal Farm Labor*, pp. 100–101.

21. Mark Day, *Forty Acres Cesar Chavez and the Farm Workers* (New York: Praeger, 1971), pp. 36–37; John Dunne, *Delano* (New York: Farrar, Straus & Giroux, 1971), pp. 73–83.

22. *Bataan News* (Sacramento, Calif.), March 20, 1967, p. 1.

23. Day, pp. 39–43.

24. Walton Bean, *California, an Interpretative History*, 2nd ed. (New York: McGraw-Hill, 1973), pp. 496–98; 501–505.

25. *El Macriado* (Delano, Calif.), April 1–15, 1969, p. 15.

26. *San Francisco Chronicle*, Dec. 29, 1970, p. 6; *San Francisco Examiner & Chronicle*, "California Living," May 13, 1973, p. 15.

27. Jose C. Alba, "Filipinos in California," *Pacific Historian*, II (1967), 39–41.

28. Munroz, *Filipinos in America*, p. 151.

29. "Filipino Businessmen and Philippine Businesses," *The Philippines in Hawaii* (Honolulu, 1948), p. 27.

30. Fuchs, *Hawaii Pono*, pp. 440–42.

31. *Filipino News* (Lihue), Feb. 11, 1955, p. 1; *Hawaiian Reporter* (Honolulu), Nov. 26, 1959, p. B–15.

32. *Hawaiian Reporter*, Nov. 26, 1959, p. A–11.

33. Ibid., p. C–5; *Honolulu Star-Bulletin*, March 29, 1974, p. 2. Others have served as state representatives: Emilio Alcon, Benjamin Cayetano, Oliver Lunasco, Rick Medina and Barney Menor. At the county level, Hawaiian Filipinos have been elected to leadership posts. Richard Caldito of Maui County in 1956 became the first Filipino to be elected to a Board of Supervisors. See *Honolulu Star-Bulletin*, Nov. 6, 1974, p. A–18; *Honolulu Advertiser*, Jan 6, 1975, p. B–1.

34. *Honolulu Star-Bulletin*, Nov. 6, 1974, p. A–18.

35. Ibid., Dec. 11, 1974, p. D–9; *Honolulu Advertiser*, Jan. 6, 1975, p. B–1.

36. *Honolulu Star-Bulletin*, Feb. 27, 1975, p. 22.

37. Benjamin Menor, pp. 48–51; *Honolulu Star-Bulletin*, April 14, 1974, p. D–2; April 15, 1974, p. 2; Feb. 27, 1975, p. 16.

38. *Honolulu Star-Bulletin*, March 29, 1974, p. 2.

39. Elisabeth H. Bell, "When Will the Filipino Become a Political Power?" *Honolulu*, IX (April 1975), 32–33, 54.

40. Felipe, "Hawaii, a Pilipino Dream," p. 35.

41. *Ka Leo O Hawaii* (Honolulu), April 21, 1972, p. 3; *Sunday Star-Bulletin & Advertiser*, Oct. 12, 1975, p. I–1.

42. *San Francisco Examiner & Chronicle*, "California Living," May 13, 1973, pp. 15–16.

43. Ibid.; *Honolulu Advertiser*, Dec. 12, 1969, p. A–6.

44. U. S. Immigration and Naturalization Service, *In-migration in Professional and Related Fields* (Washington, D. C., 1969), chart 3.

45. Munroz, p. 149. Americans were aware of the Philippine nurses following the mass strangulation of seven student nurses in Chicago in July 1966. See *Chicago Tribune*, July 14, 1966, p. 1; July 15, 1966, pp. 2, 8.

46. *San Francisco Examiner & Chronicle*, "California Living," Feb. 23, 1969, p. A–20; May 13, 1973, pp. 15–16.

47. *Honolulu Advertiser*, Nov. 22, 1971, pp. A–10–A–11.

48. Ibid.

49. *Honolulu Star-Bulletin*, Sept. 9, 1974, p. B–1.

50. Ibid., June 12, 1975, p. B–14; *Honolulu Advertiser*, Jan 11, 1971, p. A–3; Nov. 22, 1971, p. A–10—A–11; *Honolulu Star-Bulletin*, June 12, 1975, p. B–14.

Chapter VIII

1. Shannon McCune, *Korea's Heritage: a Regional & Social Geography* (Rutland, Vt.: Charles E. Tuttle Co., 1956), p. 4.

2. Clara H. Koenig, *The Republic of Korea* [Athens, Ohio: Association of Collegiate Registrars and Admissions Officers, 1958], pp. 1–2.

3. Ibid., pp. 3–5.

4. Ibid., pp. 5–6; McCune, pp. 13–15; Korea, Ministry of Culture and Information, *Facts about Korea* (Seoul, Korea, 1971), pp. 12–13.

5. McCune, pp. 17–22.

6. Koenig, p. 2.

7. McCune, pp. 67–68; *Facts about Korea*, pp. 15–16.

8. McCune, pp. 72–73.

9. Ibid., pp. 72–80; Koenig, p. 4; *Facts about Korea*, p. 21.

10. Woo-keun Han, *The History of Korea* (Honolulu: East-West Center Press, 1970), pp. 208–09; Koenig, pp. 2–3; McCune, p. 68.

11. *Facts about Korea*, pp. 26–27; McCune, p. 70.

12. *Facts about Korea*, pp. 27–28.

13. Ihan New, *When I Was a Boy in Korea* (Boston: Lothrop, Lee & Shepard Co., 1928), pp. 175–78; Mieko Wong Minn, "Hawaii's Little Orient," *Paradise of the Pacific*, LXIX (1957), 88.

14. Minn, p. 83.

15. New, pp. 126–27.

16. *Facts about Korea*, p. 30; McCune, p. 71.

17. *Facts about Korea*, pp. 115–16; McCune, pp. 74–75; Koenig, pp. 5–6.

18. Koenig, p. 5; *Facts about Korea*, pp. 117–19.

19. Han, pp. 354–57, 458, 471–72; *Facts about Korea*, p. 119.

20. Han, pp. 3–22; McCune, pp. 25–26; *Facts about Korea*, p. 33.

21. Han, pp. 111–19, 151–85.

22. McCune, pp. 27–39; *Facts about Korea*, pp. 35–39.

23. Han, pp. 475–78; Warren Kim, *Koreans in America* (Seoul: Op Chin Chui Printing Co., 1971), pp. 91–103.

24. *Facts about Korea*, pp. 41–44.

25. Ibid., pp. 47–48; 61–75; McCune, pp. 82–115.

26. *Facts about Korea*, pp. 47–50; *World Almanac, 1975*, pp. 548–49.

Chapter IX

1. Kim, *Koreans in America*, p. 3; Arthur L. Gardner, "So-Chae-P'il and the Tongnip Sinmun," M.A. thesis, Univ. of Hawaii, 1969, pp. 1–2; Hyung-Chan Kim, "Some Aspects of Social Demography of Korean Americans," *International Migration Review*, VIII (1974), 24, indicates that the first Koreans considered by the United States to be immigrants arrived in Hawaii on Jan. 15, 1900.

2. Han, pp. 463, 472, 474, 485; Kim, *Koreans in America*, pp. 3–4; Lee Houchins and Chang-su Houchins, "The Korean Experience in America," *Pacific Historical Review*, XLIII (1974), 549.

3. Wayne Patterson, Presentation, Korean Studies Seminar, Univ. of Hawaii, Honolulu, 1973.

4. Allen founded the first Western medical institution in Korea—Kwaghyewon Hospital—in 1885. He became United States Minister to Korea in 1897. See Han, p. 458, and U.S. Congress, *Congressional Directory*, 55 Cong., 2 sess. (1897), p. 263.

5. Korea, *Imperial Rules and Regulations of the Department of Emigration of the Empire of Korea* (Seoul, Nov. 16, 1902); Patterson presentation.

6. Houchins, p. 551.

7. Ibid., p. 552.

8. Ibid., pp. 552–53; Kim, *Koreans in America*, p. 10; Kim, "Aspects of Social Demography," p. 24.

9. *Honolulu Evening Bulletin*, Jan. 13, 1903, as quoted in *50 Years of Progress: Hawaii Korean Golden Jubilee Celebration* [Honolulu, 1953], pp. 8, 11, 13. There is some disagreement as to the number of emigrants from Korea to Hawaii in the first decade of the twentieth century. See Kim, *Koreans in America*, p. 10; Houchins, p. 553; Bernice Kim, "The Koreans in Hawaii," M.A. thesis, Univ. of Hawaii, 1937, p. 2.

10. Horace Allen to John Hay, Seoul, December 10, 1902; Horace Allen to Sanford Dole, Seoul, December 10, 1902, U.S. Department of State, *Despatches from United States Ministers to Korea, 1883–1905* (U.S. National Archives microfilm).

11. Kim, *Koreans in America*, pp. 10–11; Houchins, pp. 553–54.

12. Bernice Kim, "Koreans in Hawaii," *Social Science*, IX (1934), 409; Kim, *Koreans in America*, p. 11.

13. Kim, *Koreans in America*, pp. 14–20.

14. See Appendix A, Tables V & VI.

15. H. Brett Melendy, *Oriental Americans* (New York: Twayne Publishers, 1972), pp. 110–13, 203 n. 58, 59.

16. Houchins, p. 556.

17. Melendy, *Oriental Americans*, pp. 129–30.

18. Ibid., p. 205 n. 45.

19. Houchins, p. 559; Kim, *Koreans in America*, pp. 22–23.

20. Kim, "Koreans in Hawaii," M.A. thesis, p. 121.

21. Houchins, p. 558.

22. Korea, *Dr. Syngman Rhee the President of the Republic of Korea* (Seoul, [n.d.]), pp. 1–2; Robert Oliver, *Syngman Rhee* (New York: Dodd Mead, 1954), p. 126.

23. Houchins, p. 558.

24. Ibid.; Kim, *Koreans in America*, pp. 23–24.

25. Kim, *Koreans in America*, p. 24.

26. Ibid.

27. Ibid., p. 26; see Appendix A, Tables IV and V.

28. U.S. Immigration and Naturalization Service, *Annual Report, 1958*, p. 32.

29. Ibid., *1970*, pp. 59, 70; ibid., *1974*, p. 59.

30. Ibid., *1974*, p. 59; *Time*, July 5, 1976, p. 19.

31. See Appendix A, Table V; *Time*, July 5, 1976, p. 16.

Chapter X

1. Melendy, *Oriental Americans*, p. 105; Roger Daniels, *Politics of Prejudice* (Berkeley: Univ. of California Press, 1962), p. 27.

2. Herbert B. Johnson, *Restrictions of Japanese Immigration, A Reply* (San Francisco, n.p., 1905), pp. 2–4.

3. U.S. *Congressional Record*, 59 Cong., 1 sess. (1905), pp. 115, 568. McKinlay, Republican from San Francisco, introduced H.R. 3160 on Dec. 5 and Hayes, Republican from San Jose, introduced H.R. 8975 on Dec. 18, 1905.

4. Japanese and Korean Exclusion League, "Printed Form Letter," 1906, in "Japanese in California" pamphlet box, Bancroft Library, Univ. of California, Berkeley.

5. "San Francisco School Board Resolution Adopted March 13, 1907," U.S. State Dept. Numerical File 2542/48. Melendy, *Oriental Americans*, p. 106.

6. *San Francisco Chronicle*, Jan. 22, 1907, p. 4.

7. Japanese and Korean Exclusion League, *Minutes*, March 10, 1907, pp. 4–5. During 1907, Representative Burton L. French, a Republican from Moscow, Idaho, proposed that Japanese and Korean laborers be prohibited from entering the United States. See U.S. *Congressional Record*, 60 Cong., 1 sess. (1907), p. 3006.

8. Asiatic Exclusion League, *Proceedings*, Jan. 5, 1908, p. 20; May 10, 1908, p. 32.

9. *San Francisco Chronicle*, Feb. 1, 1910, p. 6.

10. U.S. *Congressional Record*, 62 Cong., 1 sess. (1911), p. 244; 63 Cong., 1 sess. (1913), p. 225; 62 Cong., 2 sess. (1911), p. 13; 64 Cong., 1 sess. (1915), p. 363.

11. "1912 State Democratic Platform," Hugh Bradford, "Scrapbook of Clippings," California Section, California State Library, Sacramento, California.

12. Kim, *Koreans in America*, pp. 55–56; Houchins, p. 561.

13. Telegram, David Lee, President, Korean National Association, to Wm. Jennings Bryan, June 30, 1913, U.S. State Dept. Decimal File 311.954 H37.

14. Memorandum, George H. Leidmore to Secretary of State, July 5, 1913, Seoul, Korea, Decimal File 811.52/186.

15. Kim, *Koreans in America*, p. 56; Houchins, p. 561.

16. See pp. 47–48; 264.

17. *Petition of Easurk Emsen Charr*, 273 Fed. 207.

18. *In re En Sk Song*, 271 Fed. 23.

19. Korean Chamber of Commerce, Los Angeles, *Korean Commerce & Industry Bulletin*, April, 1947. On Aug. 5, 1975, the Republic of Korea awarded posthumously the Order of Civil Merit Mugunghaw Medal to Joseph R. Farrington for "contributing to promoting Korean immigration into the United States through his consistent effort to bring about enactment of legislation which would amend United States immigration and naturalization laws to remove racial restrictions to Koreans." See *Honolulu Star-Bulletin*, Aug. 5, 1975, p. A–4.

20. U.S. *Congressional Record*, 79 Cong., 1 sess. (1945), pp. 671, 2077; 80 Cong., 1 sess. (1947), pp. 220, 306, 694; 80 Cong., 2 sess. (1948), p. A 3592.

21. Ibid., 81 Cong., 1 sess. (1949), pp. 17, 664, 792; 81 Cong., 2 sess. (1950), p. 11322.

22. *U.S. Statutes*, LXVI, 175, 177, 239.

23. *Nation*, CLXXI (Aug. 26, 1950), 179. In 1950, Helen Gahagen Douglas noted that House Joint Resolution 238 which had aimed at removing racial restrictions for 90,000 resident Japanese and Korean aliens which the House of Representatives adopted had been rejected by the Senate. See *Congressional Record*, 81 Cong., 2 sess. (1950), pp. A 1334–35.

24. See p. 53, *Deering's* [California] *Civil Code, 1945 Supplement* (San Francisco: Whitney-Bancroft Publishers, 1945), pp. 9–10; "A Digest of Marriage Laws," *The Commonweal*, March 16, 1945, pp. 536–37; *Perez v. Sharp*, 32 Calif., 2nd series, 711.

Chapter XI

1. Kim, "Koreans in Hawaii," pp. 136–37.

2. "Report of the Superintendent of Hawaiian Mission—Minutes, 1st Session of Hawaiian Mission of the Methodist Episcopal Church, Honolulu, Dec. 1903," as quoted in Kim, "Koreans in Hawaii," p. 139.

3. Kim, *Koreans in America*, pp. 32–33.

4. Samuel Sang Lee, ed., *50 Years of St. Luke's Church, Honolulu, Hawaii* [Honolulu: Paradise of the Pacific, 1957], pp. 3–21; Kim, *Koreans in America*, p. 33.

5. Kim, *Koreans in America*, pp. 33–34; *50 Years of Progress*, p. 39.

6. Kim, "Koreans in Hawaii," pp. 138, 147–48.

7. Ibid., pp. 140–42; Kim, *Koreans in America*, p. 42; Oliver, *Syngman Rhee*, pp. 122–23.

8. Kim, "Koreans in Hawaii," 142–43; Kim, *Koreans in America*, p. 43.

9. Kim, "Koreans in Hawaii," pp. 142–44; Kim, *Koreans in America*, p. 43; Oliver, *Syngman Rhee*, pp. 123–24.

10. *50 Years of Progress*, pp. 2, 40; Kim, *Koreans in America*, pp. 43–44.

11. *Korean Student Bulletin*, XIII (1935), 8.

12. Kim, "Koreans in Hawaii," pp. 196–97; Kim, *Koreans in America*, p. 44.

13. See Appendix A, Table VI.

14. Kim, *Koreans in America*, p. 34.

15. Ibid., pp. 36–37.

16. Helen L. Givens, "The Korean Community in Los Angeles County," M.A. thesis, Univ. of Southern California, 1939, p. 22.

17. Kim, *Koreans in America*, pp. 34–40.

18. Givens, pp. 30–31.

19. Kim, *Koreans in America*, pp. 25–27; *Korean Student Bulletin*, I (1922)–XIII (1935).

20. William C. Smith, "The Second Generation Oriental in America," preliminary paper prepared for Second General Session, Institute of Pacific Relations, July 15–29, 1927, Honolulu, p. 7.

21. *Korean Student Bulletin*, VIII (1930), 1, 5.

22. Kim, "Koreans in Hawaii," pp. 156–57.

23. The Korean Information and Educational Service of Hawaii published a bilingual magazine to promote the study of the Korean language and culture by Koreans of American ancestry. See Arthur L. Gardner, *The Koreans in Hawaii* (Honolulu: Social Science Institute, Univ. of Hawaii, 1972), pp. 11, 31 (hereafter cited as *Koreans*). In 1975, the Korean Community Council, a coalition of thirty Korean

organizations still strove to promote the Korean culture in Hawaii. See Multi-Cultural Center, *Hawaii Heritage News*, III (May, 1975), 1, 4.

24. *Bohk Dohng*, I (March 14, 1956), 8.
25. Interview with Paul Chun, Asian American Drug Abuse Program, Los Angeles County, Los Angeles, Nov. 11, 1974; interview with Rev. San Bom Woo, Korean United Presbyterian Church, Los Angeles, Nov. 11, 1974.

Chapter XII

1. Kim, *Koreans in America*, pp. 46–47, 50–51.
2. Ibid., pp. 49–50, 52.
3. Houchins, p. 558.
4. Ibid., p. 557; Kim, *Koreans in America*, pp. 80–81.
5. Kim, *Koreans in America*, pp. 81–82.
6. Ibid., pp. 83–84.
7. Ibid., pp. 52–55.
8. Ibid., p. 47; Kim, "Koreans in Hawaii," p. 126; Gardner, pp. 36–37, 52.
9. Kim, *Koreans in America*, p. 87. A special census reported that in 1915 there were eight Korean males in Hastings, Nebr. See U.S. Bureau of Census, *Special Census of Population of Hastings, Nebraska, Dec. 13, 1915*, pp. 5–6.
10. Kim, *Koreans in America*, pp. 58, 87–88.
11. Ibid., pp. 58–59; Oliver, *Syngman Rhee*, p. 122; Korea, *Dr. Syngman Rhee*, p. 4.
12. Gardner, *Koreans*, p. 76; Kim, *Koreans in America*, pp. 58–59; Kim, "Koreans in Hawaii," pp. 129–31.
13. Houchins, "Korean Experience," p. 565.
14. Oliver, *Syngman Rhee*, p. 126; Houchins, p. 567.
15. Oliver, *Syngman Rhee*, pp. 127–28; Houchins, pp. 567–68.
16. *New York Times*, March 9, 1919.
17. Houchins, pp. 570–75; Kim, *Koreans in America*, pp. 98–111.
18. Kim, *Koreans in America*, pp. 121–22.
19. *Korean Student Bulletin*, III (1925), 2; Gardner, "So Chae-P'il and the Tongnip Sinmun," pp. 2–3.
20. Houchins, pp. 572–73; Oliver, Syngman Rhee, p. 147.
21. Gardner, *Koreans*, p. 56; Kim, *Koreans in America*, p. 63. In 1975, South Korean consulates and embassies were experiencing protests from various groups relative to the Park government. In Honolulu, few Koreans participated in any demonstrations. Activists in Seoul explained this lack of interest: "Honolulu [was] a rather quiet

place where the Koreans spent much of their energy fighting among themselves." See *Honolulu Star-Bulletin*, Aug. 3, 1975, p. B–2.

22. Gardner, *Koreans*, p. 56; Kim, *Koreans in America*, pp. 63–64.

23. Gardner, *Koreans*, pp. 36–37; Kim, *Koreans in America*, pp. 63–64.

24. Kingsley K. Lyu, "Korean Nationalistic Activities in the United States and Hawaii," Document 4, Lyu Collection, Hawaiian Collection, Univ. of Hawaii Library; Gardner, *Koreans*, pp. 34–35; Kim, *Koreans in America*, pp. 64–65.

25. Kim, *Koreans in America*, p. 66; Givens, "Korean Community in Los Angeles," p. 47.

26. *Korean Pacific Weekly* (Honolulu), Sept. 16, 1944, p. 1.

27. *70th Anniversary Celebration of Korean Immigration to Hawaii* [Honolulu, 1973], p. 3 .

28. Kim, *Koreans in America,* pp. 60–61; Givens, "Korean Community in Los Angeles," pp. 40–46.

29. Eubank, "Effects . . . World War II on . . . Koreans and Filipinos. . . ." pp. 40–41.

30. *Seattle Post-Intelligencer*, Feb. 19, 1942, as quoted in Eubank, p. 41.

31. Eubank, pp. 44, 94–96; Kim, *Koreans in America*, pp. 69, 137; Morton Grodzins, *Americans Betrayed: Politics and the Japanese Evacuation* (Chicago: Univ. of Chicago Press, 1949), pp. 48, 50–54; *Grizzly Bear* (Los Angeles) LXXII (Feb. 1942), 48–54.

32. Kim, *Koreans in America*, p. 144.

33. Eubank, p. 70.

34. Hawaii, Office of Military Governor, General Orders No. 5, Dec. 8, 1941.

35. *Korean National Herald-Pacific Weekly* (Honolulu), Feb. 25, 1942, as quoted in Eubank.

36. *San Francisco Chronicle*, Dec. 29, 1941, p. 2.

37. Kim, *Koreans in America*, p. 140.

38. *Time*, Feb. 2, 1942, p. 21; Eubank, pp. 75–76.

39. Eubank, pp. 84–87.

40. Lyu Collection, Univ. of Hawaii Library, Document 17.

41. Gardner, "So-Chae-P'il and the Tongnip Sinmun," p. 3.

Chapter XIII

1. Morris Pang, "A Korean Immigrant," *Social Process*, XIII (1949), p. 19; Kim, "Koreans in Hawaii," p. 81.

2. Kim, "Koreans in Hawaii," p. 87.

3. Ibid., p. 101.

4. Pang, p. 21.

5. Kim, "Koreans in Hawaii," p. 104.

6. Kim, *Koreans in America*, p. 12.

7. Kim, "Koreans in Hawaii," pp. 105–07.

8. Ibid., pp. 113–14.

9. *Star-Bulletin & Advertiser* (Honolulu), Jan. 7, 1973, p. C–1.

10. Kim, "Koreans in Hawaii," p. 108.

11. Ibid., p. 110.

12. Ibid., p. 111.

13. Ibid., p. 110.

14. Ibid., p. 102.

15. Ivers, "Statement on Immigration," Honolulu, 1909.

16. Lind, *Hawaii's People*, pp. 76–78; *Bohk Dohng* (Honolulu), April 29, 1956, p. 3; Houchins, pp. 562–63; see Appendix A, Tables V, VI.

17. Reinecke, "The Big Lie of 1920"; Kim, "Koreans in Hawaii," p. 170.

18. Kim, "Koreans in Hawaii," p. 171.

19. *Bohk Dohng*, April 29, 1956, p. 3; Kim, "Koreans in Hawaii," pp. 158–63.

20. Kim "Koreans in Hawaii," pp. 173–77.

21. Territory of Hawaii, Bureau of Immigration, Labor and Statistics, *First Report, 1912; Second Report, 1913; Third Report, 1914; Fourth Report, 1915; Fifth Report, 1916.*

22. Houchins, p. 555. Successful vegetable farms in Oregon and a 292-acre melon farm near Logan, Utah, have been reported. See Houchins, p. 563; Kim, *Koreans in America*, p. 27.

23. Dale White, "Koreans in Montana," *Asia and America*, XLV (1946), 156.

24. Ichihashi, *Japanese in the United States*, p. 154; Lasker, *Filipino Immigration*, pp. 356–57.

25. Kim, "Koreans in Hawaii," pp. 167–68.

26. Japanese and Korean Exclusion League, *Minutes*, Jan 1, 1907, p. 16.

27. U.S. Immigration Commission, *Agriculture*, I, 62; II, 31; *Immigrants in Industry*, XXIV, 18. See Taylor, *Mexican Labor . . .*, p. 7. A major Imperial Valley agriculturalist employed some Koreans in 1914 but they did not become a permanent part of the valley's seasonal labor force.

28. Melendy, *Oriental Americans*, pp. 138–39; Houchins, p. 563.

29. Melendy, pp. 138–39; Joseph McGowan, *History of Sacramento Valley* (New York: Lewis Publishing Co., 1961), II, 202. Rice

sold per one hundred pounds at $2.75 in 1916; $4.51 in 1917; $4.95 in 1918; and $5.62 in 1919.

30. Houchins, p. 563; Kim, *Koreans in America*, p. 27.

31. Kim, *Koreans in America*, p. 26.

32. Givens, pp. 34–35.

33. Ibid., pp. 30–33.

34. Ibid., p. 35.

35. Younghill Kang, "Oriental Yankee," *Common Ground* I (1941), 59–63.

36. Richard E. Kim, *The Innocent* (New York: Ballantine Books, [1969]); *The Martyred* (New York: G. Braziller, [1964]); *Lost Names* (New York: Praeger, 1970).

37. *Honolulu Advertiser*, June 27, 1962, p. 5; *New York Times*, Aug. 6, 1948, p. 11; Aug. 3, 1952, p. V–3.

38. Korean Chamber of Commerce [Los Angeles], *Korean Commerce & Industry Bulletin*, I (Nov. 1, 1946), 1; Robert C. Schmitt, "Hawaii's Koreans, 1960," *Korean Bulletin of Hawaii*, Autumn Issue, 1960, [p. 21].

39. *70th Anniversary . . . Korean Immigration*, p. 7.

40. *Honolulu Star-Bulletin*, July 11, 1975, p. D–3.

41. *Honolulu Advertiser*, Jan. 12, 1967, p. A–10; *Los Angeles Times*, Nov. 4, 1974, p. 25.

42. *Honolulu Star-Bulletin*, May 11, 1966, p. 1.

43. *Honolulu Advertiser*, April 2, 1961, p. 8; Dec. 9, 1967, p. 1.

44. Ibid., June 13, 1957, p. 1; June 2, 1971, p. A–9; *70th Anniversary . . . Korean Immigration*, p. 6.

45. U.S. Dept. of Justice, Immigration and Naturalization Service, "Inmigration in Professional and Related Fields, Fiscal 1969."

46. Interview with Paul Chun, Los Angeles, Nov. 11, 1974.

47. *Honolulu Advertiser*, Nov. 28, 1973, p. B–1.

48. *Sunday Star-Bulletin & Advertiser*, pp. C–1 & C–7.

49. *Honolulu Star-Bulletin*, Sept. 10, 1973, p. B–1; Calif. Dept. of Industrial Relations, *Californians . . . Filipino Ancestry*, p. 180.

Chapter XIV

1. *World Almanac & Book of Facts, 1975* (New York: Newspaper Enterprise Association, 1974), pp. 144, 513, 540, 559.

2. H. G. Rawlinson, *India, a Short Cultural History*, rev. ed. (London, Cresset Press, 1952), p. 4.

3. Ibid., pp. 5–7; Times (London), *Times Atlas of the World* (Boston: Houghton Mifflin, 1967), plates 4, 5, 31.

4. Rawlinson, pp. 5–7; *Times Atlas*, plates 4, 5, 29.

5. Rawlinson, pp. 6–7; *Times Atlas*, plates 4, 5, 28.

6. Rawlinson, pp. 9–18.

7. Ibid., pp. 19–38.

8. Ibid., pp. 56–81.

9. Ibid., p. 25.

10. Ibid., p. 26.

11. Louis Renou, ed., *Hinduism* (New York: George Braziller, 1962), pp. 15–57.

12. L. S. Stavrianos, *The World to 1500* (Englewood Cliffs, New Jersey: Prentice-Hall, Inc. 1970), pp. 152–53.

13. Rawlinson, p. 46.

14. Stavrianos, p. 106.

15. Rawlinson, pp. 199–264.

16. Ibid., pp. 297–357.

17. *World Almanac, 1975*, pp. 513–14; 540–41; 559–60.

18. In the 1970's, it has been estimated that India had 453.2 million Hindus, 61.4 million Muslims, 14.2 million Christians, 10.3 million Sikhs, 3.8 million Buddhists, and 2.6 million Jainists. See *World Almanac, 1975*, p. 541.

19. Rawlinson, pp. 377–83.

Chapter XV

1. All immigrants to the U.S. from India are called East Indians in this book, regardless of whether they are Indians, Pakistani, or from Bengladesh.

2. Paul Knaplund, *The British Empire 1815–1939* (New York: Harper & Bros., 1941), pp. 244–45, 253, 271.

3. Chandra I. Jayawardena, "Migration and Social Change: A Survey of East Indian Communities Overseas," *Geographical Review*, LVIII (1968), 428–29; James F. Abbott, *Japanese Expansion and American Policies* (New York: Macmillan Co., 1916), pp. 146–56.

4. Girindra Mukerji, "The Hindu in America," *Overland Monthly* LI (April 1908), 312–13.

5. Ibid., 311; "The Hindu in America," *American Review of Reviews*, XXXVII (May 1908), 604.

6. Rajani Kanta Das, *Hindustani Workers on the Pacific Coast* (Berlin: Walter De Gruyter & Co., 1923), p. 1; Gurdial Singh, "East Indians in the United States," *Sociology and Social Research*, XXX (1945–46), 208.

7. Das, p. 10.

8. Ibid., 7–8; Harold S. Jacoby, *A Half-Century Appraisal of East Indians in the United States* (Stockton, Calif.: College of the

Pacific, 1956), p. 7; Saint N. Singh, "Asiatic Immigration: A World Question," *Living Age*, CCLXXXII (1914), 390; E. M. Wherry, "Hindu Immigrants in America," *Missionary Review of the World*, XXX (1907), 618; Gary R. Hess, "The Forgotten Asian Americans: The East Indian Community in the United States," *Pacific Historical Review*, XLIII (1974), 578.

9. U.S. Immigration Commission, *Dictionary of Races or Peoples*, 61 Cong., 3 sess. (1911), pp. 52–54, 75–76. The commission, important in the evolution of a U.S. immigration policy, was comprised of three senators, three representatives, and three presidential appointees. The bulk of the work was researched by its staff. The commission produced 42 volumes, released in 1911. While proclaimed as a scientific approach to the problem, it reflected the growing view that immigration restriction was needed as well as a literacy test. See Robert Divine, *American Immigration Policy, 1924–1952* (New Haven: Yale Univ. Press, 1957).

10. Memoranda regarding Hindus in the United States, Jan. 23, 1914, U.S. Dept. of Commerce and Labor, Bureau of Immigration and Naturalization File No. 52903/11B (hereafter cited as BIN). Das, pp. 9–12; see Appendix A, Table VII.

11. Gurdial Singh, pp. 208–09; Das, p. 3; Nand Singh Sihra, "Indians in Canada," *Modern Review*, XIII (1914), 140–49.

12. Mukerji, p. 12; William L. MacKenzie King, *Report on Mission to England to confer with the British Authorities on the subject of Immigration to Canada from the Orient, and Immigration from India in Particular*, 7–8 Edward VII (1908), p. 8.

13. Das, pp. 6–7.

14. Sushil Kumar Jain, "East Indians in Canada," *Research Group for European Migration Problems Bulletin* [The Hague, P. H. Klop], June 1971, p. 3.

15. Charles Young and Helen Reid, *The Japanese Canadians* (Toronto: Univ. of Toronto Press, 1938), pp. xx–xxii, 7–8; K. K. Kawakami, "Canada as a 'White Man's Country,'" *Current History*, XIX (1923–24), 829–32.

16. R. Brown, "White Canada," *Harper's Weekly*, LI (1907), 1447.

17. Saint N. Singh, "The Picturesque Immigrant from India's Coral Strand," *Out West*, XXX (1909), 43–44.

18. Sihra, pp. 144–46.

19. King, pp. 8–9; Das, pp. 8–9; Hess, "East Indian Community," pp. 578–79.

20. *Literary Digest,* July 18, 1914, pp. 95–96; *Outlook,* CVII (1914), 824–25; *Living Age,* CCLXXXII (1914), 310–12.

21. Tien-Fang Cheng, *Oriental Immigration in Canada* (Shanghai, China: Commercial Press, Ltd., 1931), pp. 156–57; Jain, p. 6.

Chapter XVI

1. Samuel Gompers, *Meat vs. Rice: American Manhood against Asiatic Coolieism* (San Francisco: Asiatic Exclusion League, 1908), p. 17.

2. *Outlook,* LXXXVII (Sept. 14, 1907), 51–52; Robert E. Wynne, "Labor Leaders and the Vancouver Anti-Oriental Riot," *Pacific Northwest Quarterly,* LXVII (1966), 174.

3. James Bryce to Alvey A. Adee, Sept. 12, 1907; telegram, Adee to Albert E. Mead, Sept. 16, 1907; telegram, Mead to Adee, Sept. 19, 1907, U.S. State Dept. Numerical File 8497/1. Hereafter cited as Numerical File.

4. *Outlook,* LXXXVII (Sept. 21, 1907), 89; Wynne, pp. 172, 176–77.

5. Asiatic Exclusion League, *Proceedings,* Sept. 20, 1908, p. 12.

6. Ibid.

7. Charles Reed, U.S. Marshal to Attorney General, March 26, 1910, Numerical File 24041/5.

8. James Bryce to Philander Knox, Numerical File 24041.

9. *Sacramento Bee,* Jan. 27, 1908, p. 7; *San Francisco Examiner,* Dec. 6, 1911, p. 1.

10. Asiatic Exclusion League, *Proceedings,* Feb. 16, 1908, pp. 8–10.

11. U.S. Immigration Commission, *Immigrants in Industry,* II, 198.

12. *San Francisco Chronicle,* Sept. 29, 1910, p. 1; *Survey,* Oct. 1, 1910, pp. 2–3; Gary R. Hess, "The 'Hindu' in America: Immigration and Naturalization Policies and India, 1917–1946," *Pacific Historical Review,* XXXVIII (1969), 62–63.

13. *Survey,* Oct. 1, 1910, p. 3.

14. California Board of Control, *California and the Oriental: Japanese, Chinese and Hindus* (Sacramento, 1920), pp. 101–102.

15. Emory S. Bogardus, *Immigration and Race Relations* (Boston: D.C. Heath, 1928), pp. 53–63.

16. Saint N. Singh, "Asiatic Immigration," pp. 391–92.

17. Herman Scheffauer, "The Tide of Turbans," *Forum,* XLIII (Jan.–Jun. 1910), 616.

18. Agnes F. Buchanan, "The West and the Hindu Invasion," *Overland Monthly,* LI (1908), 313.

19. Asiatic Exclusion League, *Proceedings,* Jan 16, 1910, pp. 5–9.

20. U.S. *Congressional Record*, 62 Cong., 1 sess. (1911), p. 244; 62 Cong., 2 sess. (1912), p. 13; 63 Cong., 1 sess. (1913), p. 225; 64 Cong., 1 sess. (1916), p. 363. See Chapter X, The Korean Struggle for American Citizenship, pp. 132–33.

21. Peter T. Conmy, *The History of California's Japanese Problem and the Part Played by the Native Sons of the Golden West in its Solutions* (Oakland, n. p., 1942), p. 3.

22. *New York Times*, June 20, 1913, p. 5; *San Francisco Examiner*, Dec. 6, 1913, p. 3; Dec. 7, 1913, p. 68. In 1916, the U.S. Supreme Court agreed to review the case after the circuit court upheld federal district judge Maurice T. Dooling. Judge Dooling in February, 1917, announced that his 1913 decision was in error. In theory, this made it possible for East Indians living in the Philippines to apply for entry. See *San Francisco Examiner*, Nov. 7, 1916, p. 7; Feb. 22, 1917, p. 4.

23. U.S. Commissioner General of Immigration, *Annual Report, 1913–14*, pp. 305–06.

24. Das, *Hindustani Workers . . .*, p. 18; *Congressional Record*, 63 Cong., 2 sess. (1914), pp. 4886, 5339; *San Francisco Examiner*, Jan. 24, 1914, p. 1; Feb. 14, 1914, p. 1. Caminetti's attacks gained considerable support from various elements on the Pacific Coast. See BIN File 52903/110B and Numerical File 811.52/37.

25. U.S. House, Committee on Immigration, "Hearings Relative to Restriction of Immigration of Hindu Laborers," 63 Cong., 2 sess. (1914), pp. 45–46.

26. Hess, "Hindu in America," pp. 63, 74, 90–92.

27. *U.S. Statutes at Large*, XXXIX, 874; John Higham, *Strangers in the Land* (New York: Atheneum, 1963), pp. 202–04.

28. Sudhindra Bose, "Asian Immigration to the United States," *Modern Review* (Calcutta), XXV (1919), 523.

29. U.S. Commissioner General of Immigration, *Annual Report, 1918–19*, pp. 59–60.

30. U.S. *Congressional Record*, 66 Cong., 1 sess. (1919), 7406–07.

Chapter XVII

1. U.S. Immigration Commission, *Immigrants in Industry*, I, 325–26.

2. H. A. Millis, "East Indian Immigration to British Columbia and the Pacific Coast States," *American Economic Review*, I (1911), 74. In 1906, only 24 were refused admission; in 1907 and 1908, the numbers rejected were 417 and 438. Between 1909 and 1914, 3,161 Indians were admitted while 2,087 were debarred. See Das, pp. 9–11 and BIN File 52903/110B.

Notes and References   289

3. Hess, "East Indian Community," p. 580; *Collier's*, March 26, 1910, p. 15.

4. "Directive to Commissioner of Immigration, San Francisco, April 27, 1910," BIN File 52903/110.

5. Hess, "East Indian Community," p. 580.

6. William R. Wheeler to Charles P. Neil, Commissioner of Labor, August 11, 1910," BIN File 52903/110.

7. Report, William H. Michael to State Department, August 11, 1910, Calcutta, BIN File 52903/110. Michael, writing on September 1, 1910, reported that the more stringent screening at Pacific ports was having its effect in India. He urged the continuation of a tight admission program. See Wm. H. Michael to Asst. Sec. of State, September 1, 1910, BIN File 52903/110.

8. Daniel Keefe to Commissioners of Immigration, El Paso, Honolulu, Montreal, San Francisco, and Seattle, BIN File 52903/110.

9. Samuel Bond to Charles Nagel, Secretary of Commerce and Labor, September 27, 1910; clipping, *San Francisco Examiner*, September 28, 1910; Keefe to Bond, October 6, 1910, BIN File 52903/110.

10. H. A. Millis, East Indian Immigration to the Pacific Coast," *Survey*, XXVIII (1912), 381.

11. Hess, "East Indian Community," p. 582.

12. U.S. Census, *Population, 1930*, VII, 58–59; see Appendix A, Tables VII, VIII; Calif. Board of Control, *California and the Oriental*, p. 26; U.S. Immigration Commission, *Report on Japanese and East Indians on the Pacific Coast*, p. 325. Das reported that there were 5,424 East Indians in the continental U.S. in 1910 and 362 in Hawaii. California with 2,742 and Washington with 1,414 were reported to have had the largest population. See Das, *Hindustani Workers ...*, p. 17.

13. Territory of Hawaii, Bureau of Immigration, Labor and Statistics, *First Report, 1912; Second Report, 1913; Fourth Report 1915; Fifth Report, 1916*.

14. Asiatic Exclusion League, *Proceedings*, February 16, 1910, p. 9.

15. Das, *Hindustani Workers ...*, pp. 18–21; Gurdial Singh, pp. 208, 214; "Hindu in America," *American Review of Reviews*, pp. 604–05; U.S. Immigration Commission, *Immigrants in Industry*, I, 325–30.

16. U.S. Census, *Population, 1930*, VII, 58–59; see Appendix A, Tables VII, VIII.

17. Report, Avra M. Warren, Consul, Karachi, India, Oct. 16, 1923, Decimal File 845.56/4.

18. Jacoby, A Half-Century Appraisal, pp. 7–8; Hess, "East Indian Community," p. 590; San Francisco Examiner, Aug. 28, 1928, p. 3; San Francisco Chronicle, April 24, 1933, p. 4; Feb. 19, 1940, p. 5; Lawrence A. Wenzel, "The Rural Punjabis of California," Phylon, XXIX (1968), 250.

19. See Appendix A, Tables VII, VIII, IX.

20. U.S. Congressional Records, 78 Cong., 2 sess. (1944), pp. 4415, 4479.

21. Hess, "Hindu in America," pp. 73–75.

22. Ibid., pp. 75–79.

23. Wenzel, p. 251; Jacoby A Half-Century Appraisal, p. 9; Hess, "East Indian Community," pp. 592–95; U.S. Immigration and Naturalization Service, Annual Report, 1957, p. 37; 1961, p. 43; 1970, p. 64.

24. Jacoby, A Half-Century Appraisal, p. 10.

25. See Appendix A, Table VII.

26. Ibid.

27. Jacoby, A Half-Century Appraisal, p. 11.

28. See Appendix A, Table VIII.

29. Hess, "East Indian Communities," p. 595.

30. U.S. Immigration and Naturalization Service, Annual Report, 1971, p. 54; 1974, pp. 3, 59.

Chapter XVIII

1. San Francisco Chronicle, Jan. 31, 1926, pp. 1F–2F.

2. Hess, "East Indian Community," p. 585; Kalyan K. Banerjee, Indian Freedom Movement Revolutionaries in America (Calcutta: Jijnasa, 1969), p. 8; Emily C. Brown, Har Dayal: Revolutionary and Rationalist (Tucson: Univ. of Arizona Press, 1975), p. 128.

4. Brown, pp. 111–12; 140–48; Banerjee, p. 9; Hess, "East Indian Community," p. 585. During the McCarthy era of the 1950's, the "seventh annual report on un-American activities in California found Ghadr to mean 'traitor.'" Seen Banerjee, p. 9.

5. Giles T. Brown, "The Hindu Conspiracy, 1914–1917," Pacific Historical Review, XVII (1948), 299–300; Mark Naidis, "Propagada of the Gadar Party," Pacific Historical Review, XX (1957), 252.

6. Don K. Dignan, "The Hindu Conspiracy in Anglo-American Relations during World War I," Pacific Historical Review, XL (1971), 61–62.

7. *San Francisco Examiner,* Dec. 20, 1917, p. 3.

8. Giles Brown, p. 300; Hess, "East Indian Community," p. 586. In 1917, Nawab Khan revealed in the San Francisco conspiracy trial that Jawala Singh, who had been a wealthy Sikh in the Stockton area, had established five scholarships at the University of California to prepare students as Indian revolutionaries. See *San Francisco Examiner,* Dec. 20, 1917, p. 1, and Emil Brown, *Har Dayal,* pp. 127–28.

9. Dignan, p. 73; Hess, "East Indian Community," p. 587.

10. Giles Brown, pp. 308–10; Hess, "East Indian Community," p. 586.

11. Dignan, pp. 75–76; Naidis, pp. 251, 254.

12. Sailendra Nath Ghose, "Deportation of Hindu Politicals," *Dial,* LXVII (Aug. 23, 1919), 45–47; Robert Lovett, "U.S. and India," *New Republic,* LXVI (April 1, 1931), 175–76; Alan Raucher, "American Anti-Imperialists and the Pro-India Movement, 1900–1932," *Pacific Historical Review,* XLIII (1974), 91.

13. Raucher, p. 96; U.S. Senate, Committee on Immigration, "Hearings . . . Ratification . . . Naturalization of certain persons of the Hindu Race," 69 Cong., 2 sess. (1926), p. 24.

14. Raucher, pp. 91–95; Hess, "East Indian Community," p. 587; Naeen Gul Rathore, "Indian Nationalist Agitation in the United States: A Study of Lala Lajpat Rai and the Indian Home Rule League of America, 1914–1920," Ph.D. dissertation, Columbia Univ., 1965, p. 45.

15. Dignan, p. 75.

16. Hess, "East Indian Community," pp. 587–88.

17. Raucher, pp. 96–100.

18. Hess, "Hindu in America," pp. 73–75; Hess, "East Indian Community," pp. 591–92.

19. Hess, "Hindu in America," p. 74.

Chapter XIX

1. An example of this unfairness can be seen in the restrictive covenant developed by real estate agents of Port Angeles, Washington, in January, 1913. See Joan M. Jensen, "Apartheid: Pacific Coast Style," *Pacific Historical Review,* XXXVIII (1969), 335–40.

2. Harold S. Jacoby, "More Thind against than Sinning," *Pacific Historian,* II (1958), 5; Saint N. Singh, "Picturesque Immigrant . . . ," pp. 49–50. On March 20, 1908, Abdul Hamid and Bellal Houssain received their citizenship in the New Orleans district court. In February, 1909, Abdul G. Mondul was admitted in the Galveston, Texas,

court and on May 14, 1909, Abba Dolla was granted citizenship in Savannah, Georgia, See U.S. Senate, Committee on Immigration, "Ratification and Confirmation of Naturalization of Certain Persons of the Hindu Race," 69 Cong., 2 sess. (1926), p. 1.

3. *Second Decennial Digest of the American Digest, 1906–1916* (St. Paul: West Pub. Co., 1917–23), I, 680.

4. *In re Balsara,* 171 Fed. 294; *United States v. Balsara,* 180 Fed. 103; Taraknath Das, "Stateless Persons in U.S.A.," *Calcutta Review,* 3rd series, XVI (1925), 40.

5. *Second Decennial Digest,* I, 681; *In re Akhay Kumar Mozumdar,* 207 Fed. 115; Das, "Stateless Persons," p. 41; *India Review* (Madras), XIV (1913), 520.

6. U.S. Senate, Committee on Immigration, "Ratification . . . of Certain Persons . . . , 69 Cong., 2 sess. (1926), p. 5.

7. Das, "Stateless Persons," p. 41.

8. *In re Sadar Bhagwab Singh,* 246 Fed. 496; *In re Mohan Singh,* 257 Fed. 209.

9. Melendy, *Oriental Americans,* p. 150.

10. *Ozawa v. United States,* 260 U.S. 189.

11. *In re Bhagat Singh Thind,* 268 Fed. 683.

12. *United States v. Bhagat Singh Thind,* 261 U.S. 204.

13. Ray E. Chase and S[akharan] G. Pandit, *An Examination of the Opinion of the Supreme Court of the United States deciding against the Eligibility of Hindus for Citizenship* (Los Angeles, 1926), 11; *Modern Review,* XXXIII (1923), 770.

14. U.S. Senate, Committee on Immigration, "Ratification . . . of Certain Persons . . . ," 69 Cong., 2 sess. (1926), pp. 6–7; *United States v. Ahkay Kumar Mozumdar* 296 Fed. 173; *Ahkay Kumar Mozumdar v. United States* 299 Fed. 240.

15. U.S. Senate, Committee on Immigration, 69 Cong., 2 sess. (1926), p. 2; Hess, "Hindu in America," pp. 70–71.

16. U.S. Senate, Committee on Immigration, 69 Cong., 2 sess. (1926), pp. 17–19, 43–45; Hess, "Hindu in America," p. 70.

17. U.S. Senate, Committee on Immigration, 69 Cong., 2 sess. (1926), pp. 10–12; J. W. Garner, "Denationalization of American Citizens," *American Journal of International Law,* XXI (1927), 106–107; Jacoby, "More Thind against," p. 7.

18. *United States v. Ali,* 7 Fed. 2nd, 728; *United States v. Ali,* 20 Fed. 2nd, 998; *United States v. Gokhale,* 26 Fed. 2nd, 360; *Gokhale v. United States,* 278 U.S. 662.

19. Melendy, *Oriental Americans,* pp. 119–23.

20. *Literary Digest,* March 10, 1923, p. 13.

21. Calif. Board of Control, *California and the Oriental,* pp. 47, 181.

22. U.S. Dept of State, *Papers Relating to Foreign Relations of the United States, 1924,* II, 252–59; Esme Howard to Charles Evans Hughes, June 2, 1924, U.S. State Dept. Decimal File 811.5245/6. Hereafter cited as Decimal File.

23. Charles Evans Hughes to Friend Richardson, August 16, 1924, Decimal File 811.5245/7; Richardson to Hughes, September 5, 1924, Decimal File 811.5245/10.

24. Letters and telegrams to State Department regarding rights of "Hindus" to own land, Decimal File 811.5245/11–18; Sacramento County District Attorney J. J. Henderson to State Dept., December 15, 1923, Decimal File 811.5245/3.

25. Gurdial Singh, p. 213; D. P. Panda and Mme. Kamaldevi, "Justice for Hindus in America," *Christian Century,* LVII (March 13, 1940), 357.

26. Hess, "Hindu in America," p. 68. Following the Thind case, American missionaries expressed concern about the treatment of Indian nationals in the United States. Basically, their concern was for their own efforts which were now jeopardized. See Fred B. Fisher, Methodist Church of South Asia, Calcutta, to Charles Evans Hughes, August 11, 1923, Decimal File 811.5245/1; *Nation,* CXVII (July 17, 1923), 447.

27. Stephen N. Hay, "Rabindranath Tagore in America," *American Quarterly,* XIV (1962), 457–58; L. Natarajan, *American Shadow over India* (Bombay: People's Publishing House, Ltd., 1952), p. 18.

28. Panda and Kamaldevi, p. 357; *San Francisco Chronicle,* Feb. 6, 1935, p. 2; U.S. *Congressional Record,* 75 Cong., 1 sess. (1937), p. 7165.

29. U.S. *Congressional Record,* 76 Cong., 1 sess. (1939), p. 8799.

30. Panda and Kamaldevi, p. 357.

31. U.S. House, Committee on Immigration and Naturalization, "Petitions by Natives of India for Legislation to include Natives of India Now Residing in the United States as Eligible to Naturalization," 76 Cong., 1 sess. (1939), pp. 15–16.

32. *Grizzly Bear,* LXV, (Sept. 1939), 19.

33. Hess "Hindu in America," p. 72; "Letters to Editors—Naturalization for Hindus," *Nation,* CLI (No. 23, 1940), 516.

34. Hess, "East Indian Community," p. 595.

Chapter XX

1. S. Chandrasekhar, "Indian Immigration in America," *Far Eastern Survey,* XIII (1944), 138–9; Saint N. Singh, "Picturesque Immigrant," p. 47.

2. *Victoria Daily Times* as quoted in Sihra, "Indians in Canada," p. 141.

3. Chandrasekhar, p. 139.

4. Nand Singh Sihra, Balwant Singh, and Narain Singh, "Indians in Canada," *Indian Review*, XIV (June, 1913), 453.

5. British Columbia, Legislative Assembly, *Journal*, 1927, p. 16; Das, *Hindustani Workers*, pp. 20–21.

6. Jain, "East Indians in Canada," p. 6.

7. Chandrasekhar, p. 147; Das, *Hindustani Workers*, p. 17.

8. *Tentative Findings of the Survey of Race Relations: a Canadian-American Study of the Oriental on the Pacific Coast* (Stanford Univ., 1925), p. 13.

9. Das, *Hindustani Workers*, p. 26; U.S. Immigration Commission, *Immigrants in Industry*, I, 323–33.

10. Asiatic Exclusion League, *Proceedings*, Feb. 16, 1908, p. 9.

11. Ibid.; U.S. Immigration Commission, *Immigrants in Industry*, I, 3, 336.

12. Asiatic Exclusion League, *Proceedings*, Feb. 16, 1908, p. 9; McGowan, II, 48, 140.

13. Chandrasekhar, p. 147.

14. U.S. Immigration Commission, *Immigrants in Industry*, I, 62, 87; II, 110.

15. Millis, "East Indian Immigration," *Survey*, p. 384; Das, *Hindustani Workers*, p. 35.

16. U.S. House, Committee on Immigration, Hearings . . . Restriction of Immigration of Hindu Laborers," 63 Cong., 2 sess. (1914), p. 6.

17. U.S. Immigration Commission, *Immigrants in Industry*, I, 337; II, 419–20.

18. Interview by James Wood with Mr. Cook, Bridge Land and Navigation Co. [1930], James E. Wood Collection, Bancroft Library.

19. Das, pp. 25–26.

20. Calif. Board of Control, *California and the Oriental*, p. 20.

21. Ibid., p. 47; Das, pp. 23–25; Chandrasekhar, p. 149.

22. Calif. Board of Control, *California and the Oriental*, p. 48.

23. Chandrasekhar, p. 149.

24. Calif. Board of Control, *California and the Oriental*, p. 48; Das, pp. 18, 22.

25. Das, p. 18.

26. Chandrasekhar, p. 149; Taylor, *Mexican Labor . . .* , pp. 19–20; Das, p. 96.

27. Gurdial Singh, "East Indians in the United States," p. 214.

28. Theodore Fieldbrave, "East Indians in the United States," *Missionary Review of the World*, LVII (1934), 291.

29. Z. Helen Bilder, "The East in the United States," *Great Britain and the East*, XLVIII (1937), 24; *New Yorker*, March 24, 1951, p. 36; U.S. Senate, Committee on Immigration, "Hearings ... to permit approximately three thousand Natives of India who entered the United States prior to July 1, 1924 to become naturalized," 78 Cong., 2 sess. (1944), p. 52.

30. *New Yorker*, March 24, 1951, pp. 35–37.

31. *Honolulu Star-Bulletin*, July 2, 1957, p. 22.

32. *Honolulu Advertiser*, Aug. 22, 1973, p. D–1.

33. Ibid., Sept. 3, 1944, p. 15.

34. U.S. House, Committee on Immigration and Naturalization, "Hearings," 79 Cong., 1 sess. (1945), pp. 143–45; *New York Times*. May 4, 1937, p. 20.

35. Dharam Yash Dev, *Our Countrymen Abroad* (Swaraj Bhawan, Allahabad: All Congress India Co., 1940), p. 55; U.S. House, Committee on Immigration and Naturalization, "Petitions of Natives of India...," 76 Cong., 1 sess. (1939) p. 11; Hess, "East Indian Community," p. 591.

36. U.S. Bureau of Census, *Nonwhite Population by Race, 1940*, (Washington, D.C.)

37. Gurdial Singh, p. 214; U.S. Senate, Committee on Immigration, "Hearings ... three thousand East Indians," 78 Cong., 1 sess. (1944), pp. 51–52.

38. Jacoby, "A Half-Century Appraisal," p. 22.

39. U.S. House, Committee on Immigration and Naturalization, "Hearings ... to grant a Quota to Eastern Hemisphere Indians...," 79 Cong., 1 sess. (1945), pp. 149–50; U.S. Senate, Committee on Immigration, "Hearings ... three thousand East Indians," 78 Cong., 1 sess. (1944), pp. 51–52.

40. Chandrasekhar, "Indian Immigration in America," p. 139.

41. U.S. Senate, Committee on Immigration, 78 Cong., 1 sess. (1944), pp. 39–40.

42. *Sacramento Bee*, April 27, 1956, p. 8.

43. U.S. Congress, *Biographical Directory of the American Congresses, 1774–1961* (Washington, D.C., 1961), p. 1563; Bill Smith, "California's Bearded Lions," *Fortnight*, XVIII (1955), 54; *Sacramento Bee*, April 27, 1956, p. 8; *New York Times*, April 4, 1973; p. 44.

44. U.S. Department of Justice, Immigration and Naturalization

Service, Memorandum, "In-migration in Professions and Related Fields, Fiscal 1967," chart 3; "Fiscal 1969," chart 3.

Chapter XXI

1. Hess, "East Indian Community," p. 584.
2. Annette Thackwell Johnson, "Armageddon," *Independent*, CIX (Nov. 25, 1922), 296.
3. *Review of Reviews*, XXXV (1907), 68.
4. Lee McCrae, " 'Birds of Passage' in California," *Missionary Review of the World*, XLI (1918), 910.
5. Francis J. Brown and Joseph S. Roucek, eds. *One America*, 3rd ed. (New York: Prentice-Hall, 1952), pp. 307–308.
6. Millis, "East Indian Immigration," *Survey*, p. 385.
7. Hess, "East Indian Community," p. 594.
8. Millis, "East Indian Immigration," p. 385; Calif. Board of Control, *California and the Oriental*, rev. ed. 1922, pp. 124–25.
9. Calif. Board of Control, *California and the Oriental*, rev. ed., pp. 124–25; Millis, "East Indian Immigration," *American Economic Review*, p. 75.
10. Jacoby, "A Half-Century Appraisal," p. 12; Buchanan, "The West and the Hindu Invasion," p. 311; Fieldbrave, "East Indians in the United States," pp. 291–92.
11. Jacoby, pp. 25–26; Taylor, *Mexican Labor . . .* , p. 10.
12. U.S. Senate, Committee on Immigration, "Hearings . . . Ratification . . . Naturalization of certain persons of the Hindu Race," 69 Cong., 2 sess. (1926), pp. 34–35; *San Francisco Chronicle*, Jan 31, 1936, p. 2F.
13. *Perez v. Sharp*, 32 Calif., 2nd series, 711.
14. Jacoby, pp. 12–13.
15. *San Francisco Examiner*, "California Living," Oct. 24, 1965, pp. 38, 41.
16. Saint N. Singh, "Picturesque Immigrant," p. 46.
17. George W. Hinman, *The Oriental in America* (New York: Missionary Education Movement of the United States and Canada, 1913), p. 17.
18. Clifford M. Drury, "Hinduism in the United States," *Missionary Review*, new series, XXXIV (1921), 281–83; Mukerji, pp. 312–13.
19. *Hinduism Comes to America* (Chicago: Vedanta Society, 1933), pp. 4–13; Wendell Thomas, *Hinduism Invades America* (New York: Beacon Press, 1930).
20. Fieldbrave, p. 293.
21. Saint N. Singh, "Picturesque Immigrant," p. 52; Emily C. Brown, *Har Dayal*, p. 87.

22. *Newsweek,* Aug. 2, 1971, p. 72; Stephen Rose, "Guru on Fourteenth Street," *Christian Century,* LXXXIX (Jan. 19, 1972), 67–69.

23. *San Francisco Examiner,* "California Living," Oct. 24, 1965, pp. 38, 41.

24. Jacoby, pp. 11–12, 25; Hess, "East Indian Community," p. 584.

25. Jacoby, pp. 11–12.

26. Gurdial Singh, p. 214; Jacoby, p. 24; U.S. House, Committee on Immigration and Naturalization, "Hearings . . . Restrictions of Immigration of Hindu Laborers," 63 Cong., 2 sess. (1914), p. 7; Smith, "California's Bearded Lions," pp. 52–53.

27. Smith, p. 54; Jacoby, p. 24.

28. *Sacramento Union,* Oct. 25, 1973; p. C 1; *San Francisco Chronicle,* Nov. 17, 1969, p. 3.

29. *Honolulu Advertiser,* March 30, 1974, p. A–21; *Sunday Star-Bulletin & Advertiser,* July 25, 1976, p. E–2.

30. Lawrence A. Wenzel, "East Indians of Sutter County," *North State Review,* III (1968), 15.

31. Wenzel, "Rural Punjabis of California," pp. 253–55.

32. McWilliams, *Brothers Under the Skin,* p. 249; Brown and Roucek, *One America,* p. 308.

33. Yusuf Dadabhay, "Circuitous Assimilation among Rural Hindustani in California," *Social Forces,* XXXIII (1954), 141.

34. Ibid., pp. 138–41.

35. Wenzel, "East Indians of Sutter County," p. 17; *San Francisco Examiner,* "California Living," Oct. 24, 1965, p. 38.

36. Hess, "East Indian Community," pp. 593–94.

Selected Bibliography

A. BIBLIOGRAPHIES

ALCANTARA, RUBEN R., NANCY S. ALCONCEL, and CESAR S. WYCOCO. "The Filipinos in Hawaii: an Annotated Bibliography." Honolulu: Social Science Research Institute, Univ. of Hawaii, 1972.

GARDNER, ARTHUR L. *The Koreans in Hawaii.* Honolulu: Social Science Research Institute, Univ. of Hawaii, 1970.

SAITO, SHIRO. "The Overseas Filipinos a Working Bibliography." Honolulu: East-West Population Institute Conference on International Migration from the Philippines, East-West Center, 1974.

————. *Philippine Ethnography: a Critically Annotated and Selected Bibliography.* Honolulu: Univ. of Hawaii Press, 1971.

WHITNEY, PHILIP. "Filipinos in the United States." *Bulletin of Bibliography,* XXIX (July–Sept. 1972), 74–83.

B. MANUSCRIPTS

HUGH BRADFORD. Scrapbook Pertaining to the Alien Land Law of 1913 and Other Matters. California State Library, Sacramento, Calif.

ROMAN P. CARIAGA. Filipinos at Ewa. Honolulu, 1935. Hawaiian Collection, Univ of Hawaii, Honolulu, Hawaii.

Hawaii. Office of the Military Governor. General Orders, Dec. 1941– April 1942. Hawaiian Collection, Univ. of Hawaii.

RICHARD IVERS. Statement of Immigration prepared by Mr. Ivers, President, Board of Immigration for Federal Immigration Commission, Honolulu, 1909. Hawaiian Collection, Univ. of Hawaii.

Japanese in California. Bancroft Library, Univ. of California, Berkeley, Calif.

KINGSLEY K. LYU. Korean Nationalist Activities in the United States and Hawaii, 1900–1945. Hawaiian Collection, Univ. of Hawaii.

PABLO MANLAPIT. Pablo Manlapit. Hawaiian Collection, Univ. of Hawaii.

HERBERT PROBASCO. Japanese and Filipino Labor Unions and the 1920 Plantation Strike in Hawaii. Hawaiian Collection, Univ. of Hawaii.

299

MANUEL L. QUEZON. Papers, National Library of the Philippines, Manila, Philippines.
————. Papers on Filipinos in Hawaii, 1914–1943. Hawaiian Collection, Univ. of Hawaii.
JOHN E. REINECKE. The Big Lie of 1920. Hawaiian Collection, Univ. of Hawaii.
TRINIDAD A. ROJO. Filipino-American Contacts, Bancroft Library, Univ. of California.
United States Department of Commerce and Labor. Bureau of Immigration and Naturalization. Correspondence Files. National Archives, Washington, D. C.
United States Department of State. Decimal File. National Archives. Washington, D. C.
————. Despatches from United States Ministers to Korea, 1883–1905. National Archives, Washington, D. C.
————. Numerical File. National Archives, Washington, D. C.
JAMES EARL WOOD. Miscellaneous Printed Items Relating to Filipinos in California and the United States. Bancroft Library, Univ. of California.

C. GOVERNMENT DOCUMENTS

1. *Federal*
Congressional Record, 59–90 Cong., 1905–1967.
U.S. Statutes at Large, 1902–1965.

a. Congressional Documents
55 Cong., 2 sess., 1897. *Congressional Directory.*
61 Cong., 3 sess., 1911. Senate Joint Committee on Hawaii. *Fourth Report of Commissioner of Labor on Hawaii, 1910.*
63 Cong., 2 sess., 1914. House of Representatives. *Hearings Relative to Restriction of Immigration of Hindu Laborers.*
69 Cong., 2 sess., 1926. Senate. Committee on Immigration. *Hearings on Ratification and Confirmation of Naturalization of Certain Persons of the Hindu Race.*
71 Cong., 2 sess., 1930. House. Committee on Immigration and Naturalization. *Hearings on Exclusion of Immigration from the Philippine Islands.*
————. ————. ————. *Preliminary Hearing Subject to Revision: Immigration from Countries of the Western Hemisphere.*
72 Cong., 2 sess., 1932. House. Committee on Immigration and Naturalization. *Hearings on House Joint Resolutions 549 and 577: To Return to the Philippine Islands Unemployed Filipinos.*

————. ————. ————. Report No. 1926. *Return Unemployed Filipinos to Philippine Islands.*

73 Cong., 1 sess., 1933. House. Committee on Immigration and Naturalization. Report No. 127. *Return of Certain Filipinos to Philippine Islands.*

74 Cong., 1 sess., 1935. House. Committee on Immigration and Naturalization. Report No. 622. *Emigration of Filipinos from the United States.*

————. ————. ————. Report No. 74. *Provide for Transportation to the Philippine Islands of Indigent Filipinos Resident in the United States and Territories.*

74 Cong., 2 sess., 1936. Senate. Joint Committee on Hawaii. Report No. 849. *Emigration of Filipinos from the United States.*

————. ————. Committee on Immigration. Report No. 2031. *Extend the Period for Emigration of Filipinos from the United States to the Philippine Islands.*

74 Cong., 2 sess., 1936. House. Committee on Immigration and Naturalization. Report No. 2004. *To Extend the Period for Emigration of Filipinos from the United States to the Philippine Islands.*

75 Cong., 1 sess., 1937. House. Committee on Immigration and Naturalization. Report No. 216. *To Further Extend the Period for Emigration of Filipinos from the United States to the Philippine Islands.*

————. Senate. Committee on Immigration. Report No. 427. *Further Extend the Period for Emigration of Filipinos from the United States to the Philippine Islands.*

76 Cong., 1 sess., 1939. House. Committee on Immigration and Naturalization. Report No. 198. *Providing Means by Which Certain Filipinos Can Emigrate from the United States.*

————. ————. ————. *Hearings on Petitions by Natives of India for Legislation to Include Natives of India Now Residing in the United States as Eligible to Naturalization.*

————. Senate. Committee on Immigration. Report 756. *Providing Means by Which Certain Filipinos Can Emigrate from the United States.*

————. ————. ————. *Transporting Filipinos to the Philippine Islands, 1937–Dec. 31, 1938.*

76 Cong., 3 sess., 1940. House. Select Committee to Investigate the Interstate Migration of Destitute Citizens. *Hearings.*

78 Cong., 2 sess., 1944. House. Committee on Immigration and

Naturalization. *Hearings on House Resolutions 2012, 2776, 4003, 4229, and 4826: Naturalization of Filipinos.*

————. ————. ————. Report No. 1940. *Authorizing the Naturalization of Filipinos.*

————. Senate. Committee on Immigration. *Hearings to Permit Approximately Three Thousand Natives of India Who Entered the United States Prior to July 1, 1924 to Become Naturalized.*

79 Cong., 1 sess., 1945. House. Committee on Immigration and Naturalization. Report No. 252. *Authorizing the Naturalization of Filipinos.*

————. ————. ————. *Hearings on House Resolutions 173, 1584, 1624, 1746, 2256, and 2609: Bills to Grant a Quota to Eastern Hemisphere Indians and to Make Them Racially Eligible for Naturalization.*

————. Senate. Committee on Immigration. *Hearings on S. 236, a Bill to Permit All People from India Residing in the United States to be Naturalized.*

79 Cong., 2 sess., 1946. Senate. Joint Committee on Hawaii. Report No. 1439. *Authorizing the Naturalization of Filipinos.*

87 Cong., 1 sess., 1961. House. *Biographical Directory of the American Congresses, 1774–1961.*

89 Cong., 1 sess., 1965. Senate. Committee on the Judiciary. Subcommittee on Immigration and Naturalization. *Aliens in the United States.*

91 Cong., 1 sess., 1969. Senate. Committee on the Judiciary. *Immigration and Nationality Act.* 6th ed., revised through May 1, 1969.

b. Executive Documents

Bureau of Census. *Special Census of the Population of Hastings, Nebraska, Dec. 13, 1915.*

————. *General Population Characteristics, Outlying Territories and Possessions, 1920.*

————. *General Population Characteristics, Territories, 1930.*

————. *Population, 1930.*

————. *Characteristics of the Nonwhite Population by Race, 1940.*

————. *General Population Characteristics, Hawaii, 1940.*

————. *Population, 1940.*

————. *Characteristics of the Nonwhite Population by Race, 1950.*

————. *General Population Characteristics, Hawaii, 1950.*

————. *Characteristics of the Nonwhite Population by Race, 1960.*

————. *Detailed Population Characteristics, 1960.*

————. *General Population Characteristics, 1960.*

————. *Detailed Population Characteristics, 1970.*

————. *General Population Characteristics, 1970.*

————. *Japanese, Chinese and Filipinos in the United States, 1970.*

————. *Number of Filipinos by Counties of United States, 1970.*

Bureau of Immigration and Naturalization. *Industrial Conditions in the Hawaiian Islands.* 1913.

Bureau of Insular Affairs. Report to the Secretary of War. *Filipino Emigration to the United States and Hawaii, 1932–35.*

————. *Directory of Filipino Students in the U.S.,* 1917.

————. Report to the Secretary of War. *Filipino Students in the United States, 1904–1911.*

Bureau of Labor Statistics. *Filipino in California.* Bulletin 541 (Sept. 1931), 290–91.

————. *Labor Conditions in Hawaii: Fifth Report of the Commissioner of Labor Statistics on Labor Conditions in Hawaii, 1915.*

————. *Labor Conditions in the Territory of Hawaii, 1929–30.* Bulletin No. 534.

————. *Labor in the Territory of Hawaii, 1939.*

————. *Monthly Labor Review,* 1916–1958.

Commission on Law Enforcement. Report No. 10. *Report on Crime and the Foreign Born,* 1931.

Department of Justice. Immigration and Naturalization Service. "Annual Indicator of the In-migration into the United States of Aliens in Professional and Related Occupations, Fiscal Year 1967."

————. ————. "————, Fiscal Year 1969."

————. ————. *Annual Reports, 1898–1974.*

————. Immigration Service. "The Alien Population of the State of Hawaii." 1965–1969.

Department of State. *Papers Relating to Foreign Relations of the United States, 1924.*

Federal Writers' Project. "Unionization of Filipinos in California Agriculture." Oakland, Calif., [1937].

Immigration Commission. *Immigrants in Industry, Part 25: Japanese and Other Immigrant Races in the Pacific Coast and Rocky Mountain States.* 3 vols. 61 Cong., 2 sess., 1911. Senate.

————. *Dictionary of Races or Peoples.* 61 Cong., 3 sess., 1911. Senate.

Philippine Islands. Joaquin Balmori. *Report on the Investigation Made about Conditions under Which the Filipino Laborers Are Working in Sugar Plantations in the Territory of Hawaii.* Manila, Philippines, 1912.

————. Bureau of Labor. *Report of the Director of Labor to his Excellency the Governor-General of the Philippine Islands.* Manila, 1926.

————. ————. *Activities of the Bureau of Labor.* Manila, 1930.

————. Resident Labor Commissioner's Office, Honolulu, T.H. *Authoritative Statement Relative to Filipino Laborers in Hawaii.* Honolulu, 1924.

c. Judicial Documents

Ahkay Kumar Mozumdar v. United States. 299 Fed. 240.

Gokhale v United States. 278 U.S. 662.

In re Akhay Kumar Mozumdar. 207 Fed. 115.

In re Alverto. D.C. 198 Fed. 688.

In re Balsara. 171 Fed. 294.

In re Bautista. 245 Fed. 765.

In re Bhagat Singh Thind. 268 Fed. 683.

In re En Sk Song. 271 Fed. 23.

In re Geronimo Para. 269 Fed. 643.

In re Lampitoe. D.C. 232. Fed. 382.

In re Mohan Singh. 257 Fed. 209.

In re Rallos. D.C. 241 Fed. 686.

In re Rena. 50 Fed. 606.

In re Sadar Bhagwab Singh. 246 Fed. 496.

Morrison v. California. 291 U.S. 82.

Ozawa v. United States. 260 U.S. 189.

Petition of Easurk Emsen Char. 273 Fed. 207.

Roque Espiritu De La Yala v. United States. 77 Fed. 988.

Toyota v. United States. 268 U.S. 402.

United States v Akhay Kumar Muzumdar. 296 Fed. 173.

United States v. Ali. 7 Fed. 2nd, 728.

United States v. Ali. 20 Fed. 2nd, 988.

United States v. Balsara. 180 Fed. 103.

United States v. Balsara. 180 Fed. 694.

United States v. Bhagat Singh Thind. 261 U.S. 204.

United States v. Gokhale. 26 Fed. 2nd, 360.

2. State

California. *Statutes,* 1901–1933.

————. *Journal of the Senate of the State of California.* Sacramento, 1929.

————. Board of Control. *California and the Oriental.* Sacramento, 1920.

————. ————. *California and the Oriental.* rev. ed. Sacramento, 1922.

————. Bureau of Labor Statistics. *The Alaska Salmon Canneries. Appendix to Legislative Journals,* III. 40 Sess., 1913.

————. Department of Employment. Farm Placement Service. *California Annual Farm Labor Report, 1961.* Sacramento, 1962.

————. Department of Industrial Relations, *Facts about Filipino Immigration into California.* Sacramento, 1930.

————. ————. State Fair Employment Practices Commission. *Californians of Japanese, Chinese and Filipino Ancestry.* San Francisco, 1965.

————. Mason, Paul, comp. *Constitution of the State of California. Annotated.* Sacramento, 1946.

————. *Perez v. Sharp.* 32 Calif. 2nd Series, 711.

————. *Rolden v. Los Angeles County.* 129 Calif. 267.

Hawaii. Board of Immigration. *First Report of the Board of Immigration to the Governor of the Territory of Hawaii.* Honolulu, 1907.

————. ————. Labor and Statistics. *First Report to the Governor of the Territory of Hawaii.* Honolulu, 1912.

————. ————. ————. *Second Report* . . . . Honolulu, 1913.

————. ————. ————. *Third Report* . . . . Honolulu, 1914.

————. ————. ————. *Fourth Report* . . . . Honolulu, 1915.

————. ————. ————. *Fifth Report* . . . . Honolulu, 1916.

————. Commission on Manpower and Full Employment. State Immigration Service Center. *Report.* Honolulu, 1972.

————. ————. ————. *Report on Immigrant Services and Problems, 1973.* Honolulu, 1973.

————. ————. ————. *Immigrants in Hawaii, 1965–1975.* Honolulu, 1975.

————. Committee on Agriculture and Immigration. *Report of Committee on Agriculture and Immigration of the House of Representatives, Legislature of the Territory of Hawaii, Session of 1911, in response to a Resolution requiring Inquiry into the Question of Filipino Immigration.* Honolulu, 1911.

————. Governor's Conference on Immigration. *Proceedings.* 2 vols. Honolulu, 1969.

Minnesota. Governor's Interracial Commission. *The Oriental in Minnesota.* St. Paul, Minn., 1949.

3. *City Documents*

Honolulu, Hawaii. Office of Human Resources. *Profile of Oahu's Aging Population.* Honolulu, 1973.

4. *Foreign Documents*

Canada. Department of Labour. *Report of W. L. Mackenzie King on Mission to England to Confer with the British Authorities on the Subject of Immigration to Canada from the Orient and Immigration from India in Particular.* Ottawa, Canada, 1908.

————. British Columbia. Legislative Assembly. *Report on Oriental Activities within the Province.* Victoria, British Columbia, 1927.

Japan. Consulate-General, San Francisco. *Documentary History of Law Cases Affecting Japanese in the United States, 1916–1924.* 2 vols. San Francisco, Calif., 1925.

Korea. *Dr. Syngman Rhee The President of the Republic of Korea.* Seoul, Korea, [n.d.].

————. *Imperial Rules and Regulations of the Department of Emigration of the Empire of Korea.* Seoul, Korea, Nov. 16, 1902.

————. Ministry of Culture and Information. *Facts about Korea.* Seoul, Korea, 1971.

————. Office of the Educational Attaché, Korean Embassy. *Korean Scholars and Students in the United States, 1961–1970.* Washington, D. C., 1970.

D. NEWSPAPERS

Bataan News (Sacramento)
Bohk Dohng (Honolulu)
Chicago Tribune
El Malcriado (Delano, Calif.)
Filipino Informer (San Francisco)
Filipino News (Lihue, Hawaii)
Hawaiian Reporter (Honolulu)
Honolulu Advertiser
Honolulu Evening Bulletin
Honolulu Star-Bulletin
Ka Leo O Hawaii (Honolulu)
Los Angeles Times
Monterey Peninsula Herald (Monterey, Calif.)
New York Times
Pahayag (Honolulu)
Sacramento Bee
Sacramento Union
San Francisco Call
San Francisco Chronicle
San Francisco Examiner
San Francisco Examiner & Chronicle

San Jose Mercury
Stockton Record (Stockton, Calif.)
Sunday Star-Bulletin & Advertiser (Honolulu)
Western Worker (San Francisco)

E. PERIODICALS

American Monthly Review of Reviews
Asia and the Americas
Asian Student
Collier's
Filamerican (Honolulu)
Filipino Nation (Los Angeles)
Filipino Outlook (Honolulu)
Filipino Student Bulletin (New York)
Filipino Students' Magazine (Berkeley, Calif.)
Grapevine (New York)
Grizzly Bear (Los Angeles)
Harper's Weekly
Hawaii Heritage News (Honolulu)
India Review (Madras, India)
Korean Bulletin of Hawaii (Honolulu)
Korean Pacific Weekly (Honolulu)
Korea Review (Philadelphia)
Korean Student Bulletin (New York)
Literary Digest
Living Age
Missionary Review of the World
Modern Review (Calcutta, India)
Nation
New Republic
New Yorker
Newsweek
Outlook
Pacific Citizen (Salt Lake City)
Paradise of the Pacific (Honolulu)
Philippine American Advocate (Washington, D. C.)
Philippine Quarterly (Chicago)
Philippines Journal (Honolulu)
Pilipino Progress (Pearl City, Hawaii)
Review of Reviews
Seamen's Journal
Social Process in Hawaii (Honolulu)

Survey
Time
United States of India (San Francisco)
U. S. News & World Report
Wagayway (Honolulu)

F. ALMANACS AND HANDBOOKS

Deering's [California] *Civil Code, 1945 Supplement.* San Francisco:
    Whitney–Bancroft Publishers, 1945.
Second Decennial Digest of the American Digest, 1906–1916. St.
    Paul, Minn.: West Publishing Co., 1917–1923.
Third Decennial Digest of the American Digest, 1916–1926. St.
    Paul, Minn.: West Publishing Co., 1928–1929.
*Fourth Decennial Digest of all Decisions of the State and Federal
    Courts as Reported in the National Reporter and the State Re-
    ports.* St. Paul, Minn.: West Publishing Co. [1937–1938].
Federal Reporter. St. Paul, Minn.: West Publishing Co. 1922.
*Statistical History of the United States from Colonial Times to the
    Present.* Stamford, Conn.: Fairfield Publishers, 1965.
Times Atlas of the World. Boston: Houghton Mifflin Co., 1967.
World Almanac and Book of Facts. New York, 1966–1975.

G. TRANSACTIONS

Asiatic Exclusion League. *Proceedings.* San Francisco, 1908–1910.
Commonwealth Club of California. "Filipino Immigration." *Transac-
    tions.* XXIV (1929).
East-West Center Population Institute. *Proceedings of Conference on
    International Migration from the Philippines.* Honolulu: East-
    West Center, 1975.
Japanese and Korean Exclusion League. *Minutes.* San Francisco,
    1906–1907.
Korean Community of Southern California. *Yearbook, 1964.* Holly-
    wood, California, 1964.
Supreme Fraternal Council Legionnaires Del Trabajo in America
    Inc. *L D T Blue Book.* Stockton, California, 1949.

H. BOOKS

ABBOTT, JAMES F. *Japanese Expansion and American Policies.* New
    York: Macmillan Co., 1916.
ADAMS, ROMANZO. *Intermarriage in Hawaii.* New York: Macmillan
    Co., 1937.

BANERJEE, KALYAN KUMAR. *Indian Freedom Movement: Revolutionaries in America*. Calcutta. Jijnasa, 1969.

BEAN, WALTON. *California: an Interpretative History*. New York: McGraw–Hill Co., 1968.

BOGARDUS, EMORY S. *Immigration and Race Attitudes*. Boston: D. C. Heath, 1928.

BOURNE, EDWARD G. *Spain in America, 1450–1580*. New York: Harper & Bros., 1904.

BROWN, EMILY C. *Har Dayal: Hindu Revolutionary and Rationalist*. Tucson: Univ. of Arizona Press, 1975.

BROWN, FRANCIS J. and JOSEPH S. ROUCEK, eds. *One America*. 3rd ed. New York: Prentice–Hall, 1952.

BUAKEN, MANUEL. *I Have Lived with the American People*. Caldwell, Idaho: Caxton Printers, 1948.

BULOSAN, CARLOS. *America Is in the Heart*. New York: Harcourt, Brace and Co. [1941].

————. *The Laughter of My Father*. New York: Harcourt, Brace and Co. [1944].

————. *Sound of Falling Light; Letters in Exile*. Dolores Feria, ed. Quezon City, Philippines: n. p., 1960.

BURMA, JOHN H. *Spanish–Speaking Groups in the United States*. Durham, N.C.: Duke Univ. Press, 1954.

CARIAGA, ROMAN P. *The Filipinos in Hawaii: Economic and Social Conditions 1906–1936*. Honolulu: Filipino Public Relations Bureau, 1937.

CHANDRA, KANANUR V. *Racial Minorities in Canada: Asian Minorities*. San Francisco: R and E Research Associates, 1973.

CHENG, TIEN–FANG. *Oriental Immigration in Canada*. Shanghai, China: Commercial Press, 1931.

CRESSEY, PAUL G. *The Taxi-Dance Hall*. Chicago: Univ. of Chicago Press, 1932.

DANIELS, ROGER. *Politics of Prejudice*. Berkeley: Univ. of California Press, 1962.

DAS, RAJANI KANTA. *Hindustani Workers on the Pacific Coast*. Berlin: Walter DeGruyter & Co., 1923.

DAY, MARK. *Forty Acres: Cesar Chavez and the Farm Workers*. New York: Praeger Publishers, 1971.

DEV, DHARAM YASH. *Our Countrymen Abroad*. Swarji Bhawan, Allahabad: All India Congress Co., 1940.

DE WITT, HOWARD. *Anti–Filipino Movements in California: a History, Bibliography and Study Guide*. San Francisco: R and E Research Associates, 1976.

310 ASIANS IN AMERICA

DIVINE, ROBERT. *American Immigration Policy, 1924–52.* New Haven: Yale Univ. Press, 1957.

DOBBY, ERNEST H.G. *Southeast Asia,* 7th ed., London: Univ. of London Press, 1960.

DUNNE, JOHN. *Delano.* New York: Farrar, Straus & Giroux, 1971.

FISHER, LLOYD H. *The Harvest Labor Market in California.* Cambridge, Mass.: Harvard Univ. Press, 1953.

FUCHS, LAWRENCE H. *Hawaii Pono: a Social History.* New York: Harcourt, Brace & World, Inc., 1961.

GRODZINS, MORTON. *Americans Betrayed: Politics and the Japanese Evacuation.* Chicago: Univ. of Chicago Press, 1949.

GRUNDER, GAREL A. and WILLIAM E. LIVEZEY. *The Philippines and the United States.* Norman, Okla.: Univ. of Oklahoma Press, 1951.

HAN, WOO-KEUN. *The History of Korea.* Kyung–shik Lee, trans. Grafton K. Mintz, ed. Honolulu: East–West Center Press, 1970.

HESS, GARY R. *America Encounters India, 1941–47.* Baltimore: Johns Hopkins Press, 1971.

HIGHAM, JOHN. *Strangers in the Land.* New York: Atheneum, 1963.

Hinduism Comes to America. Chicago: Vedanta Society, 1933.

HINMAN, GEORGE W. *The Oriental in America.* New York: Missionary Education Movement of the United States and Canada, 1913.

HUNDLEY, NORRIS, JR., ed. *The Asian American: the Historical Experience.* Santa Barbara, Calif.: Clio Press, 1976.

HUNTER, ALLEN A. *Out of the Far East.* New York: Friendship Press, 1934.

ICHIHASHI, YAMATO. *Japanese in the United States: a Critical Study of the Problems of the Japanese Immigrants and Their Children.* Stanford, Calif.: Stanford Univ. Press, 1932.

JOSEPH, P. T. *The Amiable American.* Trivandrum, India: St. Joseph's Press, 1963.

KANG, YOUNGHILL, *East Goes West.* New York: Chas. Scribner's, 1937.

————. *The Grass Roof.* New York: Chas. Scribner's, [1931].

KIM, RICHARD. *The Innocent.* New York: Ballantine Books, [1969].

————. *Lost Names.* New York: Praeger, 1970.

————. *The Martyred.* New York: G. Braziller, [1964].

KIM, SUNG YONG. *United States–Philippine Relations, 1946–1956.* Washington, D. C.: Public Affairs Press, 1968.

KIM, WARREN Y. *Koreans in America.* Seoul, Korea: Po Chin Chai Printing Co., 1971.

KNAPLAND, PAUL. *The British Empire, 1815–1939.* New York: Harper & Bros., 1941.

KONDAPI, C. *Indians Overseas, 1838–1939*. New Delhi: Indian Council of World Affairs, 1951.

KONVITZ, MILTON R. *The Alien and the Asiatic in American Law*. Ithaca, N. Y.: Cornell Univ. Press, 1946.

LASKER, BRUNO. *Filipino Immigration to Continental United States and to Hawaii*. Chicago: Univ. of Chicago Press, 1931.

LIEM, CHANNING. *America's Finest Gift to Korea: the Life of Philip Jaisohn*. New York: William–Frederick Press, 1952.

LEMERT, EDWIN M. and JUDY ROSBERG. *The Administration of Justice to Minority Groups in Los Angeles County*. 2 vols. University of California Publications in Culture and Society. Berkeley: Univ. of California Press, 1948.

LEWIS, HENRY T. *Ilocano Rice Farmers*. Honolulu: Univ. of Hawaii Press, 1971.

LIND, ANDREW W. *Hawaii's People*, 3rd ed. Honolulu: Univ. of Hawaii Press, 1967.

MANZON, MAXIMO C. *The Strange Case of the Filipinos in the United States*. New York: American Committee for the Protection of Foreign Born, 1938.

McCUNE, SHANNON. *Korea's Heritage: a Regional & Social Geography*. Rutland, Vt.: Charles E. Tuttle Co., 1956.

McGOWAN, JOSEPH. *History of Sacramento Valley*. 3 vols. New York: Lewis Publishing Co., 1961.

McWILLIAMS, CAREY. *Brothers under the Skin*, rev. ed. Boston: Little, Brown & Co., 1951.

————. *Factories in the Field*. Boston: Little, Brown & Co., 1939.

MELENDY, H. BRETT and BENJAMIN F. GILBERT. *The Governors of California: Peter H. Burnett to Edmund G. Brown*. Georgetown, Calif.: Talisman Press, 1965.

MELENDY, H. BRETT. *The Oriental Americans*. New York: Twayne Publishers, 1972.

MUKERJI, DHAN GOPEL. *Caste and Outcast*. New York: E. P. Dutton & Co., 1923.

MUNROZ, ALFREDO N. *The Filipinos in America*. Los Angeles: Mountainview Publishers, 1971.

NATARAJAN, L. *American Shadow over India*. Bombay: People's Publishing House, Ltd., 1952.

NEW, IHAN. *When I Was a Boy in Korea*. Boston: Lothrop, Lee & Shepard Co., 1928.

NICANOS, PRECIOS M. *Martyrs Never Die*. New York: Pre–Mer Publishing Co., 1968.

————. *Profiles of Notable Americans in the USA*. New York: Pre-Mer Publishing Co., 1963.

OLIVER, ROBERT T. *Syngman Rhee: the Man behind the Myth*. New York: Dodd Mead, 1954.

PALMER, ALBERT W. *Human Side of Hawaii: Race Problems in the Mid Pacific*. Boston: Pilgrim Press, 1924.

————. *Orientals in American Life*. New York: Friendship Press, 1934.

The Philippines in Hawaii. Honolulu, Hawaii, n. p., 1948.

PORTEUS, STANLEY D. and MARJORIE E. BABCOCK. *Temperament and Race*. Boston: Gorham Press, 1926.

PRATT, JULIUS W. *America's Colonial Experiment*. New York: Prentice–Hall, 1951.

RAWLINSON, H. G. *India, a Short Cultural History*, rev. ed. London: Cresset Press, 1952.

RENOU, LOUIS, ed. *Hinduism*. New York: George Braziller, 1962.

RITTER, ED, HELEN RITTER and STANLEY SPECTOR. *Our Oriental Americans*. St. Louis, Mo.: McGraw–Hill, 1965.

ROLLAND, ROMAIN. *The Life of Vivekananda and the Universal Gospel*. Calcutta, India: N. Mukherjee, 1931.

ROMULO, CARLOS P. *I Walked with Heroes*. New York: Holt, Rinehart and Winston, 1961.

SCAFF, ALVIN H. *The Philippine Answer to Communism*. Stanford: Stanford Univ. Press, 1955.

SCHMITT, ROBERT C. *Demographic Statistics of Hawaii, 1778–1965*. Honolulu: Univ. of Hawaii Press, 1968.

SCHWARTZ, HARRY. *Seasonal Farm Labor in the United States*. New York: Columbia Univ. Press, 1954.

SINGH, KHUSHWANT. *The Sikhs*. London: Geo. Allen & Unwin, Ltd., 1953.

SINGH, PARDAMAN. *Ethnological Epitome of the Hindustanis of the Pacific Coast*. Stockton, Calif.: Pacific Coast Khalsa Diwan Society, 1922.

SPENCE, HARTZELL. *Marcos of the Philippines*. New York: World Publishing Co., 1969.

STEVENS, SYLVESTER. *American Expansion in Hawaii, 1842–1898*. Harrisburg, Pa.: Archives Publishing Co. of Penn., Inc., 1945.

STRAVIANOS, L. S. *The World to 1500*. Englewood Cliffs, N. J.: Prentice–Hall, 1970.

SUTHERLAND, WILLIAM A. *Not by Might*. Las Cruces, New Mexico: Southwest Publishing Co., 1953.

TAYLOR, PAUL S. *Mexican Labor in the United States Imperial Valley*.

University of California Publications in Economics. Berkeley: Univ. of California Press, 1928.

WELTY, PAUL THOMAS. *The Asians*, 3rd ed. Philadelphia: J. B. Lippincott, 1970.

THOMAS, WENDELL. *Hinduism invades America*. New York: Beacon Press, [1930].

UCLA ASIAN AMERICAN STUDIES CENTER. *Letters in Exile: an Introductory Reader on the History of Pilipinos in America*. Los Angeles: Univ. of California, 1976.

WENTWORTH, EDNA CLARK. *Filipino Plantation Workers in Hawaii*. San Francisco: American Council Institute of Pacific Relations, 1941.

WERNER, EMMY E., JESSIE M. BIERMAN and FERN E. FRENCH. *The Children of Kauai*. Honolulu: Univ. of Hawaii Press, 1971.

YOSHINO, MASATOSHI M., ed. *Water Balance of Monsoon Asia*. Honolulu: Univ. of Hawaii Press, 1971.

YOUNG, CHARLES H. and HELEN R.Y. REID. *The Japanese Canadians*. Toronto: Univ. of Toronto Press, 1938.

I. ARTICLES

ALBA, JOSE C. "Filipinos in California," *Pacific Historian*, II (1967), 37–41.

ALCANTARA, RUBEN R. "The Filipino Wedding in Waialua, Hawaii," *Amerasia Journal*, I (1972), 1–12.

ALLEN, KATHRYN M. "Hindoos in the Valley," *Westways*, XXXVII (April 1937), 8–9.

ANTHONY, DONALD E. "Filipino Labor in Central California," *Sociology and Social Research*, XVI (Sept. 1931–June 1932), 149–56.

BALLARD, WALTER J. "Filipino Students in the United States," *Journal of Education*, LXVII (1908), 272.

BELL, ELISABETH H. "When Will the Filipinos Become a Political Power?" *Honolulu*, IV (April 1975), 32–3, 54–55.

BILDER, Z. HELEN. "The East in the United States," *Great Britain and the East*, XLVIII (1937), 24.

BOGARDUS, EMORY S. "American Attitudes towards Filipinos," *Sociology and Social Research*, XIV (Sept.–Oct. 1929), 59–69.

————. "Citizenship for Filipinos," *Sociology and Social Research*, XXIX (Sept.–Oct, 1944), 51–54.

————. "Filipino Immigrant Attitudes," *Sociology and Social Research*, XIV (May–June 1930), 469–79.

————. "The Filipino Immigrant Problem," *Sociology and Social Research*, XIII (May–June 1929), 472–79.

————. "The Filipino Press in the United States," *Sociology and Social Research*, XVIII (Sept. 1933–April 1934), 581–85.

————. "Filipino Repatriation," *Sociology and Social Research*, XXI (Sept.–Oct. 1936), 67–71.

————. "Foreign Migrations within United States Territory: the Situation of the Filipino Peoples," *Proceedings of the National Conference of Social Work*, 1929, pp. 573–79.

————. "Immigration Quota for India," *Sociology and Social Research*, XXVIII (Sept. 1943–Aug. 1944), 479–83.

————. "Racial Reactions by Regions," *Sociology and Social Research*, XLIII (Sept. 1958–Aug. 1959), 286–90.

————. "What Race are Filipinos?" *Sociology and Social Research*, XVI (Jan.–Feb. 1932), 274–79.

BOSE, SUDHINDRA. "American Impressions of a Hindu Student," *Forum*, LIII (1915), 251–57.

————. "Asian Immigration in the United States," *Modern Review* (Calcutta), XXV (1919), 523–26.

BOWLER, ALIDA C. "Social Hygiene in Racial Problems—the Filipino," *Journal of Social Hygiene*, XVIII (1932), 452–56.

BOYD, MONICA. "Oriental Immigration: the Experience of the Chinese, Japanese, and Filipino in the United States," *International Migration Review*, V (1971), 48–61.

BROWN, GILES T. "The Hindu Conspiracy, 1914–17," *Pacific Historical Review*, XVII (1948), 299–310.

BUAKEN, IRIS BROWN. "My Brave New World," *Asia and the Americas*, XLIII (1943), 268–70.

————. "You Can't Marry a Filipino Not if You Live in California," *Commonweal*, XLI (March 1945), 534–37.

BUAKEN, MANUEL. "Life in the Armed Forces," *New Republic*, CIX (Aug. 30, 1943), 279–80.

————. "Our Fighting Love of Freedom," *Asia and the Americas*, XLIII (1943), 357–59.

————. "Where Is the Heart of America," *New Republic*, CIII (Sept. 23, 1940), 410.

BUCHANAN, AGNES FOSTER. "The West and the Hindu Invasion," *Overland Monthly*, LI (1908), 308–13.

BULOSAN, CARLOS. "As Long as the Grass Shall Grow," *Common Ground*, IX (1949), 38–43.

BURMA, JOHN H. "The Background of the Current Situation of Filipino–Americans," *Social Forces*, XXX (Oct. 1951), 42–48.

————. "Interethnic Marriage in Los Angeles, 1948–1959," *Social Forces*, XLII (Dec. 1963), 156–65.

CARIAGA, ROMAN. "Some Filipino Traits Transplanted," *Social Process,* II (1936), 20–23.

CATAPUSAN, BENICIO T. "The Filipino Labor Cycle in the United States," *Sociology and Social Research,* XIX (Sept.–Oct. 1934), 61–63.

————. "Filipino Intermarriage Problems in the United States," *Sociology and Social Research,* XXII (Jan.–Feb. 1938), 265–72.

————. "Filipino Repatriates in the Philippines," *Sociology and Social Research,* XXI (Sept. 1936–Aug. 1937), 72–77.

————. "Filipino Immigrants and Public Relief in the United States," *Sociology and Social Research,* XXIII (Sept. 1938–Aug. 1939), 546–54.

————. "The Filipinos and the Labor Unions," *American Federationist,* XLVII (1940), 173–76.

————. "Leisure–time Problems of Filipino Immigrants," *Sociology and Social Research,* XXIV (Sept. 1939–Aug. 1940), 541–49.

————. "Problems of Filipino Students in America," *Sociology and Social Research,* XXVI (Sept. 1941–Aug. 1942), 146–53.

CHANDRASEKHAR, S. "The Indian Community in the United States," *Far Eastern Survey,* XIV (June 6, 1945), 149–49.

————. "Indian Immigration in America," *Far Eastern Survey,* XIII (July 26, 1944), 138–44.

CLIFFORD, MARY DORITA. "The Hawaiian Sugar Planters' Association and Filipino Exclusion," *The Filipino Exclusion Movement, 1927–1935* (Quezon City, Philippines: Institute of Asian Studies, Occasional Papers No. 1, 1967), pp. 11–29.

————. "Motivation for Ilocano Migration," *Proceedings of Conference on Internation Migration from the Philippines, June 10–14, 1974* (Honolulu: East–West Center, 1975), pp. 24–26.

CORPUS, SEVERINO F. "Second Generation Filipinos in Los Angeles," *Sociology and Social Research,* XXII (Sept. 1937–Aug. 1938), 446–51.

DADABHAY, YUSUF. "Circuitous Assimilation among Rural Hindustanis in California," *Social Forces,* XXXIII (Dec. 1954), 138–41.

DIGNAN, DON K. "The Hindu Conspiracy in Anglo–American Relations during World War I," *Pacific Historical Review,* XL (1971), 57–76.

DAS, TARAKNATH. "Stateless Persons in U.S.A.," *Calcutta Review,* 3rd series, XVI (1925), 40–46.

DAYAL, R. "The Disabilities of Indians Abroad," *Modern Review* (Calcutta), XLI (1927), 161–68.

"Digest of Marriage Laws," *Commonweal*, XLI (March, 1945), 536–37.

DRURY, CLIFFORD M. "Hinduism in the United States," *Missionary Review of the World*, new series, XXXIV (April 1921), 281–83.

EISENBERG, PHILIP. "Historical Perspectives of Korean Dress," *Korean Survey*, V (1956), 3–6.

FERARU, ARTHUR. "Korean Students in the United States," *School and Society*, LXXXVI (Feb. 1, 1958), 60–62.

FERIA, R. T. "War and the Status of Filipino Immigrants," *Sociology and Social Research*, XXXI (Sept.–Oct. 1946), 48–53.

FIELDBRAVE, THEODORE. "East Indians in the United States," *Missionary Review of the World*, LVII (1934), 291–93.

"Filipino Labour in Hawaii," *International Labour Review* (Geneva), XV (1927), 581–86.

FOSTER, NELLIE. "Legal Status of Filipino Intermarriage in California," *Sociology and Social Research*, XVI (May–June 1932), 441–54.

GARNER, J. W. "Denationalization of American Citizens," *American Journal of International Law*, XXI (1927), 106–107.

GHOSE, SAILENDRA NATH. "Deportation of Hindu Politicals," *Dial*, LXVII (Aug. 23, 1919), 145–47.

GOETHE, C. M. "Filipino Immigration Viewed as a Peril," *Current History*, XXXIV (June 1931), 353–54.

GONZALO, D. F. "Social Adjustments of Filipinos in America," *Sociology and Social Research*, XIV (Nov.–Dec. 1929), pp. 166–73.

HART, DONN V. "American Filipinana: Current Filipino-American Serial Publications in the United States," *Southeast Asia; International Quarterly*, II (1972), 531–34.

HAY, STEPHEN N. "Rabindranath Tagore in America," *American Quarterly*, XIV (1962), 439–63.

HAYDEN, RALSTON. "The United States and the Philippines," *Annals of the American Academy of Political and Social Science*, CXXII (Nov. 1925), 26–48.

HAYNER, NORMAN S. "Social Factors in Oriental Crime," *American Journal of Sociology*, XLIII (July 1937–May 1938), 908–19.

HESS, GARY. "The 'Hindu' in America: Immigration and Naturalization Policies and India, 1917–1946," *Pacific Historical Review*, XXXVIII (1969), 59–79.

————. "The Forgotten Asian Americans: the East Indian Community in the United States," *Pacific Historical Review*, XLIII (1974), 576–96.

"The Hindu in America," *American Review of Reviews,* XXXVII (May 1908), 604.

"The Hindu, the Newest Immigration Problem," *Survey,* XXV (Oct. 1, 1940), 2–3.

HOUCHINS, LEE and CHANG–SU HOUCHINS. "The Korean Experience in America," *Pacific Historical Review,* XLIII (1974), 548–75.

INEZ, DORTENO B. "The Question of Race Pops Again," *Commonwealth Chronicle* (1936), p. 8.

JACOBY, HAROLD S. "More Thind Against than Sinning," *Pacific Historian,* II (Nov. 1958), 1–2, 8.

JAYAWARDENA, CHANDRA I. "Migration and Social Change a Survey of Indian Communities Overseas," *Geographic Review,* LVIII 1968), 426–49.

JENSEN, JOAN M. "Apartheid: Pacific Coast Style," *Pacific Historical Review,* XXXVIII (1969), 335–40.

JOHNSON, ANNETTE T. "Armageddon," *Independent,* CIX (Nov. 25, 1922), 296–98.

————. "'Rag Heads'–a Picture of America's East Indians," *Independent,* CIX (1922), 234–35.

JONES, GEORGE HEBER. "The Korean Abroad," *World Outlook,* II, (July 1916), 25–26.

JONES, IDWAL. "Mr. Har Chand," *Westways,* XXXI (Sept. 1939), 16–17.

KANG, YOUNGHILL. "Oriental Yankee," *Common Ground,* I (1941), 59–63.

KAWAKAMI, K. K. "Canada as a 'White Man's Country,'" *Current History,* XIX (Oct. 1923–March 1924), 829–34.

KEELY, CHARLES B. "Philippine Migration: Internal Movements and Emigration to the United States," *International Migration Review,* VII (1973), 177–87.

KIM, BERNICE. "Koreans in Hawaii," *Social Science,* IX, (1934), 409–13.

KIM, HYUNG–CHAN. "Some Aspects of Social Demography of Korean Americans," *International Migration Review,* VIII (1974), 23–42.

KINLOCH, GRAHAM C. "Race, Socio–economic Status and Social Distance in Hawaii," *Sociology and Social Research,* LVII (Oct. 1972–July 1973), 156–67.

KINLOCH, GRAHAM C. and JEFFREY A. BORDERS. "Racial Stereotypes and Social Distance among Elementary School Children in Hawaii," *Sociology and Social Research,* LVI (Oct. 1971–July 1972), 368–77.

KIRK, GRAYSON. "The Filipinos." *Annals of the American Academy of Political and Social Science*, CCXXIII (July 1942), 45–48.

KITE, ELIZABETH. "An American Criticism of 'The Other Side of the Medal,'" *Modern Review* (Calcutta), XLI (1927), 168–170.

LAMBERT, RICHARD D. and MARVIN BRESSLER. "Indian Students and the United States: Cross–cultural Images," *Annals of the American Academy of Political and Social Science*, CXCV (Sept. 1954), 62–72.

LASKER, BRUNO. "In the Alaska Fish Canneries," *Mid–Pacific Magazine*, XLIII (1932), 335–38.

LAWRENCE, JAMES R. "The American Federation of Labor and the Philippine Independence Question, 1920–1935," *Labor History*, VII (1966), 62–69.

LIND, ANDREW. "Interracial Marriage as Affecting Divorce in Hawaii," *Sociology and Social Research*, XLIX (Oct. 1964–July 1965), 17–26.

LORD, VIRGINIA and ALICE W. LEE. "The Taxi Dance Hall in Honolulu," *Social Process*, II (1936), 46–49.

LOVETT, ROBERT MOSES. "The United States and India: a Footnote to Recent History," *New Republic*, LXVI (April 1, 1931), 175–76.

McCRAE, LEE. "'Birds of Passage' in California," *Missionary Review of the World*, XLI (1918), 910.

McWILLIAMS, CAREY. "Exit the Filipinos," *Nation*, CXLI (1935), 265.

––––––. "Thirty–five Thousand New Aliens," *Pacific Weekly* (Carmel, Calif.), V (Aug. 24, 1936), 19–21.

MALCOM, ROY. "Immigration Problems on the Pacific Coast," *Current History*, XXXIII (Oct. 1930–March 1931), 720–728.

MELENDY, H. BRETT. "California's Discrimination against Filipinos, 1927–1935," *The Filipino Exclusion Movement, 1927–1935* (Quezon City, Philippines: Institute of Asian Studies, Occasional Papers No. 1, 1967), pp. 3–10.

––––––. "Filipinos in the United States," *Pacific Historical Review*, XLIII (1974), 520–47.

MENOR, BENJAMIN. "Filipino Plantation Adjustments," *Social Process*, XIII (1949), 48–51.

MINN, MIEKO WONG. "Hawaii's Little Orient," *Paradise of the Pacific*, LXIX (Nov. 1957), 71–88.

MILLIS, H. A. "East Indian Immigration to British Columbia and the Pacific Coast States," *American Economic Review*, I (1911), 72–76.

————. "East Indian Immigiration to the Pacific Coast," *Survey*, XXVIII (1912), 379–86.

MUKERJI, GIRINDRA. "The Hindu in America," *Overland Monthly*, LI (1908), 308–41.

NAIDIS, MARK. "Propaganda of the Gadar Party," *Pacific Historical Review*, XX (1951), 251–60.

"Naturalization of Filipinos," *Far Eastern Survey*, XIV (Jan. 17, 1945), 9–10.

PALMER, ALBERT W. "Who are the Orientals in America?" *Missionary Review of the World*, LVII (1934), 263–65.

PANDA, D. P. and MME. KAMALDEVI. "Justice for Hindus in America," *Christian Century*, LVII (March 13, 1940), 357.

PANG, MORRIS. "A Korean Immigrant," *Social Process*, XIII (1949), 19–24.

PERNIA, ERNESTO M. "The Question of the Brain Drain from the Philippines," *International Migration Review*, X (1976), 63–72.

PERRY, DONALD R. "Aliens in the United States," *Annals of the American Academy of Political and Social Science*, CCXXIII (Sept. 1942), 1–9.

PHILLIPS, HUBERT. "The Oriental on the Pacific Coast," *Nation*, CXXXII (1931), 12–14.

PIVAR, DAVID J. "The American Federation of Labor and Filipino Exclusion: 1927–1934," *The Filipino Exclusion Movement 1927–1935* (Quezon City, Philippines: Institute of Asian Studies, University of the Pilippines, Occasional Papers No. 1), pp. 30–39.

PONCE, DANILO E. "The Filipinos in Hawaii," Nancy Foon Young, ed., "Searching for the Promised Land: Filipinos and Samoans in Hawaii," Univ. of Hawaii College of Education General Assistance Center [1973], pp. 1–22.

QUINTO, DOLORES. "Life Story of a Filipino Immigrant," *Social Process*, IV (1938), 71–78.

RAUCHER, ALAN. "American Anti–Imperialists and the Pro–Indian Movement, 1900–1932," *Pacific Historical Review*, XLIII (1974), 83–110.

RICHARDS, EUGENE S. "Attitudes of College Students in the Southwest toward Ethnic Groups in the United States," *Sociology and Social Research*, XXXV (Sept. 1949–Aug. 1950), 22–30.

RIGGS, FRED W. *U.S. Legislation Affecting Asiatics*, part II, *Far Eastern Survey*, XVI (May 21, 1947), 115–17.

RISDON, RANDALL. "A Study of Interracial Marriages Based on Data for Los Angeles County," *Sociology and Social Research*, XXXIX (Nov.–Dec. 1954), 92–95.

ROJO, TRINADAD A. "Social Maladjustments among Filipinos in the United States," *Sociology and Social Research*, XXI (May–June 1937), 447–57.

ROSE, STEPHEN. "The Guru on Fourteenth Street," *Christian Century* LXXXIX (Jan. 19, 1972), 67–69.

SANTOS, BIENVENIDO N. "Filipinos in War," *Far Eastern Survey*, XI (Nov. 30, 1942), 249–50.

SCHARRENBERG, PAUL. "Filipinos Demand Special Privileges," *American Federationist*, XLVI (1939), 1350–53.

SCHEFFAUER, HERMAN. "The Tide of Turbans," *Forum*, XLIII (Jan.–June 1910), 616–18.

SCHISBY, MARIAN. "Hindus and American Citizenship," *Proceedings of the National Conference of Social Work* (Chicago: Univ. of Chicago Press, 1927), pp. 579–81.

SCHMITT, ROBERT C. "Hawaii's Koreans, 1960," *Korean Bulletin of Hawaii*, pp. 20–22.

SCOTT, JAMES BROWN. "Japanese and Hindus Naturalized in the United States," *American Journal of International Law* XVII (1923), 328–30.

SIHRA, NAND SINGH. "Indians in Canada," *Modern Review* (Calcutta), XIV (July–Dec. 1913), 140–49.

SIHRA, NAND SINGH, BALWANT SINGH and NARAIN SINGH. "Indians in Canada," *Indian Review* (Madras), XIV (1913), 453–56.

SINGH, GURDIAL. "East Indians in the United States," *Sociology and Social Research*, XXX (Sept. 1945–Aug. 1946), 208–16.

SINGH, SAINT NIHAL. "Asiatic Immigration: a World Question," *Living Age*, CCLXXXII (Aug. 15, 1914), 387–92.

—————. "The Picturesque Immigrant from India's Coral Strand," *Out West*, XXX (1909), 43–54.

SMITH, BILL. "California's Bearded Lions," *Fortnight*, XVIII (Sept. 1955), 52–54.

SMITH, PETER. "A Demographic Overview of Outmigration from the Philippines," *Proceedings of Conference on International Migration from the Philippines, June 10–14, 1974* (Honolulu: East–West Center, 1975), pp. 11–13.

SMITH, WILLIAM C. "Minority Groups in Hawaii," *Annals of Academy of Political and Social Science*, CCXXII (July 1942), 36–44.

—————. "The Second Generation Oriental in America," Preliminary paper prepared for second general session, July 15–19, 1927, Institute of Pacific Relations, Honolulu, 1927, pp. 1–36.

"Social Hygiene and Racial Problems," *Journal of Social Hygiene,* XVIII (1932), 456–57.

TAGGAOA, FERNANDO A. "No Cause for Regret," *Asia,* XLII (1942), 567.

THOMPSON, DAVID. "The Filipino Federation of America, Incorporated: a Study in the Natural History of a Social Institution," *Social Process,* VII (1941), 24–35.

WENZEL, LAWRENCE A. "The East Indians of Sutter County," *North State Review* (Chico, Calif.) III, (April 1968), 15–25.

––––––. "The Rural Punjabs of California: a Religio–Ethnic Group," *Phylon,* XXIX (1968), 245–56.

WHARTON, DON. "They Are Forging a New Link with India." *Reader's Digest,* LXXIV (Feb. 1959), 167–70.

WHERRY, E. M. "Hindu Immigrants in America," *Missionary Review of the World,* XXX (Dec. 1907), 918–19.

WHITE, DALE. "Koreans in Montana," *Asia and the Americas,* XLV (1946), 156.

WYNNE, ROBERT E. "American Labor Leaders and the Vancouver Anti–Oriental Riot," *Pacific Northwest Quarterly,* XLVII (1966), 172–79.

TSUCHIYA, IWAO. "Fluctuations of Rainfall in Southeast Asia," *Water Balance of Monsoon Asia,* Masatoshi M. Yoshino, ed. (Honolulu: Univ. of Hawaii Press, 1971), pp. 217–39.

J. PAMPHLETS

BOGARDUS, EMORY S. *Anti–Filipino Race Riots: a Report made to the Ingram Institute of Social Science of San Diego.* San Diego: Ingram Institute, May 15, 1930.

CHASE, RAY E. and S[AKHARAN] G. PANDIT. An *Examination of the Opinion of the Supreme Court of the United States Deciding against the Eligibility of Hindus for Citizenship.* Los Angeles, n. p., 1926.

DIZON, NICOLAS C. *The "Master" vs. Juan de la Cruz.* Honolulu: Mercantile Press, 1931.

DUCKWORTH-FORD, R. A. *Report on Hawaiian Sugar Plantations and Filipino Labor.* Manila, n. p., 1926.

50 Years of Progress Hawaiian Korean Golden Jubilee Celebration. [Honolulu, n. p. 1973].

GOMPERS, SAMUEL and HERMAN GUTSTADT. *Meat vs. Rice: American Manhood against Asian Coolieism.* San Francisco: Asiatic Exclusion League, 1908.

INSTITUTE OF LABOR ECONOMICS, UNIVERSITY OF WASHINGTON. *Job Opportunities for Racial Minorities in the Seattle Area.* Seattle, [Univ. of Washington], 1948.

JACOBY, HAROLD S. *A Half–Century Appraisal of East Indians in the United States.* Sixth Annual College of the Pacific Faculty Research Lecture, May 23, 1956.

JAIN, SUSHIL KUMAR. "East Indians in Canada," *R.E.M.P. Bulletin* (Research Group for European Migration Problems). [The Hague: P. H. Klop], June, 1971.

JAPANESE AND KOREAN EXCLUSION LEAGUE. *Japanese Immigration, Occupations, Wages, etc.* San Francisco, n. p., 1907.

JOHNSON, HERBERT B. *Restriction of Japanese Immigration: a Reply.* [San Francisco], 1905.

KOENIG, CLARA H. *The Republic of Korea: A Guide to the Placement of Students from the Republic of Korea in United States Educational Institutions.* [Athens, Ohio: Association of Collegiate Registrars and Admissions Officers, 1958].

KOREAN AMERICAN CULTURAL ASSOCIATION, INC. *The Culture of Korea.* Los Angeles, n. p., 1946–47.

KOREAN CHAMBER OF COMMERCE. *Korean Commerce & Industry Bulletin.* Los Angeles, n. p., 1946–47.

KOREAN CIVIC ASSOCIATION. *We Who Fight the Common Enemy.* Honolulu, n. p., 1945.

KRISHNAYYA, G. S. and J. M. KRISHNAYYA. *Going to U. S. A.: a Guide Book for Students and Other Visitors.* Bombay: S. Raru, [1952].

LEE, SAMUEL SONG, ed. and compiler. *50 Years of St. Luke's Church Honolulu, Hawaii in Commemoration of Consecration of the Church Building.* [Honolulu, n. p., Oct. 1957].

MACINNES, TOM. *Oriental Occupation of British Columbia.* Vancouver, British Columbia: Sun Publishing Co., 1927.

MANLAPIT, PABLO. *Filipinos Fight for Justice: Case of the Filipino Laborers in the Big Strike of 1924 Territory of Hawaii.* Honolulu: Kumalae Publishing Co., 1933.

MILLER, SLATOR M. *Report to Mr. H. A. Walker, President Hawaiian Sugar Planters' Association on 1945–1946 Filipino Emigration Project.* [Honolulu, n. p., 1946].

MONCADO, HILARIO C. *Filipino Labor Conditions in the Territory of Hawaii.* Honolulu, n. p., 1936.

PLATT, SANFORD L. *Immigration and Emigration in the Hawaiian Sugar Industry,* Honolulu, n. p., 1950.

RESPICIO, F. A. *Hawaii's Filipinos and Their Part in the War.* Honolulu, n. p., 1945.

ROBERTS, W. K. *The Mongolian Problem in America.* San Francisco, n. p., 1906.

70th Anniversary Celebration of Korean Immigration to Hawaii. [Honolulu, n. p., 1906].

SINGH, RATTAN. *Brief History of the Hindustan Gadar Party.* [San Francisco, n. p.], 1929.

Survey of Race Relations. Stanford [Stanford Univ. Press], 1925.

SURVEY OF RACE RELATIONS. *Tentative Findings of the Survey of Race Relations: a Canadian–American Study of the Oriental on the Pacific Coast.* Stanford [Stanford Univ. Press], April 13, 1925.

WEINGARTEN, VICTOR. *Raising Cane: a Brief History of Labor in Hawaii.* Honolulu: International Longshoremen's & Warehousemen's Union, Sept. 1946.

Mimeographed Pamphlets

CONMY, PETER T. "The History of California's Japanese Problems and the Part played by the Native Sons of the Golden West in its Solution." [Oakland] July 1, 1942.

ESPERANZA, FREDDIE A. "A Study of the General Attitudes and Knowledge of the Filipino Immigrant in Kalihi and Wahiawa toward Public Assistance." Paper, Univ. of Hawaii School of Social Work, 1972.

GALEDO, LILLIAN, LAURENA CABANERO and BRIAN TOM. "Roadblocks to Community Building: a Case Study of the Stockton Filipino Community Center Project." Davis, Calif. Univ. of California Asia American Studies Division: Asian American Research Project, Working Publication No. 4, 1970.

GALEDO, LILLIAN and THERESA MAR. "Filipinos in a Farm Labor Camp." "Asia in America." Davis, Calif.: Univ. of California American Studies Division: Asian American Research Project, Working Publication No. 3, 1970.

INTER-CHURCH FEDERATION OF HONOLULU. "Filipino Life in Honolulu." [Honolulu], May 1936.

JOHNS, WATSON L. "The Hindu in California." Univ. of Oregon, Seminar paper, 1941.

KOREAN COMMUNITY COUNCIL OF HAWAII. "Newsletter." [Honolulu], 1964.

LASMAN, LAWRENCE, OFELIA J. BULURAN, JEFFERY NOLAN and LINNERA O'NEIL. "A Study of Attitudes of Filipino Immigrants about Hawaii." Univ. of Hawaii School of Social Work group project, May 1971.

MAYER, ADRIAN C. "Report on the East Indian Community in Vancouver." Univ. of British Columbia, Institute of Social and Economic Research Working Paper, [1959].

"Report of Hawaiian Interracial Committee on Filipino Importation." [Honolulu, 1945].

SOCIAL SCIENCE INSTITUTE, FISK UNIVERSITY. "Orientals and Their Cultural Adjustment." Nashville, Tenn., 1946.

YOUNG, NANCY FOON, ed. "Searching for the Promised Land: Filipinos and Samoans in Hawaii." Univ. of Hawaii College of Education General Assistance Center, [1973].

K. THESES AND DISSERTATIONS

AGBAYANI, ADEUDATO J. "The Resident Commissioner of the Philippines to the United States." Dissertation, Univ. of Santo Tomas, Manila, 1941.

ALCANTARA, RUBEN R. "The Filipino Community in Waialua." Dissertation, Univ. of Hawaii, 1973.

AQUINO, VALENTIN R. "The Filipino Community in Los Angeles." Thesis, Univ. of Southern California, 1952.

AVE, MARIO. "Characteristics of Filipino Organizations in Los Angeles," Thesis, Univ. of Southern California, 1956.

CARIAGA, ROMAN R. "The Filipinos in Hawaii: a Survey of the Economic and Social Conditions." Thesis, Univ. of Hawaii, 1936.

CATAPUSAN, BENICO T. "The Social Adjustment of Filipinos in the United States." Dissertation, Univ. of Southern California, 1940.

CLIFFORD, MARY DORITA. "Filipino Immigration to Hawaii." Thesis, Univ. of Hawaii, 1954.

COLOMA, CASIANO P. "A Study of the Filipino Repatriation Movement." Thesis, Univ. of Southern California, 1939.

EUBANK, LAURIEL E. "The Effects of the First Six Months of World War II on the Attitudes of Koreans and Filipinos toward the Japanese in Hawaii." Thesis, Univ. of Hawaii, 1943.

GARDNER, ARTHUR L. "So Chae-P'il and the Tongnip Sinmun." Thesis, Univ. of Hawaii, 1969.

GIVENS, HELEN LEWIS. "The Korean Community in Los Angeles County." Thesis, Univ. of Southern California, 1939.

JUNASA, BIENVENIDO. "Study of Some Social Factors Related to the Plans and Aspirations of the Filipino Youth in Waipahu." Thesis, Univ. of Hawaii, 1961.

JURIKA, STEPHEN, JR. "The Political Geography of the Philippines." Dissertation, Stanford Univ., 1962.

LAMB, HELEN BOYDEN. "Industrial Relations in the Western Lettuce Industry." Dissertation, Radcliffe College, 1942.

KIM, BERNICE BONG HEE. "The Koreans in Hawaii." Thesis, Univ. of Hawaii, 1937.

MARIANO, HONORANTE. "The Filipinos Immigrants in the United States." Thesis, Univ. of Oregon, 1933.

OBANDO, AQUINO B. "A Study of the Problems of Filipino Students in the United States." Thesis, Univ. of Southern California, 1936.

PROVIDO, GENEROSO P. "Oriental Immigration from an American Dependency," Thesis, Univ. of California, Berkeley, 1931.

RATHORE, NAEEM GUL. "Indian Nationalist Agitation in the United States: a Study of Lala Lajpat Rai and the India Home Rule League of America, 1914–1920." Dissertation, Columbia Univ. 1965.

WALLOVITS, SONIA E. "The Filipinos in California." Thesis, Univ. of Southern California, 1966.

L. INTERVIEWS AND PRESENTATIONS

Interview with Paul Chun, Asian American Drug Abuse Center, Los Angeles County, Los Angeles, Nov. 11, 1974.

Interview with James Misahon, Honolulu, Hawaii, Dec. 18, 1972.

Interview with the Rev. San Bom Woo, Korean United Presbyterian Church, Los Angeles, Nov. 11, 1974.

Presentation by Wayne Patterson, Korean Studies Seminar, Univ. of Hawaii, 1973.

Index

Index

329

330 ASIANS IN AMERICA

nos, 46, 47, 54-57, 66; against Koreans, 132, 133
Exeter, California, 54, 232

Fair Oaks, California, 194
Farrington, Joseph B., 137, 279
Farrington, Wallace R., 91
Feather River Canyon, California, 228
Federalistas, 25
Fieldbrave, Theodore, 232
Figueras, Jose, 92-93
Filipino Agricultural Laborers Association, 100-101
Filipino-American Coordinating Conference, 102
Filipino-American Political Association, 102
Filipino Businessmen's Association of Hawaii, 103
Filipino Club of Stockton, 102
Filipino Federation of America, 87-88, 89
Filipino Higher Wage Movement, 90
Filipino immigration: *see* Immigration: Filipinos
Filipino Labor Supply Association, 80, 81
Filipino Labor Union, 80, 81, 89
Filipino Nation, 87
Filipino Naturalization Act of 1946, 28, 50
Filipino old-timers: California, 98-99; Hawaii, 106
Filipinos as American nationals, 26, 46-48
Filipinos: in Alaska, 81-82; in California, 41-47, 58-81, 95, 97-102; in Hawaii, 33-41, 68-69, 85-94, 96, 103-106
First Filipino Infantry Regiment, 50, 51, 52, 103, 105
Fong, Hiram, 170
Fordham University, 104
Free Hindustan, 209
French, Burton L., 278
Friar lands, Philippines, 25
Friends of Freedom for India, 213

Fresno, California, 94, 199, 228, 232
Furuseth, Andrew, 83

Galang, V. S., 103
Gambling: Filipinos, 60, 64-67, 78, 99, 100, 106; Koreans, 163
Gandhi, Mahatma, 179, 181
Ganges River, 176, 177, 178, 183
Garden Grove, California, 168
Gare-Hawes-Cutting Bill of 1932, 26
Garrison, Lindley M., 83
Gentlemen's Agreement, 74, 126, 127, 133, 188, 197
Ghadr Party, 210, 211, 213, 290
Ghose, Sailendra Nath, 212, 213, 220
Glenn County, California, 231
Georgetown University, 213
George Washington University, 128
Gobind, 182
Gobind Day (East Indians), 244
Goethe, C. M., 61
Gokhale, Shankar Laxman, 220
Gompers, Samuel, 192
Gonzalo, D. F., 59
Grass Roof, 168
Great Northern Railroad, 165
Gridley, California, 231
Grizzly Bear, 224
Gujarat, India, 183, 185
Gujarti, 178, 207
Gupta, Heramba Lal, 210-11
Guru, 242

Haan, Kilsoo, 155, 156
Hackfeld & Company, 121
Hamid, Abdul, 291
Hana, Maui, 169
Hand, Learned, 212
Hanford, California, 232
Han'gul, 113-14
Hare Krishna, 242
Harrison, Francis B., 25, 36, 37
Hart, Fred J., 67
Harvard University, 33, 128, 234; Law School, 170
Hastings College, 144
Hastings, Nebraska, 150, 281